The Frontlines of Peace

ALSO BY SÉVERINE AUTESSERRE

Peaceland:
Conflict Resolution and the Everyday Politics of International Intervention

The Trouble with the Congo:
Local Violence and the Failure of International Peacebuilding

Further Praise for *The Frontlines of Peace*

"Peacebuilding rests on the courage and wisdom of those people closest to conflict, and we must invest in them in ways that dignify their work and commitment. Autesserre's book makes clear how to do this. *The Frontlines of Peace* is a must-read."

—John Paul Lederach, Professor Emeritus of International
Peacebuilding, University of Notre Dame

The Frontlines of Peace

An Insider's Guide to Changing the World

SÉVERINE AUTESSERRE

OXFORD
UNIVERSITY PRESS

Oxford University Press is a department of the University of Oxford. It furthers
the University's objective of excellence in research, scholarship, and education
by publishing worldwide. Oxford is a registered trade mark of Oxford University
Press in the UK and certain other countries.

Published in the United States of America by Oxford University Press
198 Madison Avenue, New York, NY 10016, United States of America.

CIP data is on file at the Library of Congress
ISBN 978–0–19–753035–1

DOI: 10.1093/oso/9780197530351.001.0001

1 3 5 7 9 8 6 4 2

Printed by LSC Communications, United States of America

Published with the support of the Gerda Henkel Foundation, Duesseldorf.

To Monique Alligier and André Autesserre, who gave me life

And to Philippe, Fanny, Ariane, Ayten, Elisabeth, Leigh, Catherine &
Alan, Kim & Jack, and my medical team, who helped me keep it

Contents

Foreword

by Leymah Gbowee, 2011 Nobel Peace Prize Laureate

As I read this book—one telling the story of ordinary individuals who successfully opposed violence—the word "hope" kept coming to mind, as it reminded me of my own journey. More specifically, I am reminded of hope's pertinence in creating a movement powerful enough to end Liberia's civil war.

And much like some characters you will encounter in this book, my experience with violence was intimate and intense. As a 17-year-old, I watched bewilderedly as armed men—engaged in a power struggle—drove bullets through my envisioned future, and the political became personal.

I watched for many months as every glimmer of hope of a successful resolution to the ongoing conflict faded. I grew sick of international donors tossing money at the problem, and greedy politicians brawling, when they could have been endeavoring to secure peace.

As each day went by, my children's future looked gloomy. Men who sat at peace conferences returned with no solution to our problems. All the while, women sat idly at home, oblivious to treaty conversations.

Frustrated by the stagnancy of peace efforts, we women—of all ages, means, religions, and tribes—united to champion our cause and that of our children. We resorted to every possible tactic we could imagine: street protests, sit-ins, pickets, prayers, fasting, and vigils. We also employed sex strikes in an effort to get our partners to heed our requests for peace.

All aforementioned tactics did not garner the needed attention to bring the rebels and government officials to one accord. So, we formed a human barricade to prevent our politicians from exiting the ongoing peace talks. And when that didn't work, we threatened to rip our clothes off. In many African cultures, it's considered a terrible curse for men to see their mothers naked—and so they backed off. Eventually, on August 18, 2003, they finally signed the peace agreement that ended our 14-year-long conflict.

My story speaks to this simple truth: the people whom foreign interveners are ostensibly trying to save—mothers, rural villagers, inner-city dwellers, etc.—have the precise know-how and motivation to bring a deadly conflict to an end. This reflects the conclusion Séverine has reached through her 20 years of *extraordinary work: her deep dive in today's major conflict hot spots, her access to the hallways and dining rooms of world leaders, and her willingness to speak truth to power.*

Though this truth is simple, its enormous implications require overhauling the entrenched peacebuilding procedures that the United Nations, diplomats, and politicians have used for decades. And this is no easy feat, as you will learn through the many tales of outcast peacebuilders and aid interveners who dared to do things differently.

I've seen Séverine speak to students, activists, and Nobel laureates. While we may come from different worlds, we are warriors who place our trust in the same weapons and have the same core beliefs at heart. Her research findings resonate with my personal journey. The principles on which she stands are those at the center of the Gbowee Peace Foundation Africa and the Women, Peace, and Security program at Columbia University. When we speak, and when we write, both of us want to take our audience on a transformative journey, which is precisely what The Frontlines of Peace *will do for you.*

In this book, you will read the untold stories of individuals who effectively fight for peace every day across the globe. You'll see how the residents of Idjwi have avoided falling prey to the terrible violence that has engulfed their neighbors in the rest of eastern Congo. You'll become familiar with other communities that have established peace amid devastating armed conflicts, like in Somaliland and Colombia. You'll discover a new approach to peace that can work for conflicts around the world, including where you live. And you'll understand how an ordinary individual like me could build lasting peace, and win the Nobel Peace Prize!

By reading this book, you'll grasp what you can personally do to build peace around you, whether or not you live and work in conflict zones. Because a victim of rape in Liberia feels the same pain as one in Europe. The tears of parents losing sons and daughters to gun violence fall just as hard in the inner cities of America as they do in Syria. The trauma of young children forced to fight in Burundi reflects that of all youth forced to grow up under systems of violence across the globe. Violence affects us all, and the alternative peacebuilding strategies outlined in The Frontlines of Peace *can be applied to any of its forms.*

For the longest time, the kind of "bottom-up, insider-led" approach to resolving conflict that Séverine advocates for was disdained and overlooked in international circles. To an extent, it still is today. Local peacebuilding strategies are indeed starting to receive significant attention from individual practitioners and researchers—in part thanks to Séverine's trailblazing scholarship on this matter, as well as the work of the individuals and organizations she portrays in this book. But today, too many powerful actors around the globe still consider grassroots peacebuilding a sideshow—that it is a profoundly controversial enterprise. Most of the fabulous local initiatives I see around me remain unreported, undocumented, and unsupported. At the same time, our leaders and the media focus all their attention on warlords, corrupt politicians, and international elites. Plus, the idea of "putting locals in the driver's seat" continues to alarm and anger many foreign aid experts.

Numerous books and articles have been written on peacebuilding and international interventions, but their negativity often irks me. Analysts consistently emphasize the problems with our work; they keep telling us how and why we get things wrong, but they rarely explain what we can and do get right. Admittedly, it is easy to sit in the confines of one's home and point out the wrongs, so I am thankful for Séverine's book as its focus on success and its objective yet constructive approach are so important.

The Frontlines of Peace *gives us a pathway forward following the costly, devastating failures of internationally-led, top-down peace efforts in so many conflicts around the world. Through her stories (some funny, some heartbreaking, some gut-wrenching), Séverine uncovers exactly what it takes to build peace from the ground up. And she compellingly assesses how politicians, military leaders, and foreign interveners can both assist and undermine such efforts.*

Don't get me wrong: Foreign and national elites do have a role to play in peacebuilding. In Liberia, my fellow activists and I gratefully enlisted the help of the United Nations peacekeepers. Likewise, Séverine's "model interveners" are perfect examples of how foreign peacebuilders can support locals. In Liberia, we ordinary activists put pressure on President Taylor and rebel leaders until they reached a peace agreement. By the same token, the Somalilanders who have built an autonomous peace and the American activists who have decreased gun violence in their cities show us how bottom-up and top-down peace efforts can be effectively united.

The Frontlines of Peace *is not just another book about international politics. It's a book that will change the way you see the world around you. This is not another book about war and failure. It's a book about fostering peace in the darkest and most desperate situations, and a hopeful and inspiring story about humanity's successes in containing violence. And this is not another book about lovely but naïve and impractical ideas. It's a book about real-life stories that everyone can relate to, and about pragmatic solutions that everyone can use.*

So whoever you are and wherever you live, The Frontlines of Peace *is a book for you. Everybody can use Séverine's ideas to make a difference, anywhere, any day. We all have what it takes to build peace in our own communities. You, too, can be one of the insiders changing the world. You, too, can make your voice heard and achieve peace and safety in your community, just like I did. Now, it's your opportunity to read on and discover how.*

The Frontlines of Peace

Preface

War, Hope, and Peace

When I was 17, my father brought me a tape recording of exploding bombs from Sarajevo. He was a sound technician for the French state radio, and he traveled the world reporting on wars, presidents' visits, and revolutions. On the nights he returned home, he would always lay out the presents and memorabilia he had collected during his trip on our big wooden table. Then he would hold up each item and explain what it was, how he came by it, and what it meant. He would let me sample all of the strange food he had brought back (Japanese crackers, South African jerky, Lebanese pastries, American gummy burger candies) and he would laugh at the faces I made when I didn't like the taste. Through these moments with my dad, I discovered new cuisines, new countries, new people, new cultures—each more fascinating than the one before.

The presents were fantastic, but his stories were even better: tales of him riding the Orient Express to Vladivostok, participating in the Algerian Revolution, escaping his kidnappers in Iran, walking miles with Rwandan refugees in Congo, dodging death in Yugoslavia, flying around the world on the French presidential supersonic jet. At every dinner party, every reception, my father was the center of attention. I was so proud of him. Neither of my parents had finished high school, and yet all of these people who were much more educated, and much wealthier, would cling to my dad's every word.

Of course, there was a dark side to all of that. My earliest memory is of my mom sitting in our weathered armchair, looking pensive, and explaining to me that my father would not be back for Christmas. He was covering the war between Iran and Iraq, and he was unable to leave. I was three, and I didn't understand that he might never return.

As I grew older, I began to realize that my father often stretched the truth. Maybe he was not one of the leaders of the Algerian Revolution after all. Maybe he was not best friends with French presidents François Mitterrand, Jacques Chirac, and their respective prime ministers. Maybe he did not save his colleagues from a horrendous death in Iran.

Still, by that time, I was hooked. My father led an exciting life, and I wanted the same. He had helped countless people across the world—or maybe he hadn't, but I would.

I had my heart set on working in international news just like him, but quickly realized that it was not quite the life I imagined. My first reality check came during the competitive exam I took to enter journalism school. I passed the written examination, but failed the oral one. When I asked what I had done wrong, the director told me that journalists were not meant to help people, they were meant to report. The selection committee thought I was better suited to a humanitarian vocation, not a journalistic one.

I was furious. So I made a plan and got to work building a résumé that would make it impossible for them to reject me the next time I applied. I gained admission to a master's program in communications at the prestigious Sciences Po university, and spent my summers volunteering in India (for local charities) and South Africa (for the community radio Voice of Soweto).

Everything was going according to plan. And then, one afternoon in October 1998, in a suburb of Johannesburg, I saw the local police destroy an illegal township. They forced hundreds of poor families out of their homes and set fire to the houses to prevent the inhabitants from returning. I was outraged and horrified. I couldn't stand watching from the sidelines. I wanted to rush in and side with the residents who were confronting the policemen, but my colleagues reminded me that this was not my role. As a journalist, I had to watch and report—I was not to get involved.

That day, I realized that the jury who had failed me on my oral exam had been right, and I switched career tracks. After graduating from Sciences Po, I spent two months digging latrines and teaching English as part of a development project in Nicaragua, and I was awarded a Fulbright Scholarship to complete a second master's degree in international affairs at Columbia University in New York. I then applied to doctoral programs in political science, assuming that more education would make me a better aid practitioner. I took a gap year and went to work with one of my favorite aid organizations, Doctors of the World, in Kosovo. I was on track to become the kind of humanitarian activist I idolized.

And then my love-hate relationship with the Democratic Republic of Congo (henceforth, Congo) started. After my six months in Kosovo, I went to Barcelona on vacation with my then-boyfriend (my now-husband). One of his colleagues from Médicos Sin Fronteras (Doctors Without Borders) invited us to a New Year's Eve party. That night, after months of grueling work, we blew off steam. Several drinks in, at two or three in the morning, someone said: "Hey, by the way, I'm looking for two French speakers to go on an exploratory mission in Congo. Are you up for it?" In the heat of the moment, we said yes.

This was in early 2001, at the peak of the war in Congo. My job was to help my team understand the political, military, and humanitarian situations on the ground. During my time there, I asked everyone I met to explain to me what was going on. At the end of each briefing I was left more confused than I had been coming in. The explanations I received never seemed to fully elucidate who was fighting whom, and why. Whenever I believed that I had an analytical framework to explain the conflict, I would find numerous cases that didn't fit, and eventually the whole structure would crumble. After six months there, I still felt that I—and all of the diplomats, peacekeepers, and aid workers I had talked to—did not understand what was going on in Congo. I thought that this would make a fascinating research topic for the doctorate that I began at New York University in late 2001, so I decided to focus my studies on understanding the war there, and others around the world.

It was through my many subsequent trips to Congo, and a side mission to Afghanistan, that I started seeing the problems with the aid industry. I was increasingly shocked by the behavior of my humanitarian peers. One day, for instance, I was having lunch as usual with my team—our country director from Switzerland, our medical coordinator from Guatemala, and our administrator from Spain—and they started complaining about our Congolese assistants:

"They are *so* lazy."
"Oh, and stupid too, did you hear what the driver told me?!"
"You can't trust them. They are all corrupt. All of them. They'll steal whenever they can."
"And they'll lie to you too. All. The. Time."

This was unfortunately one discussion among many, too many, the likes of which I had also heard in Afghanistan and Kosovo. There, too, my humanitarian colleagues often branded local people as backward, corrupt, untrustworthy, incompetent, you name it, and treated them as such. Some of them yelled at their local colleagues in a degrading way. Others forgot basic manners when interacting with national authorities. We all drove so fast on dirt roads that we sprayed bystanders with dust or water.

My teammates were not heartless individuals; they had sacrificed their career prospects, their material comfort, and, for some of them, even their family lives, all in order to help perfect strangers. I wondered what had happened to transform these well-meaning human beings into such a prejudiced group.

I was also frustrated by the distance I was forced to keep from the very people I wanted so badly to support. I hated the three months I spent in Afghanistan. The situation in Kabul was so dangerous that I was not allowed to walk around, which to me is the only way to get a feel for a new place. Instead, I had to be driven everywhere—and I hate cars; I always get motion sickness. I also resented being cooped up in the cramped townhouse that doubled as our office and felt that all of the security restrictions I had to respect prevented me from doing my job. How could I understand the political, military, and security conditions well enough to help design our humanitarian strategy? The only people I met were foreign soldiers, aid workers, and Afghan officials, and all I saw was within the walls of my compound and the few administrative buildings Doctors Without Borders deemed safe enough for me to enter!

On top of that, I began to tire of addressing the consequences of violence, rather than the causes. All of the humanitarian aid workers present in Afghanistan, Congo, and Kosovo spent a tremendous amount of money, time, and energy doing incredibly important work. We responded to cholera epidemics, took care of orphans, provided health care to wounded people and rape survivors, gave temporary shelter to displaced populations, and made sure civilians caught in the crossfire would have clean water to drink and something to eat. In many places, we foreign aid workers were the only ones with the training and resources to save lives. But we did not do anything to actually prevent entire populations from starving, children from being orphaned, women from being raped, and civilians from being displaced.

The last straw came in Congo, when I attended a large meeting with a high-ranking diplomat representing the European Union. She had flown from Brussels, spent a few days in the Congolese capital Kinshasa and, upon arriving in Goma (a large town in eastern Congo), convened the representatives of all of the aid organizations funded by the European Union. She lectured us for two hours: "You should stop thinking as if you're in a war zone," she said. "Remember, the presidents and the rebel leaders have signed an agreement. You're in a time of peace now. You have to start acting accordingly." She told us to ignore the battle frontlines and cross them, while we knew we would be shot if we tried. She emphasized that the war had now ended, while my team and I had worked 16 hours a day for the past few weeks responding to a massive emergency: Tens of thousands of civilians had just fled their homes due to a fresh outbreak of fighting between rebels and the government. She seemed completely out of touch. She believed Congo had finally entered a post-conflict, peaceful phase. Meanwhile, I was confronting violence, torture, and despair on a daily basis—and aid workers continue to encounter similar conditions today, nearly two decades later.

After years of research, I finally began to understand. The European Union diplomat had been trained to analyze conflict from the top down, so she was using the tools she viewed as appropriate: working with governments and national elites. When the Congolese leaders signed an agreement, she genuinely believed that this would end the war. What was happening on the ground did not enter into her analysis of the situation. In short, she was an adept at what I now call "Peace, Inc.": the conventional way to end wars.

In this approach, foreign peacebuilders run the show. But they don't get immersed in complicated local issues or develop in-depth knowledge of the history, politics, and cultures of the countries in which they work. Instead, they interact with political and military leaders, rely on external expertise and resources, and use the same kind of solutions all over the world. This top-down, outsider-led way of working remains the status quo for numerous reasons: It emphasizes the need for only generalist knowledge, and it offers speed, broad applicability, the glamour of collaborating with elites, etc. It is also so ingrained in peacebuilding circles that most interveners don't even think they could proceed differently; it is part of their very identity.

My experiences with Peace, Inc. made me realize that we as a group—aid workers, diplomats, peacekeepers—rarely understand the causes of violence, whether in Afghanistan, Congo, Kosovo, or in other conflict situations. We also know precious little about what does and doesn't work to combat war. And we make so many mistakes in trying to help and intervene on the ground. Sometimes, we even aggravate the situation. I felt that we could and should do better—and after my years of research, I thought I was in a position to help make this happen.

I believe that the best way to understand anything is through immersion, so I've done a lot of what scholars call "participant observations," meaning participating in the same phenomenon you're researching. I've patrolled the Congolese countryside with Indian and South African peacekeepers, at times translating for them. I've gathered information on human rights and violence with United Nations officials in Congo, Colombia, and the Palestinian territories. I've attended parties, lunches, dinners, funerals, weddings, and official ceremonies all over the world. I've flown in tiny planes used for arms trafficking, and in old, massive, Soviet-era ones whose pilots spent most of the night drinking to try to forget how scared they were that they might crash the next day. I've met at least a dozen men who told me they worked for their countries' intelligence services and, every time, I wondered why they volunteered that information: Isn't the whole point of being a spy that no one knows your identity? I quite memorably spent my 34th birthday camping in the middle of the Congolese jungle with policemen and soldiers—although I've never understood the appeal of camping (too many childhood memories of tents collapsing on me in the middle of the night!).

In short, I've tried to fully immerse myself in what I call "Peaceland": the world of aid workers who spend their lives hopping from conflict zone to conflict zone. I've seen the world through their eyes, known their joys and pains, and struggled with the same challenges, fears, and frustrations. I now intimately understand why they act the way they do. And, more importantly, I've realized how we can start changing this.

A United Nations military observer interviews weary-looking residents of Katale (Congo) about recent security incidents. In typical participant observation fashion, I (the first person on the left) mirror the peacekeeper's behavior.
Photo credit: Philippe Rosen, 2011

This kind of life can be dangerous and difficult, and sometimes I've had to rely on dumb luck to stay safe. In Malakal, South Sudan, I left my hotel just a few hours before heavy fighting broke out there. In North Kivu, Congo, I found a driver who had "brothers" and "cousins" in all of the rebel groups and army units deployed in the area, so he always made sure we would be safe on the road. I trusted him with my life, literally.

I've become relatively good at protecting myself. I've found out that bulletproof vests are heavy and uncomfortable, and not really made for slight women like myself—especially when you put them on backward, as I did the first time. In fact, the vests mark me as a potential target, so I never wear them. Instead, I've learned to develop an adequate understanding of the area I'm in, to build a sufficient network to avoid ending up in the wrong place at the wrong time, and to establish contingency plans in the event I don't come back from one of my meetings or visits. I also listen to my gut, and leave when something looks suspicious—as I did the day I met with a Congolese lieutenant whose leery smile, slurred speech, and aggressive talk made me nervous, or the evening one rebel leader told me point-blank he "knew" I was a spy for the French government. And I have a go-to answer for the state officials who start flirting instead of answering my questions—"Miss or Mrs. Autesserre?" "It's Professor!"

Sometimes things end up going sour anyway. I've had a couple of close calls in Congo. In Bukavu, I found myself caught in the midst of heavy fighting, with bombs falling and rifles firing all around me. I'm still thankful to my humanitarian friends and the United Nations peacekeepers for helping me get out of there unharmed.

In Nyunzu, my back gave out after too much time riding a motorcycle on dirt roads riddled with potholes. I was temporarily paralyzed from the waist down, while Rwandan rebels prepared to attack the town. Thankfully, a friend came to get me in a tiny humanitarian plane. To ensure that my body could handle the trip, my roommates loaded me up on so much morphine (a narcotic in addition to a painkiller) that I found the whole experience a-ma-zing and couldn't stop laughing until I was back to safety.

In Kalemie, my car hurt a biker, provoking a riot. I can still feel the arms of Seti, our local logistician, wound securely around my shoulders, and the warmth of his chest against my back. I can still hear him whispering: "Don't move. Don't talk. Don't be afraid: I'll protect you." I was calm and detached at the time, although I had nightmares for years afterward.

But what scared me most was not the potential stoning, the flying ammunition, or the guns pointed at me when I crossed checkpoints, because I knew
that it was all just temporary: For me, safety was just a plane ride away. No,
what scared me was the dangers that the people I abandoned had to face. I felt
guilty, almost physically sick, every time I had to leave.

I've spent years of my life working or conducting field research in 12
different war and postwar zones, including today's major hot spots. I've
interviewed more than 800 peacebuilders, warlords, victims, survivors,
politicians, and ordinary citizens. I've used all of this research to write two
books and two dozen articles on why international interventions so often fail
to end violence. My publications have won multiple awards, some of them
very prestigious. I get invited to lecture in universities, think tanks, and
the headquarters of peacebuilding organizations all over the world, and to
appear on TV and radio shows.

For the longest time, I believed I had it all figured out: I was helping
people change their perceptions of war and revise their approaches to
peace. In the early 2000s, when I was doing research for my doctoral dissertation, the diplomats, United Nations staff, non-governmental organization officials, and other peacebuilders I interviewed were baffled by the
notion of supporting bottom-up peacebuilding in Congo. The very concept
of working at the grassroots to address tensions that may affect only a few
hundred people (but are connected to broader conflicts) was utterly foreign
to them. So was the idea that the individuals most affected by violence—and
not outsiders—should figure out what it would take for them to feel safe and
how they can achieve this goal.

When I started presenting my findings and recommendations for local conflict resolution, my hosts, colleagues, book reviewers, and audience members
called me "provocative," "groundbreaking," "revolutionary," and "dangerous."
Jean-Marie Guéhenno, the former head of United Nations Peacekeeping,
found my criticisms of his organization so offensive that, the first time he
heard me speak, he compared me to Libyan president Colonel Gaddafi. In
public. Heat rushed to my cheeks as I blushed a dark shade of red—I was
humiliated and furious. And then, a few years and a few chats later, I ended up
with Guéhenno again on a panel, where he advocated for the very ideas that
I had promoted and that he used to hate: Peacekeepers should start from the
bottom up, and work with grassroots organizations rather than pursuing the
typical top-down, outsider-led approach, which is fundamentally flawed.

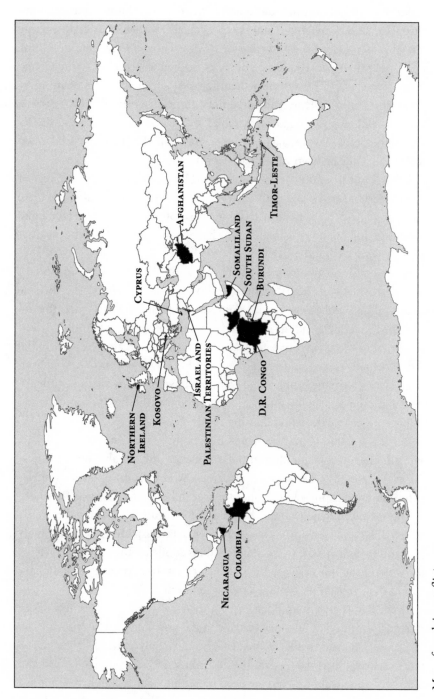

Map of work in conflict zones

More than a hundred diplomats, international bureaucrats, philanthropists, and activists—from entry-level aid workers to high-ranking ambassadors—asked me to brainstorm with them as they were designing or revising their peacebuilding strategies or their approaches to the Congo crisis. Sometimes I would meet them formally, in their offices or in mine, other times informally over lunch, dinner, or drinks. I traveled to Australia, Austria, Belgium, Canada, Colombia, Congo, France, Kenya, Mexico, the Netherlands, Sweden, Timor-Leste, the United Kingdom, the United States: It felt like my own version of a world tour.

When I was promoted to full professor at Barnard, the women's college of Columbia University, less than ten years after starting on faculty, I felt like I'd made it. And then I realized that I too was committing a huge error. I had been focusing on failures, issues, and challenges, instead of looking at what actually works to build peace.

My friends and family view many of the places I research—like South Sudan or Israel and the Palestinian territories—as lost causes. They believe peacebuilding will never work. Many of the politicians I've met, the aid workers I've trained, and the inhabitants of the conflict zones I've interviewed worry about the same thing. They know something is really wrong with the way we usually try to build peace after wars, but they don't know how to fix it. I hate seeing so many brilliant and committed people—my friends, students, peacebuilding colleagues—who are convinced that they can't do anything to change the state of the world they live in.

But when I talk about the hopeful cases that I've seen, people get very excited. They find inspiration in the experience of Leymah Gbowee, a destitute single mother living with her parents who went on to create a movement powerful enough to help end the war in her native Liberia. They keep asking for more details about the island of Idjwi in Congo and the region of Somaliland in East Africa, where residents have established astonishingly peaceful societies in the midst of horrendous conflicts. They get motivated by the work of the Life & Peace Institute, which has developed a revolutionary approach to grassroots, bottom-up peacebuilding.

These stories give them hope and, for those who work or plan to work in foreign aid, it finally provides them with the possibility for success they so badly need. Former students and readers are already putting my ideas into practice, in all kinds of organizations and ministries, all around the world. But they need more support, and we need more individuals like them—not just abroad, but in our own communities. That is why I decided to write this book.

What follows is the story of what I've learned over the past 20 years regarding how best to end violence. It is the tale of the ordinary yet extraordinary individuals and communities who have found effective ways to combat wars, and build peace.

"My Son Now Wants to Hold a Pencil Instead of a Gun"

Let me tell you the one story that gave me the energy to keep researching for this book, at a time when I had lost hope and felt that this project was going nowhere. In June 2017, I was looking for cases of international peacebuilding success in Congo and failing to find any: Everybody I met kept talking about violence and intervention failure. This didn't come as a surprise. By then, I had completed more than 350 interviews in Congo alone. I knew full well that the country was home to the deadliest conflict since World War II. I had written extensively about the fact that, despite the presence of the largest United Nations peace operation in the world— and one of the most expensive—the Congolese wars had destabilized most of Central Africa and triggered one of the world's worst humanitarian crises of the past 20 years. That's precisely why I kept searching. I thought that if I could find a positive story even in these most unlikely circumstances, it would mean that there are indeed seeds of hope hidden in the ugliness of war, and that perhaps we could learn how to foster them all across the globe.

Thankfully, three of my peacebuilder friends kept telling me that I absolutely had to meet an Indian-American woman named Vijaya Priyadarshini Thakur, because the work she did was game-changing. So I had tea with her one afternoon, in a beautiful garden overlooking the bright turquoise waters of Lake Kivu, surrounded by so many lush trees, colorful flowers, and chirping birds that it was easy to forget the dusty, noisy town around us. There, Vijaya told me the story of Justine* and her son Luca*—a story that upended her life, and that she couldn't share without tearing up.

Like tens of thousands of children in conflict zones around the world, Luca was kidnapped and forced to work for an armed group. He was only five years old when the militia abducted him, and he was so small that he couldn't

---

* Asterisks identify pseudonyms on first use.

even hold a rifle, so his commanders would march him up front, as a human shield.

Luca survived, and in 2007, after three years with the armed group, he was released and sent back home. (About 130,000 children have similarly been set free in the past 20 years, including more than 51,000 in Congo alone.) But Luca had trouble assimilating. He hated school; he had missed so many years that he was put in a class with kids much younger than him, which he found demoralizing. His mom didn't have much money, so he was often hungry. Plus he still believed what his commanders had drilled into him: that the only way to survive was to use violence.

So for the next few years, Luca kept running away to join his former militia. The only time that he thought he would ever be heard was when his voice was backed by the power of a gun. Only then did he feel safe. He was eight, and this was the only life he knew.

Meanwhile, at Bryn Mawr College in Pennsylvania (United States), Vijaya was writing her bachelor's thesis on war and peace in the African Great Lakes region. In parallel, she started working as an activist for various organizations that focused on genocide prevention. Within a few years, she grew disenchanted with the advocacy world. Her colleagues used the traditional, elite-focused approach to peacebuilding, and they relied on outsiders' skills and expertise. As a result, the organizations' diplomatic successes actually ended up harming the very people they wanted to help.

In particular, most activists at the time viewed the illegal exploitation of natural resources by armed groups as the primary cause of violence in Congo (when in reality there were a multitude of causes that I'll discuss later in the book), so they spent their time and energy advocating for new laws on conflict minerals. Sadly, their efforts to help regulate the illegal trade of minerals backfired, because the resulting legislation did nothing to destroy the actual power base of armed groups. In the absence of any broader political, economic, or social reforms, local military leaders managed to maintain their status as the principal powerbrokers in rural areas. In some cases, they even expanded their mining operations. Vulnerable populations lost their livelihood, and many of the newly unemployed young men joined rebel militias as a way to get by.

Vijaya remembers this period as a dark time in her life. She felt scared. She didn't want to acknowledge how badly she and her colleagues were doing with their Peace, Inc. approach, because that's all she knew how to do. She couldn't face the idea that she had sacrificed so much of her time and energy to something that was actually causing harm. On paper, though, things were going well for her. United States officials and activists were noticing her; she had become "a legislative hotshot," but the evidence kept mounting that Congolese people's lives were getting worse while her career was getting better.

In 2007, Vijaya won a small research grant, which she used to travel to Congo and ask ordinary people there what *they* believed would lead to peace. She mulled over the answers for a year, and eventually decided to start a pilot project in the eastern province of South Kivu—in the very village where Justine and Luca were living.

Vijaya linked up with local activists to organize lengthy meetings and workshops in which residents developed their own analysis of the conflict they faced, found a consensus on what the causes of violence were, and decided what the best responses would be. After more than a year of discussions, the villagers came up with a plan for how to build peace and prosperity in their own community.

The first step of that plan was for Vijaya and her fellow activists to raise some funds—less than $5,000 USD, half of which came from Vijaya's savings and the other half from an American philanthropist—and give out business microloans. Justine, for instance, received $40 to start a brickmaking factory. Her neighbors got similar amounts to bake donuts, sell bananas, brew beer, refine cassava flour, or breed goats. These enterprises took off, and soon Justine and her neighbors had enough money to repay their loans.

The money that participants reimbursed did not go back to Vijaya and her colleagues. Instead, it went into a communal pot, which the villagers used to invest in their communities and implement the rest of their plans. They installed taps for clean drinking water, and they rebuilt the roof of the local school. They organized trainings for the teachers to learn how to curb ethnic tensions instead of fueling them. They convinced the local chief to allocate a piece of land to displaced people who had taken refuge in their village, so that these families could farm for subsistence rather than resorting to violence. Eventually, they lobbied provincial authorities and the neighboring units of the Congolese police and army for protection and better services. They all worked together, people from all of the ethnic groups that had until then been fighting each other.

In the village of Jomba (Congo), a tailor named Immaculée T. sews a baby outfit. Immaculée received a microloan and three months of training from Vijaya Thakur and her peacebuilding organization, the Resolve Network. With these resources, she launched a successful business, became a leading voice in her community, and helped decrease violence around her.
Photo credit: Daniella Zalcman, 2016

These efforts, in Vijaya's words, led to "subtle but immense changes" in the lives of children like Luca: He now had three meals a day, shoes without holes, and role models who did not use violence to survive and gain power. His friends had big dreams for the future, like going to study computer science at the university in Goma. Plus, all the villagers were safer and healthier—no more obvious signs of malnutrition, and no more pneumonia due to leaky roofs. They were able to buy soap and improve their hygiene, so they weren't embarrassed to participate in community events anymore. Even their way of walking changed. Now, they squared their shoulders and held their heads high.

The whole time, the activists organized regular dialogue sessions in order to get feedback from participants and troubleshoot problems as they arose. Vijaya recalled a conversation she had with Justine a year after she started her brick-drying business:

Justine kept using the word "success." It was the first time that I had heard any of our beneficiaries do that, so I asked her what she meant, and when she first knew she was succeeding. She told me it was Luca: At 13, for the first time in his life, he was speaking in the future tense.

I did not understand what it meant at that time. I did not know that child soldiers have the highest recidivism rate for any crime in the world.

And then Justine said a sentence that stopped my heart: "My son now wants to hold a pencil instead of a gun."

Luca had stopped trying to run away all the time. He finally had a viable alternative to violence. He was starting to make plans, peaceful plans, within his community.

Vijaya knew that she was on to something, and that her approach could help other communities. But there was a hitch. Every aid agency to which she pitched her idea liked it, but none wanted to devote time, effort, and resources to something so unconventional. From their point of view, it was too participatory, too complex, too time-consuming, too locally-driven—too risky.

Indeed, there are big differences between the way most peacebuilding organizations work (the Peace, Inc. approach) and what Vijaya does. To start, Vijaya decided to resolve conflict from the grassroots, instead of focusing on elite leaders in capital cities. Even more importantly, Vijaya did not come and impose her beliefs. She constantly questioned all of the ideas that most aid workers take for granted—about peace, peacebuilding, war, violence, Congo, and the like—so as to avoid doing more harm than good. Unlike so many before her, Vijaya was humble, respectful, and she put ordinary citizens in the driver's seat.

If Vijaya wanted to continue using this strategy, she realized, she couldn't do so under the umbrella of an existing agency. So, for a long time, she was torn. She was 22, and the idea of creating her own organization was terrifying.

And then she had that conversation with Justine.

Shortly afterward, she quit her job in Washington, D.C. and said goodbye to her cushy life and several career prospects. A year later, the Resolve Network was born: a grassroots nonprofit organization whose mission is to build peace by using the very principles that worked so well in Justine and Luca's village.

Since its first pilot project in 2009, Resolve has worked with close to 8,000 people—all individuals at risk of being recruited by armed groups, and more than half of them former combatants like Luca. Even though militias have formed and reformed in Congo throughout the past decade, even though the pressure to remobilize has been enormous, not a single one of those participating in the Resolve programs has engaged in or gone back to fighting.

Benjamin C. (left), a farmer in the village of Binza (Congo), discusses with Vijaya Thakur (right) how to decrease violence in his community. Both are the kinds of remarkable peacebuilders whose models we should follow—the insiders changing the world.
Photo credit: Daniella Zalcman, 2016

The rest of this book suggests ways to emulate people like Vijaya and Justine to support individuals like Luca. Throughout, you'll discover a type of "peace" and "success" that is qualitatively different from the kind politicians usually try to sell us. It's not about love and harmony between world leaders and country elites; it's not what outsiders usually think peace or success should look like. Instead, it is something more realistic, more pragmatic, and much more attainable. It's something that already exists, and that you can see if you know where to look.

The peace and success you'll read about are what inhabitants of conflict zones and on-the-ground peace practitioners view as such, based on what *they* feel and experience. By this standard, peace and success take multiple forms and arrive through many different means, including beliefs in magic and other practices that many outsiders would qualify as backward or bizarre. They are localized, ad-hoc, at times even only temporary. They are not perfect or ideal and they don't garner universal praise, but they are tremendously important: They are starting points, both at home and abroad, that put us in a better position to address the broader issues that fuel violence, like the global arms trade, military aggression, neo-colonial or paternalist practices, climate change, and gender discrimination. They help us to take things into our own hands as everyday peacebuilders, rather than wait for elite leaders to get it right. They are the seeds of a potential revolution in world affairs—but a peaceful one.

A New Peace

Afghanistan, Colombia, Congo, Iraq, Myanmar, Somalia: The names of these countries evoke a story we've all heard over and over. There was violence, the United Nations got involved, donor countries pledged millions in assistance, warring parties called for ceasefires, signed agreements, held elections, and the headlines praised peace. Then a week or two later, sometimes just days later, violence flared up again. Often it had never actually ended; in many cases, it lasted for years after.

In just the past five years, wars have spawned the worst refugee crisis since World War II. They have cost more than $10 trillion annually—that's 13 percent of the world's GDP, or $4 a day, every day, for each and every one of us. They wreak havoc on the two billion people who live in over 50 conflict zones across the planet.

Even stable societies in the West are becoming increasingly polarized, facing acts of domestic terrorism and growing violence between oppositional social movements. Hate crimes and nationalist political parties have surged throughout Europe and North America.

The COVID-19 pandemic has further worsened the situation in most countries. It has exacerbated many causes of ongoing violence, such as poverty and inequality, government repression, and discrimination. The crisis has also reinforced distrust and suspicion between ethnic, political, and social groups.

Thankfully, around the world, countless people dedicate their lives to resolving conflict. Peacebuilding as an idea is as old as war: Any time certain individuals have used violence, others have tried to stop them. Peacebuilding as we know it, however, is a global industry that started in the wake of World War II, grew during the second half of the 20th century, and exploded after the end of the Cold War. Today, the United Nations alone stations roughly 100,000 peacekeepers around the globe—the second largest force deployed abroad after the United States military. Also trying to maintain domestic and international peace are diplomats and aid workers from all of the world's countries, massive institutions such as the World Bank and the African Union, as well as hundreds of thousands of non-governmental organizations, grassroots associations, and research institutes. Donors spend billions on international aid, including roughly $22 billion a year on peacebuilding.

On the one hand, these peace efforts have ended mass violence in Cambodia, Liberia, Namibia, Sierra Leone, and Timor-Leste. On the other hand, half of all ongoing wars have already lasted for more than two decades. Battle deaths have skyrocketed 277 percent in the past 15 years. The world devotes 106 times more money to military efforts than to resolving conflicts. And the COVID-19 pandemic has made international aid even trickier, due to restrictions on travel, repatriation of foreign staff, and decreased funding from donors who now have their own economic disruptions to address. One thing is clear: Our templates and techniques for building lasting peace just don't work.

There has been plenty of discussion about what has gone wrong—how we've failed to stop the genocides in Bosnia and Rwanda, the massacres in Syria and Myanmar, the horrors in Afghanistan and Colombia, the endless bloodshed in Israel and the Palestinian territories. But it is now time to ask: What has gone right?

It should seem obvious that building on what works is as important as learning from what fails. Yet, until recently, this hasn't been the focus of much attention. In the words of my friend Loochi Muzaliwa, a peacebuilder from Congo, we are "like the man who sees a white painting with a small black dot, and when you ask him what the painting is, he has seen only a small black dot, and he forgets all of the white."

When we pause to think about it, the most puzzling question is not why our conflict-resolution efforts fall flat in the face of such daunting obstacles, but why they sometimes triumph. It's not simply that success is the flip side of failure. For instance, we know that a lack of funding often leads to botched peace initiatives, but throwing money at problems is not the solution either—it can actually make things even worse.

It turns out that elections don't build peace, and democracy itself might not be the golden ticket—at least not in the short term. Contrary to what most politicians preach, building peace doesn't require billions in aid or massive international interventions. Real, lasting peace requires giving power to ordinary citizens. There have been many successful examples of peacebuilding in the past few years, all involving grassroots initiatives led by local people, at times supported by foreigners, and often using methods shunned by the international elite.

Rather than focusing on handshakes between presidents, abstract peace agreements, and negotiations between governments and rebel leaders, I chronicle the concrete, everyday actions that make a difference on the ground. Some of these are bizarre, some are creative, some involve time-tested traditions, and some are just good old-fashioned common sense. And most importantly, they promise a new peace in communities all over the world—from Idjwi in Congo to Chicago in the United States.

In the following chapters, I explain how peacebuilding can actually work, so that it can finally improve the lives of billions of people. Throughout this book, you'll meet individuals who will make you cringe, others who will make you furious—and many, many others who will inspire you. They show that, to end violence from war—and address lesser conflicts at home—we have to fundamentally change the way we view and build peace.

PART I
PEACE POSSIBLE

1

Island of Peace

In 2015, a militia leader named Chance Pay Rusiniku tried to set up yet another insurgent group in Congo. He decided to use Idjwi, an island in the middle of Lake Kivu, near the border between Congo and Rwanda, as his base. This was the kind of movement that had spiraled into massive fighting in other parts of the country. But that is not what happened in Idjwi. Apart from a handful of individuals, the inhabitants refused to follow the would-be militia leader. They were afraid and did not like the idea of violence starting on their island. Chance murdered three local chiefs and blackmailed the neighboring residents, threatening to kill them if they did not give him money or aid, but his strategy backfired. His crimes united everyone, including ordinary citizens, local elites, and state officials, against him. Hunted by the Congolese army, and finding no support on Idjwi, Chance fled to the neighboring town of Goma on the mainland, where he was subsequently arrested.

Among Congolese people, Idjwi's biggest claim to fame is its delicious pineapples. But the island's 300,000 inhabitants deserve to be known for something else: their ability to create a sanctuary of peace amid a conflict that has claimed up to five million lives.

Journalists and United Nations officials often call Congo the "rape capital of the world." News reports focus on war, violence, and chaos. Politicians and researchers emphasize how deeply intractable the conflict is: Even the largest United Nations peacekeeping mission in the world, with its billion-dollar annual budget and more than 18,000 troops, has failed to stem the bloodshed.

I have traveled to Congo regularly since 2001. I have gone to all of the most violent provinces and have interviewed 400 people. I have worked both in the bustling capital city and in areas so remote that the children there had never seen a white person before. But until I started focusing on peace rather than war, and peacebuilding success rather than peacebuilding failure, it had never occurred to me that I might want to spend time in Idjwi.

When I visited the island in 2016 and then again in 2019, the people I spoke to did not focus on the latest massacre or bout of fighting, as they so often do in other parts of eastern Congo. Idjwi's inhabitants go about their daily lives without the fear I saw and felt just a few miles away in neighboring provinces.

Idjwi is striking not for destroyed villages and houses, the all too common marks of war in the Kivu provinces, but rather, for the beauty of its lush vegetation and lakeside scenery. Were it not for the poverty visible everywhere—in the rags too many children wear, the run-down houses, the constant power cuts, the scarcity of items available at the markets—Idjwi could look like a paradise lost. Roughly the size of Malta, it boasts a varied ecological backdrop inhabited by diverse ethnic and political groups. Friendly people in vibrant red, green, yellow, and blue garb amble down dirt roads, which they share not with cars (there are fewer than a dozen on the island) but with goats, chickens, dogs, and the occasional pig. Music is everywhere, usually coming from blasting radios, but also, on festive occasions, from traditional drums that get everyone dancing.

Residents of Bugarula (Idjwi island's largest town) wash their laundry in Lake Kivu. I've seen these kinds of lush trees, colorful garments, and beautiful sceneries all over eastern Congo, but only in Idjwi have I felt a sense of calm, peace, and safety.

Photo credit: Séverine Autesserre, 2019

You may find the conditions on Idjwi to be distant and foreign, and chances are, you are reading this book far, far away from Congo. Yet all of us have more in common with Congolese citizens than we may realize. Congolese people face challenges similar to those faced by the inhabitants of Baltimore, Paris, Rio de Janeiro, and elsewhere: They want to decrease community tensions and prevent violence. In Congo, as in many other parts of the world, such longed-for harmony often seems like a pipe dream, but the story of Idjwi shows us that oftentimes local community resources can build peace better than any outside intervention. All in all, Idjwi's atypical ability to control violence shows how effective it is to build peace from the bottom up as well as from the top down, and how important it is to put local people in the driver's seat.

The Deadliest Conflict Since World War II

To understand just how extraordinary Idjwi is, it helps to remember that, in Congo, a combination of local, provincial, national, regional, and international agendas has fueled extensive violence over the past 25 years.

Congo gained independence in 1960 after 75 years of Belgian colonial rule, and then went through five years of turmoil followed by three decades of dictatorship. In the 1990s, political, economic, social, and ethnic tensions escalated into a series of civil and international wars that eventually involved Congo's nine neighboring countries as well as countless rebel groups.

From the colonial era to today, access to land and power has motivated many of the conflicts in the eastern provinces—the most violent part of the country and the area where Idjwi is located. In addition, Burundian, Rwandan, and Ugandan combatants have regularly entered Congo and allied with the national army or Congolese militias to control territory, fend off enemies, and at times, wage war on their home countries. All of these groups illegally exploit Congo's massive natural resources like charcoal, diamonds, and gold to help fund their operations.

This all results in horrible violence. In Kavumu (a couple of hours away from Idjwi, on the mainland), for instance, a group of inhabitants I met at the local market revealed that they fear being murdered in their sleep by bandits wanting to steal the few dollars they earned the previous day. The parents of baby girls worry constantly that their infants will be kidnapped, raped, and subjected to genital mutilation, as happened to nearly 40 children in their village between 2013 and 2016. I have heard similar stories of fear, torture, and despair throughout eastern Congo.

Unsurprisingly, Congolese people consistently rank peace and security as their top priorities. Universal issues like poverty and unemployment; a lack of access to education, food, and land; and governance problems, most notably corruption and injustice, are also of great concern.

Congo is the 11th least-developed country in the world. Here is what this means if you're born there: There is a good chance that you will not have enough to eat during the first few years of your life (more than 42 percent of children under the age of five suffer from malnutrition). Then, you may have to work to survive or help your family (child labor between ages 5 and 17 averages 27 percent). You may go to school for a few years (seven is typical), but you will most likely only attend elementary school (less than 50 percent of Congolese people have gone further in their studies). Odds are that you will live on less than $2 per day (like 77 percent of your fellow citizens). If you are a woman, you will probably experience some form of gender-based violence (like 51 percent of Congolese women). And, no matter your gender, you won't live that long: Life expectancy is roughly 60 years.

Many Congolese citizens learn not to depend on the state, as it is barely present outside of the main cities. This means no schools, no health centers, no reliable police or army, and no roads, except when a foreign donor or association decides to help out. In fact, 70 percent of Congolese people actively distrust their government, and my friends often cross the street when they see soldiers and police officers, because they associate them with abuse, not protection. Indeed, until recently, Congolese law and order forces were responsible for even more rapes, killings, and lootings than the rebels and militiamen they combat.

A national government that focuses on peace and development would be ideal to address these challenges. But the overwhelming majority of the elite jockeying for power place their own interests in wealth, influence, and authority above the well-being of their fellow citizens. Besides, the capital Kinshasa is too disconnected from the rest of the country for the central government to be able to do much, even if it wanted to. And none of the recent general elections ever produced a national leadership that focused on stability or progress.

In 2006, Congo held its first democratic elections since independence in 1960. Congolese citizens voted again in 2011, but accusations of fraud marred the process. Both times, President Joseph Kabila and his party won the majority of the votes. General elections were scheduled to take place in 2016, but the president rescheduled them multiple times under various pretexts.

Each delay generated massive popular protests, all of which the state violently repressed. The Kabila regime harassed, threatened, and, at times, arrested, tortured, and killed opposition figures and grassroots activists in order to suppress resistance. Ordinary people became wary of discussing elections. During my 2016 and 2017 trips to Congo, most of my friends and colleagues would lower their voices when talking about the political crisis. Others would first look around to make sure nobody was listening.

The ongoing violence further impeded democracy. Perpetual fighting means no freedom of expression and no freedom of movement—the very conditions that are necessary for free and fair elections. Criminal and armed groups make it easier for the ruling apparatus to oppress opponents, as governing elites can always blame disappearances and murders on someone else.

In 2018, Congolese people were so disappointed with the performance of their government that most of them voted for political opponents. Sadly, Kabila's camp manipulated the results in order to install a puppet president, Félix Tshisekedi, who was happy to compromise with them, thereby placing power in the hands of the old leadership. In short, the electoral process generated massive violence and didn't produce even a semblance of democracy.

Most Congolese people view electoral concerns, peace and security issues, and economic problems as inextricably linked. In the run-up to elections, politicians usually mobilize supporters by promising land, money, jobs, and the like, and then pit them against their opponents' supporters. In many of the towns and villages I've visited, the inhabitants kept asking for development programs to extend employment opportunities to their sons, nephews, neighbors—even themselves—so that they wouldn't join armed groups. Likewise, many of the militia members I talked to emphasized the very practical concerns that led them to enlist: They had no better job prospects and needed to find a way to survive—not to mention that, once they became combatants, they finally enjoyed some respect and power. The catch-22 is that violence prevents the very development initiatives that could provide alternative economic opportunities from succeeding or even starting in the first place.

This kind of vicious cycle is not specific to Congo; I've seen it at work in Colombia, Northern Ireland, Somaliland, and Timor-Leste. It is particularly obvious in the Palestinian territories: When I was there in 2012 and 2018, activists and officials kept lamenting how ever-decreasing funds for schools and industries in the refugee camps left young men with nothing to do and no future, making them easy recruits for militant and terrorist movements. Ostensibly peaceful countries have their own version of the problem. In the United States, for instance, high levels of shootings in certain neighborhoods scare away potential businesses, depriving residents of economic opportunities and increasing their desperation. Without job prospects available, young people find "employment" in the drug and gang world, further exacerbating gun violence.

So, given a dysfunctional state, an authoritarian government, extreme poverty, aggressive neighboring countries, and a host of local, national, and regional tensions, how have the people of Idjwi succeeded in maintaining their peaceful way of life?

Unlikely Peace

The only episode of mass violence that Idjwi has experienced in the recent past was right after the genocide in neighboring Rwanda. In 1994, the Rwandan government, its army, and allied youth militias massacred over 800,000 ethnic Tutsis and moderate Hutus. A Tutsi-led rebel movement eventually seized power, prompting large groups of Hutu combatants, along with 40,000 Rwandan civilians, to take refuge in Idjwi. The militants set up military camps, recruited local youth, and launched attacks on neighboring Rwandan towns. But virtually all of the Hutu soldiers, militiamen, and refugees left the island in 1996, chased out by the new Rwandan army and the Congolese rebel group it supported. Since then, through countless bouts of fighting between Rwanda and Congo, and through the multiple Congolese rebellions that have ravaged the mainland, Idjwi has remained remarkably peaceful.

Certainly, Idjwi has its share of problems. Domestic violence, police abuse, public brawls, and thefts are all too commonplace. But this is all small-scale criminality when compared to the organized fighting by large armed groups or militias that we see in other parts of Congo. For its inhabitants, and among the people from neighboring provinces, Idjwi has a reputation as a haven of peace.

Idjwi's unique situation is all the more surprising considering that the island has all of the same ingredients that have caused generalized fighting in the rest of Congo. Additionally, none of the usual explanations for peace in other parts of the world—and none of the reasons that people in Congo gave when I asked them about Idjwi—can explain why there is no mass violence there.

Idjwi is situated right on the border between Congo and Rwanda, which have been at war for most of the past 25 years. The provinces of the Kivus, where the island is located, are the epicenter of violence in Congo.

Nearly all of the Congolese people I talked to about Idjwi attributed its atypical peace to its geography. So did the few peacekeepers and foreign aid workers who had heard of the place. "It's an island," they all explained. "It's isolated and difficult to access, so armed groups have trouble getting there. And they would be trapped if they did." But many other islands—such as Rukwanzi, located between Congo and Uganda on nearby Lake Albert, and Lamu off the coast of Kenya—have been besieged by violence. And as we just saw, being an island certainly didn't protect Idjwi in 1994 during the Rwandan genocide.

Furthermore, armed groups have set up camps in the most unlikely locations throughout Congo, including on hilltops that one can access only by walking for days in the jungle, and on a remote peninsula on Lake Tanganyika. By contrast, the southernmost tip of Idjwi is so close to the Rwandan mainland that you can hold a discussion across Lake Kivu—you have to shout, of course, but you can hear and see the other side.

"But there is nothing useful or interesting on the island; there aren't even minerals to exploit," my Congolese and foreign associates would answer, "so who would bother?" Well, in the past, various rulers *did* bother. There was the famed Rwandan king Rwabugiri, who attacked Idjwi repeatedly between 1865 and 1895 and managed to occupy it for a decade. Then there were the Belgian and German colonizers, who fought over the island several times in the early 20th century. And finally, there were the Congolese and Rwandan armies in the mid-1990s.

Indeed, 25 miles in length with an area of 116 square miles (310 square kilometers), Idjwi offers a valuable swath of territory to control. In addition, from a strategic point of view, an island is easy to defend. And an island located right at the border between two countries at war makes for a fabulous stronghold. Idjwi has even been used as a platform for troop movements and arms trafficking in the past 20 years, and I've heard many unconfirmed reports that it is still at the center of various smuggling networks.

Moreover, my associates were wrong. There are in fact valuable resources on the island—such as coltan, much sought after for its use in mobile phones— which both local inhabitants and foreign companies are actively exploiting.

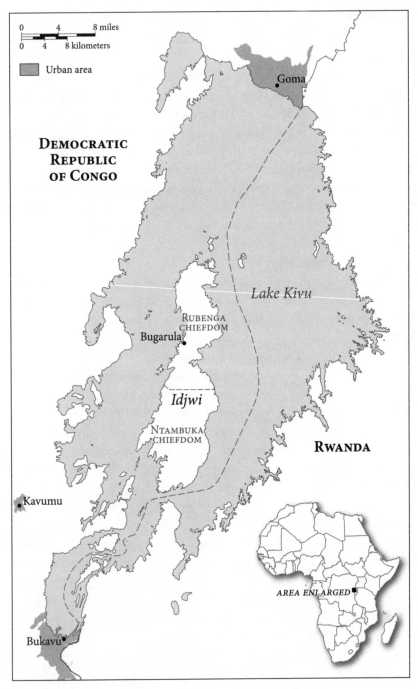

Map of Idjwi in Central Africa

The people I spoke with would usually retort that there is a simple explanation for Idjwi's peace: There is only one ethnic group there (Havu people), so the residents don't fight over ethnic issues as they so often do elsewhere in Congo. In fact, this is patently false. Enormous tensions divide the Havu majority—which includes 90 percent of the island's inhabitants—from the Pygmies, the second largest resident group, which comprises approximately 15,000 people, or 5 percent of Idjwi's population. (Scholars often view the word "Pygmies" as derogatory, but it is the name that Pygmies use to refer to themselves in Congo; they don't see anything wrong with it.)

Livingston Charles Shaniavu—a slim man in his 50s with a point to prove and an attitude fit for the task—is the leader of Idjwi's Pygmies. Persistent, intense, and bearing a clear chip on his shoulder, he reminded me of a French union leader on the eve of a strike.

Livingston Charles Shaniavu, the leader of Idjwi island's Pygmies, enjoys a beer in a local restaurant while giving me the latest news from his community. Just like every time I tried to take a picture of him, he stopped talking and smiling so that he would look authoritative in the photo.
Photo credit: Séverine Autesserre, 2019

He organized a meeting for me with the population of his village, which was attended by approximately 60 people. We all sat under a tree, talked for a couple of hours, and then visited their mud huts with thatched roofs. They treated me like a VIP, giving me and my translator wooden chairs while everybody else sat on the ground. They then started the meeting with an elaborate discourse thanking the "important professor from New York" for taking the time to speak with them. But I felt awful—powerless—as I often do when I conduct research among very destitute communities.

I type on my laptop while listening to the residents of Mafula (Idjwi, Congo), who sit on the ground opposite me and tell me about their daily life. Like all of the Pygmies I met on the island, they suffer from utter poverty, lack of access to education, and constant discrimination from their Havu neighbors.

Photo credit: Kalegamire Bahozi Kaer, 2016

My hosts explained that they face a daily struggle to survive. They don't own land and can't find other employment, so they have no money to buy food or clothes. Only 4 percent of Pygmy children are enrolled in primary schools, compared to more than 70 percent for other ethnic groups. They kept asking for my help, but there was little I could do.

In fact, the discussions I had with Livingston and his fellow villagers, and later on with other Pygmies living on the island, were eerily reminiscent of the research I had conducted 13 years before in Nyunzu, a rural town in eastern Congo. In both Nyunzu and Idjwi, Pygmies have no right to land or power. They live separately from the other communities—usually on the periphery of towns or villages. When I talked to members of the majority ethnic group (Havus in Idjwi, Bantus in Nyunzu), they would tell me: "Pygmies are lazy, dirty, and rude." "They are violent." "They stink." "They are stupid." "They don't work. Instead, they steal."

Onesphore Sematumba, the research director for a Congolese think tank, put these comments in context:

> In our mind, Pygmies are insignificant. They have always worked for us. For compensation we would give them old clothes, food that we do not want to eat. I know a man who married a Pygmy, and that was a huge scandal because... Frankly, you don't even eat with Pygmies. If you have a drink with other people, and there are Pygmies in the group, you'll give them a separate glass, just for them, and the rest of the people will share the same glass.

In fact, the prejudices are such that Havus often view and treat Pygmies as sub-humans—as animals. And the problem is more than just social discrimination: It can mean the difference between life and death. Both in Idjwi and in Nyunzu, I heard multiple stories of doctors refusing to touch or treat Pygmies, who then died from lack of care.

So, if Idjwi is prone to such extreme ethnic divisions, why hasn't it descended into violent conflict, as one might expect? "In Idjwi the Pygmies are so outnumbered," my interviewees offered, "that they know they would be exterminated if they were to rebel." But Pygmies in Nyunzu took up arms despite comprising a similarly small minority. In the mid-1990s, as Rwandan and Congolese rebel groups spread throughout the country, Nyunzu's Pygmies decided it was their opportunity to finally improve their position. They allied with Rwandan and Congolese rebels and fought their Bantu oppressors. This led to 20 years of rape and killing on both sides, resulting in the displacement of more than half a million people, a death toll in the tens of thousands, and the incineration of entire villages. By contrast, the most serious consequences of the ethnic tensions in Idjwi have been six deaths (in 2012), a few houses burned, and a few isolated incidents of beating, looting, and rape—terrible, but very different in scale.

We can't use the conventional approaches to peacebuilding, with their focus on governmental institutions, elite politics, development, and foreign intervention, to explain Idjwi's unique peace. State institutions are weaker there than in the rest of Congo. Kinshasa-based elites have historically found the eastern provinces difficult to control, plus Idjwi is an island, making it trickier to administer from the mainland. Far from resenting the state's absence, Idjwi's inhabitants have long welcomed it, priding themselves on their independence from any kind of outside power. They've also done their best to protect it. During Belgian rule, for instance, local residents would hide when colonial officials visited and refuse to provide them with food, timber, labor, or taxes. From the late 18th century onward, Idjwi became a refuge for those fleeing other regions of Rwanda and Congo, and the new arrivals further reinforced the residents' reluctance to let any central power control their destiny.

Today, only local public authorities pay attention to Idjwi, but they lack the funding to make a substantial impact. Besides, just like elsewhere in Congo, the island's inhabitants view what little state bureaucracy, police, and justice systems exist as inefficient, abusive, and highly corrupt—certainly not the key to peace or prosperity.

The same can be said for the local kings. Indeed, the patterns of migrations to Idjwi, its internal politics, and the intricacies of royal succession have generated significant hostilities around traditional power. These frictions led to several bouts of fighting and massacres in the 18th, 19th, and early 20th centuries. They enabled the Rwandan invasion of the island 150 years ago and facilitated the subsequent colonial rule by Belgium. Their most salient manifestation today is an entrenched antagonism between Idjwi's northern and southern halves. These two regions have their own *mwamis* (kings, or traditional chiefs), both of whom claim to be the legitimate ruler of the whole territory. Each leader also supports his own candidates in local and national elections and tries to keep any jobs or perks available for his own citizens. Besides, residents from each part have developed their own network of alliances with Congolese and Rwandan groups on the mainland surrounding Lake Kivu. While these simmering hostilities haven't led to mass violence recently, they make it difficult to believe the claims I heard from the kings, their advisers, and their cronies: that it is primarily thanks to the *mwamis* that the island is so peaceful.

To make matters worse, land is scarce. Together, three wealthy families and the Catholic Church own more than 75 percent of the island. This leaves approximately 30 square miles (80 square kilometers) for the other 300,000 inhabitants, in a place where farming is one of the only means of survival. Not surprisingly, access to land is the main source of contention in Idjwi. And again, none of the usual suspects help to resolve these tensions. State agricultural services are so expensive that local people avoid them, and local traditional authorities are too biased to be of help. In fact, the two *mwamis* belong to the families who control most of Idjwi's land.

As a result, poverty is omnipresent in Idjwi, where 82 percent of the island's inhabitants survive on less than $1 per day. The average life expectancy is 27 years, and only 6 percent of individuals live past age 40.

Unlike neighboring territories in eastern Congo, few foreigners have tried to make up for the state deficiencies. German, Japanese, and United Nations donors, along with non-governmental organizations and missionaries, have rehabilitated the main port as well as a few bridges, schools, health centers, and state buildings. They have also constructed a couple of factories, coached a handful of human rights activists and peace mediators, staged theatrical plays to promote social cohesion, provided some logistical and administrative support to local groups, organized a few anti-sexual violence trainings, and sent the occasional doctor, nurse, or agricultural specialist. That's it. These efforts are minuscule compared to the typical scale of international intervention in nearby territories. There, plenty of roads, buildings, and state services display billboards and logos broadcasting the support of dozens of nongovernmental organizations, foreign donors, and United Nations agencies.

The lack of international aid compared to the mainland is such that Idjwi's inhabitants kept bringing it up during our discussions. My research assistant Kalegamire Bahozi Kaer—a committed young man with razor-sharp intelligence and a great sense of humor—remarked:

> People say that Idjwi has never been at war, so the government forgets about us and the international community forgets about us. I wonder if they are trying to have us start a war so that we finally get aid projects!

To Kaer and his friends, fighting seemed like the only way to attract foreign donors and their income-generating programs to their home. As a Congolese from the mainland put it, "Idjwi is an island that suffers because there is no war there."

But Kaer did not take up arms, nor did the Pygmies, nor did any of the other inhabitants of Idjwi—not even those whom Chance tried to recruit. This is quite remarkable because the combination of poverty, land scarcity, state weakness, political tensions, ethnic discrimination, and geostrategic location that is found on the island has led to extensive violence throughout Congo and in many other parts of the world. But not in Idjwi.

It's not the fact that Idjwi is an island. It's not the fact that it lacks ethnic tensions. Nor is it the fact that a majority greatly outnumbers a minority. And it's not as if the state or other well-meaning outsiders help. No, there is something else going on in Idjwi.

Pathways to Peace

Here's what the rest of the world can learn from Idjwi: The island is peaceful not because of the government or any foreign intervention, but because of the actions of its own citizens, including the poorest and least powerful ones.

Idjwi's inhabitants have fostered what they proudly call a "culture of peace." I kept hearing this phrase—along with its companion, "we are a peaceful people"—from all kinds of acquaintances, whether Havus or Pygmies. One of the island's intellectuals explained: "We are all educated in the belief that we are special. There is a strong local identity. My grandfather always said that Idjwi has been an oasis of peace for more than 200 years." Ordinary citizens emphasized, "It's always been like that." Human life is sacred, there is a strong taboo against bloodshed, and traditional customs "dictate that we should love each other." From a young age, children learn to shun violence. And as adults, they choose to uphold and protect the culture of peace.

This nonviolent outlook shapes their political involvement. "We are a pacifist people," Idjwi's representatives declared during a large conflict-resolution conference in Goma in 2008. "We don't want any noise or any conflict." Representatives of other ethnic groups recalled finding this position quite "naïve."

It may appear simplistic, but it works. Take the perennial problem of abusive state officials, which is present throughout Congo and often leads to fighting. In Idjwi, nonviolent opposition is the norm. David Newbury, a renowned historian who spent years living on the island, recalled "a government authority who abused the population by demanding goats, food, and women." In return, local inhabitants boycotted him. They "simply refused to provide him with food, water, or social interaction—he was ostracized. And he quickly relented." Likewise, Kaer and his friends boasted that, by participating in peaceful youth protests, they managed to get rid of a public prosecutor and a territorial administrator who were harassing the population.

Many effective grassroots organizations also help maintain peace. When there is a conflict that individuals or families cannot resolve by themselves, instead of calling the police or the army or resorting to violence, people reach out to religious networks, traditional institutions, youth groups, elders' groups, women's groups, and so on.

The local church is particularly important. Most of Idjwi's inhabitants are Catholic, and—like in the rest of Congo—going to Mass is the main Sunday activity. Priests are thus very influential. But while the bishops and leaders within the local church hierarchy have fueled conflict and violence in the neighboring Kivus and during the 1994 Rwandan genocide, preachers in Idjwi focus on the daily lives of their congregations, and their sermons often emphasize living together in peace. When two families start fighting over land boundaries, presumed thefts or rapes, unpaid debts or dowries, children born out of wedlock, marriage issues, or destruction of crops by cattle, they often call on their priest to resolve the conflict. In fact, the priests receive so many such demands that the big parishes have set up Peace and Justice Commissions staffed by both clergy and laypeople.

Then there are the various traditional chiefs called the *mwamis*, especially the two local kings who, despite their tendency to fuel tension between the island's northern and southern halves, play a strong role in maintaining peace within their own territories. Such authorities still carry a lot of influence in Idjwi's conservative society. By custom, their functions include mediating disputes between their subjects, whether Havus or Pygmies. Accordingly, each of them holds court regularly, so that any resident can come and request their help. Both leaders also try to resolve conflicts indirectly, through their large network of representatives, lesser chiefs, and strongmen.

Marriage also works well as a peacekeeping tool. To this day, it has been the favorite way for the two royal families of the island to keep their rivalry under control, as well as to cement alliances with potentially threatening groups from the mainland.

As we know, the kings also often stoke disputes to pursue their own political ambitions, and their competitiveness generates significant tensions between northern and southern residents. So when the *mwamis* act as troublemakers rather than peacebuilders—or when they and their cronies do nothing—ordinary people take over.

Village elders, along with the village chiefs, have historically helped to assuage local tensions. So have ordinary residents of Idjwi, from healers and teachers to religious leaders and farmers. Over the years, these men and women have progressively gained the trust and respect of their neighbors, eventually becoming go-to mediators in case of problems.

In recent years, everyday citizens have also formed dozens of small clubs and community organizations, and they have done so without any funding. Although these associations were originally meant to promote human rights, development, or gender parity, they often ended up mediating local clashes and promoting better relationships between Havus and Pygmies. And just like the church committees, elders, and *mwamis*, they have a huge advantage over the state justice system: They provide free services. The gratis work of these associations is particularly significant in a country in which the bribability of the official judiciary often exacerbates, rather than mitigates, conflicts.

Surrounded by such a strong network, each citizen helps maintain the stability of his or her village by keeping tabs on potential rabble-rousers. People report any suspicious activities to the local chief—even if it means getting a member of their own family arrested. The island's inhabitants also watch over any outsider who comes to their neighborhood. They educate newcomers about the local norms, customs, and ways of life, and they keep an eye on those who might be up to no good. Whenever they see something wrong, they work with local leaders to prevent issues from escalating into violence.

When ordinary people can, they also take action on their own. A few years ago, for instance, my friend and research assistant Kaer started to worry about some younger kids and teenagers in his neighborhood. They were rude and disrespectful of authority; they used drugs and drank alcohol; they even tended to fight amongst themselves and tried to rape girls. So Kaer and his classmates set up a soccer club to give these would-be miscreants something better to do in their spare time. They acted as mentors, providing the kids with nonviolent role models. And so far, these efforts have proven effective—such delinquent acts are far less frequent these days.

Kalegamire Bahozi Kaer, my research assistant, stands on one of Idjwi's dirt roads while children run away playfully. He and I walked everywhere on the island without fearing for our security, even at night—something that would be unthinkable in other parts of eastern Congo.
Photo credit: Séverine Autesserre, 2019

Spats between spouses; quarrels between parents and children; squabbles among siblings, cousins, and relatives; disputes between residents and local chiefs or administrators; arguments between local people and outside authorities: All of these have the potential to generate village-, district-, province-, or even country-wide fighting, as we've seen over and over again in the rest of Congo.

You may well think that this idea is a bit far-fetched, but consider the terrible violence between Pygmies and Bantus in Nyunzu over the past few years. In one version of the story, the conflict started when a Pygmy man found his wife having an affair with a Bantu man. Other residents say that it was because Pygmies slaughtered cattle belonging to Bantus, or because Pygmies refused to pay taxes on caterpillars (a prized delicacy) they sold at a Bantu market, or because Pygmies provided information to help the Congolese army fight the local secessionist movement led by Bantus. Whatever the original reason might have been, all versions of the story agree on what happened next: The injured party asked local militias for help addressing their personal problem, and this triggered a whole cycle of massacres and counter-massacres.

Besides, banal incidents like this have led to conflicts not just in Congo, but all over the world throughout history. Are you also thinking about Helen of Troy and the Trojan War? I did—but I know, it's mythological by most accounts. However, in 532 AD, fans of two chariot racing teams (the Blues and the Greens) protested against the imprisonment of two of their fellow supporters by Emperor Justinian in Constantinople. This sparked a week-long riot that resulted in 30,000 deaths and the destruction of nearly half the city. In 1827, the Ottoman ruler of Algeria lost his temper during a dispute over a minor business transaction and struck the French consul with his fly-whisk. This gesture inadvertently triggered the French invasion of Algeria, 132 years of occupation, and a devastating seven-year-long battle for independence. In 1859, the United States and Great Britain deployed their militaries for several months over the shooting of a pig in the San Juan Islands. In 1925, Greece and Bulgaria went to war over a stray dog that a soldier had accidentally chased across the border. And in 1969, the Salvador-Honduras qualifying games for the soccer World Cup triggered a military confrontation between the two countries. The result: More than 3,000 people were killed and over 300,000 displaced. In each of these instances, like in Congo, otherwise unexceptional episodes resulted in massive armed conflict.

So Idjwi's inhabitants try to nip these problems in the bud. Adversaries reach out to local arbitrators, at times on their own initiative, and other times because of a gentle nudge from their neighbors, friends, and families, or a recognized mediator. Then local communities often oversee the arbitration process itself, make sure it reflects a wide consensus, and help implement the agreed-upon solutions.

In short, what keeps Idjwi peaceful is its inhabitants. Through their daily commitment to a culture of peace—the norms, customs, and values that have helped them mediate conflicts over the years—they have been able to maintain stability. I've seen ordinary people use this kind of approach—with variations of course—all throughout the world: in Colombia, Israel and the Palestinian territories, Somaliland. There, as in Idjwi, stability comes not through police cameras, guns, and ammunition, but through local participation.

Alternative Peacebuilding

Although foreign and Congolese elites often deride superstitions and magical beliefs as backward and seek to eliminate them, these strong beliefs actually support peace on the island of Idjwi. They help deter violence by both insiders and outsiders, just as different spiritual and religious systems help prevent violence in other countries.

For centuries, blood pacts have linked the main families of Idjwi. A middle-aged islander and human rights activist recalled:

> While I was growing up, when three elders of the neighborhood got together in a house in the evening, young children would come over, especially the boys, and we would start to talk. The old people would tell us how our ancestors used to live and how we should live now to enjoy peace and tranquility.
>
> They would especially tell us about the blood pacts. It's a friendship pact, in which you commit to never fire at someone and never cut him with a lance. For instance, if you and I became friends, to cement the friendship, you would cut my skin, pour my blood in a cup, and drink my blood. Then I would cut your skin and drink your blood, as a way to promise that I will never betray you. It's a traditional ceremony that is highly respected—although we have not used it too much these past ten years, due to concerns of hygiene and modernity and globalization.

This practice may have decreased in recent times, but the existing pacts remain in effect. And elders continue to teach children the meaning of these formalized friendship ties: Death will take those who harm members of the many other families with whom they are linked. The resulting fear is so strong that young people fled the Rwandan combatants who arrived in the mid-1990s—not necessarily because Idjwi inhabitants were afraid of the soldiers, but because they worried that the Rwandans would harass one of their blood-pact relations and somehow get them involved, bringing death upon them.

Furthermore, among the inhabitants of the surrounding provinces, Idjwi enjoys a mystic aura of fear and power. Of course, Congolese people are a bit embarrassed to discuss that with foreigners. But a group of human rights activists I met in the neighboring town of Goma finally clarified what my associates had hinted to me many times. After ten minutes of wishy-washy answers to my question "Why is Idjwi peaceful?," it was a woman, named Faulestine, who finally came clean:

> Since I was born, I've known that going to Idjwi meant looking for trouble. You can't go there for no reason. Idjwi has so many talismans! If you do

something wrong today, you'll be sent to Idjwi. Everybody is afraid to go there. Even the perpetrators . . . If you steal something, you'll be dead by the end of the day. Even the rebels don't want to go there . . . It's clear in our head that if you go to Idjwi, you're looking for death.

Everybody around the table agreed: Idjwi is the place where the guardians of the ancestral power live. And this does wonders to keep the island safe.

Historically, Idjwi was the "land of the damned," the "island of the pariahs." It's the place where, in past centuries, villagers from the mainland would send women who became pregnant out of wedlock. Today, in the eyes of people from the surrounding provinces, Idjwi is home to sorcerers who control lightning, have a privileged relationship with the spirits, and create powerful *jujus* (the local word for talismans). These magicians can cast protection upon you, but they can also harm you if you try to invade or disturb their island. For instance, in one of the many stories I heard, government officials tried to sell off a large piece of Idjwi's land, but their plane crashed en route. So, of course, local people credited the accident to Idjwi's sorcerers— these powerful adversaries who wanted to protect their territory.

While suspicions of sorcery and use of blood pacts may be unique to Idjwi, we can find similar convictions in almost all cultures. Religious beliefs and the fear of divine retribution promote nonviolence and peace activism in various sects—like the Quakers and the Jains—and have even halted deadly combats. During World War I, the German and British armies had to declare a short truce at the end of 1914 for no other reason than that it was Christmas and their troops were fraternizing between the trenches. In 2018, the Afghan government and the Taliban did the same to celebrate the end of Ramadan. Also in Afghanistan, a stranded American Navy SEAL owes his life to the *Pashtunwali*, an informal but powerful code that commands ethnic Pashtuns to assist and defend anyone in need—even their enemies.

In Liberia, as Leymah Gbowee told you, it's considered a curse for men to see their mothers naked. Thus, when push came to shove, threatening to rip their clothes off gave female peace activists the leverage they needed over male negotiators who wanted to leave ongoing peace talks. Further afield, in Papua New Guinea, the inhabitants of Bougainville Island rely on traditional rituals, at times merged with Catholic sacraments, to heal the wounds of their decade-long civil war. In Timor-Leste, they've used the *Tara Bandu* practice to that effect, and in Sierra Leone, *Fambul Tok* ceremonies. In Somaliland, the clan honor code serves a similar purpose, and in

Mozambique, ex-combatants perform purifying washing rites. The list goes on. Every culture has beliefs and traditions that insiders and outsiders can use to promote peace.

The lessons of Idjwi are clear. The most effective paths to peace include understanding and making the most of local belief systems, promoting an active culture of nonviolence, relying on grassroots associations, and strengthening community bonds.

Beyond Idjwi

It seems obvious that building on what works is as important as learning from what fails. And yet, this hasn't been the case until now. Most Congolese and foreign peacebuilders don't give Idjwi a second thought—after all, it's already peaceful, so why should they care? But there is so much that we can learn from the island.

The followers of Peace, Inc. usually try to address tensions in places like Congo through projects and aid programs—resources that come from the outside. And they interact primarily with elites: presidents, governments, rebel leaders, intellectuals, and state bureaucrats. Very few focus on tapping into and unleashing the talent and potential that local residents possess.

From looking at the basic facts of Idjwi—severe poverty, ethnic divisions, dysfunctional state bureaucracy, authoritarian government, surrounding violence—you would never guess that this place could become a haven of peace. Admittedly, north-south rivalries and Havu-Pygmy antagonisms still create a fertile ground for mass violence. But the very fact that Idjwi's residents have avoided generalized fighting for more than 20 years despite these underlying tensions is in itself a huge achievement.

What the island shows us is that no region is a lost cause. And if our usual expectations of who can stop violence—and how—don't apply to Idjwi, then why should we assume that they apply across the globe?

Every place is unique, and a multitude of factors specific to each context influence potential paths to peace. As you've seen, Idjwi's stability results from an organic, contingent process, rooted in its particular location, history, culture, and internal politics. It would be impossible—and absurd—to try to reproduce these unique factors all over the world. Just imagine the faces my Cypriot or Colombian friends would make if I were to advocate for blood pacts with their enemies as the key for peace in their regions! Rather than a boilerplate template, what we can learn from places like Idjwi is a set of principles that directly challenge some of the main assumptions underlying international peacebuilding efforts.

Contrary to what most politicians and interveners preach, outside experts, national leaders, and top-down approaches are not the only means to reestablishing peace. Bottom-up initiatives can also make a difference, and ordinary people have the capacity to address some of the deeper roots of their country's problems. Idjwi's inhabitants have done so. At their own local levels, they have found ways to address the challenges that we all face in our daily lives. And they have succeeded in the most difficult of circumstances.

Of course, grassroots achievements are fragile. Idjwi's peace wouldn't survive an invasion by a powerful armed group, whether from Rwanda or Congo, whether backed by the governments or by rebels. So top-down peacebuilding remains crucial, because it can help perpetuate the achievements of local residents. But, in the meantime, it's well worth it to invest time and resources in also building peace from the ground up.

If foreign peacebuilders want to help Congo and other war-ridden countries resolve their ongoing issues—and if Western citizens wish to decrease the tensions that divide their own communities—they should support the exceptional individuals who engage in these kinds of everyday conflict-resolution activities. They should pay more attention to the other cases of unlikely peace throughout the world—like Somaliland (which I'll discuss in depth later) and parts of Afghanistan, Colombia, and Iraq. They should seek out, build upon, and, if appropriate, encourage the alternative peacebuilding techniques that they usually disdain or combat, like Idjwi's blood pacts and magical beliefs. When designing their programs, they should involve not only the elites, who are typically based in national capitals, but also local leaders, intended beneficiaries, and ordinary citizens.

2

Role Models

When I asked Vijaya (the Indian-American woman who helped Luca turn away from his life as a child soldier) if she knew about cases of successful international peacebuilding in Congo, she didn't start out by describing her own achievements. Instead, she immediately brought up the Life & Peace Institute, often called by its acronym, LPI. "I admire their long-term vision," she said, "their truly participatory approach." LPI was a model that she used when she set up the Resolve Network and worked with Justine and Luca.

Her answer made me smile—I found a kindred spirit in Vijaya. When I advise foreign peacebuilders about making changes to the way they work, one of their first questions is often: "Is there an organization that did things right? A model we can follow?" And I too bring up LPI.

I typically start with the usual caveats: I have not yet found an agency or an individual that has avoided every possible mistake, detrimental assumption, and analytical error inherent to the standard approach that I call Peace, Inc. However, people and organizations are constantly finding innovative ways to move forward and avoid the mistakes of the past. Vijaya is one such person, and LPI is one such organization—one that, in my view, successfully works on the frontlines of peace.

In 1983, a group of religious activists came together in Sweden to brainstorm how to support churches in their conflict-resolution initiatives around the world. This conference led to the creation of a research institute, LPI, two years later. For the first decade, the staff conducted studies and advocacy projects around wars in the Horn of Africa, eventually devoting most of their efforts to the situation in Somalia. In the 1990s, they partnered with Somali and foreign scholars, and fully embraced the mantra of Dr. John Paul Lederach (a professor so influential that I think of him as the pope of peacebuilding), who believes that the best solutions to any conflict come from the very people experiencing it. Through its action in Somalia, and then in other parts of Africa, LPI progressively developed a new way to confront violence. This became their hallmark—a back-seat, bottom-up, flexible approach completely different from Peace, Inc.'s outsider-led, top-down, standardized strategy.

Today, LPI's work varies from place to place, as do its strengths and weaknesses. Even in a specific country, its programs shift depending on many factors: the personalities of successive leaders and employees, donors' requirements, local politics, etc. So, I won't discuss LPI's initiatives in general. Instead, I will focus on a country close to my heart, a country where LPI has proven that, contrary to popular belief, local peacebuilding *can* succeed even in the most divided societies, and outsiders *can* support grassroots efforts— you guessed it: Congo.

The Early Years

It all started with Hans Romkema, a Dutch man in his late twenties— friendly, open, and passionate. Hans went to Rwanda as a humanitarian worker for Save the Children in 1996 and moved to eastern Congo in 1998. When I interviewed him a few years later, he told me that his job in the Kivu provinces was fascinating but frustrating. He remembered that "there were always windows of opportunity remaining for peace at the local level," even in the places most affected by violence. He also found many villages where inhabitants were trying to resolve conflicts on their own. He wanted to boost these grassroots initiatives, but he never had enough time, money, or resources. With the help of his largest donor, the Swedish International Development Cooperation Agency, he started looking for an organization that wished to support local peace efforts, and he discovered LPI.

Hans conducted research for a year before officially launching LPI's programs in Congo, becoming its first representative there in 2002. He hired smart, innovative, and promising Congolese staff members like Déo Buuma—an ambitious and self-driven high school teacher. Unusually tall and increasingly plump (every year a bit more so, as being fat is a sign of beauty, wealth, and success in eastern Congo), Déo has the kind of contagious smile that, no matter your mood, always makes you grin in return. He had attended teacher-training academy, and then, in his free time from his high school job, taught himself how to drive, operate a computer, and speak English. Eventually, he used these skills to secure a job with an international agency helping Rwandan refugees. He then climbed organizational ladders, eventually working with Hans as the head of Save the Children's Bukavu office. Later, when Hans left Save the Children to start LPI's Congo program, he made sure that Déo would join him.

Together, Hans, Déo, and their colleagues defined how LPI would approach the Congolese conflict—in a markedly different way than most of the other aid agencies did in the early 2000s. To start, LPI would focus on the *causes* of violence rather than its consequences, and thus work on building peace rather than delivering humanitarian aid. Furthermore, its staff wouldn't follow the Peace, Inc. approach that virtually all peacebuilders were using at the time and that centered on governmental elites and rebel leaders. Instead, they would work at the grassroots with civil society activists. From the start, bottom-up work was LPI's trademark. Its staff would always try to address local issues in addition to the relevant national and international sources of tension.

Hans, Déo, and their team gained a deep understanding of local peace-building by contacting experts on the topic and attending training sessions on negotiation techniques. They compiled a list of ongoing grassroots peace efforts in the Kivu provinces, and then convinced the donor agencies of various European states to support these initiatives. Next, the group identified reliable Congolese partners and provided them with funding, logistical support, and training. They implemented projects ranging from peace talks between local elites to soccer matches between youths from communities in conflict, to micro-credit cooperatives for women from rival clans and ethnic groups. Hans also worked directly with armed group leaders to facilitate ceasefires and disarmament. At the time, LPI was one of the dozen or so aid agencies present on the rebel side of the frontline, one of the select few focusing on peacebuilding, and one of two with the ability to access the pockets of land controlled by Congolese self-defense militias and Rwandan rebels.

LPI's efforts paid off. In several villages of the Walikale, Masisi, and Rutshuru territories, native militias and rebel soldiers stopped fighting. In other towns and rural areas, warring communities resumed talking to each other and started designing strategies for reconciliation. It wasn't much, and it wasn't peace, but it was further than anybody had gotten before.

Deciding to work from the bottom up was an innovative and bold move at the turn of the millennium. And thus, as is so often the case with trailblazers, Hans and his colleagues faced a lot of criticism. When I met Hans, he struck me as the kind of person I could easily adopt as a role model, but he had many more foes than friends. Congolese people, highly distrustful of this foreigner who acted so out of the norm, accused him of anything and everything. Depending on who you spoke to, he was either a collaborator with the Rwandan army or with the Rwandan rebels, or a spy for the Congolese insurgents or for their opponents. He received death threats, and two rebel leaders actually tried to get him killed. He did not even have much support among other interveners. The diplomats and United Nations peacekeepers I talked to branded him as corrupt, unreliable, naïve, and dangerous. They accused him of trafficking arms and diamonds, fraternizing with the worst human rights violators, and so on. These accusations were unfounded and rooted in people's suspicions of anybody who dared disrupt the entrenched system of Peace, Inc. So Hans fought back. Then, progressively, he lost hope. And finally, in July 2004, he left LPI and went back home to the Netherlands, where he has worked as a freelance political consultant ever since.

I personally think that Hans's departure was a huge loss for LPI—and for Congo. The first time I interviewed him, he spent hours explaining the ins and outs of local politics in South Kivu. He went into so much detail that I got lost in his rapid-fire monologue. By 10 p.m. that night, my hand hurt from five hours of non-stop writing and my back ached from sitting for far too long—but he was giving me such incredible information that I still didn't want to end our discussion.

His network of local contacts was also amazing. In March 2004, for instance, a local militia kidnapped a Swedish evaluator subcontracted by LPI, along with his Congolese assistant. The perpetrators took their rings and valuables, even their shoes, and forced them to walk barefoot in the forest for hours. Had the abductees worked for any other organization, they would have spent weeks or months in captivity, with a high likelihood of torture, death, or both. (In December of the same year, for instance, a United Nations consultant and three of his local colleagues were kidnapped in a neighboring province, physically abused, tossed in a nearby lake, and held for two long weeks.) But thankfully, in this case, Hans was in charge. He reached out to his local and foreign contacts and got the two men released the very evening of their kidnapping. The ordeal was certainly traumatic for them, but it lasted less than a day, and they were not beaten, or injured, or killed—all thanks to Hans.

Admittedly, there *was* something wrong with Hans's work. But it was not the idea of focusing on bottom-up initiatives, nor his alleged wrongdoings. Rather, it was the very common idea that outsiders can lead the peacebuilding process. It took more than five years, countless problems, and two successive country directors for LPI to realize its mistake.

Taking Stock and Starting Again

In 2006, Alexandra Bilak began working for LPI in Congo. I couldn't help feeling slightly envious when we met, as she represented everything I wanted to be at the time. A French-English dual citizen, her command of both languages was perfect. She had already spent several years in Congo and Rwanda, so she knew the situation inside-out. She was also smart, dynamic, rigorous, no-nonsense, and more than willing to ruffle some feathers. She was obviously overwhelmed with work, yet she took hours to answer all of my questions and then look into her archives and send me tons of documents she thought would be useful for my research.

Alexandra quickly became concerned by her colleagues' practices: LPI claimed that it worked only in support of local partners, but in fact, its staff was directly in charge of countless mediation processes. Like any outsiders, LPI's teams had neither the knowledge, nor the skills, nor the networks to be fully effective. Additionally, the support they did provide to their Congolese partners was so thinly spread—over more than 40 local organizations—that it did little good. At the behest of one of their donors, Alexandra launched an in-depth evaluation, and soon thereafter came to the grim realization that LPI's programs had little long-term impact. In response, she started the lengthy process that transformed LPI from an agency working from the bottom up—but with the same tired relationship between insiders and outsiders—to one with an approach so effective that it now offers a model for international action.

Alexandra decided that LPI should stop implementing projects directly so that it would truly put local partners in the driver's seat. Furthermore, she resolved that it should aim for quality instead of quantity. From then on, it would focus on a handful of selected organizations, to which it would provide whatever support they needed. To link grassroots efforts to broader peace initiatives, it would follow Professor Lederach's advice and serve as an intermediary. It would help its urban-based local partners connect with both rural communities and national and international powerbrokers.

Rather than assuming that its staff or partners knew what the problems were and how to fix them, LPI would adopt the Participatory Action

Research approach. This was the pet strategy of André Bourque, a veteran consultant from Canada whom various LPI staff members described as "a kind of hippie with a white beard, who always wore colorful shirts" and covered the walls with giant, equally colorful Post-its scrawled with ideas from his never-ending brainstorms. This approach, which has been used to drive social change in all kinds of fields and organizations, relies on two core tenets. First, outside researchers, project implementers, and intended beneficiaries work together to understand problems and resolve them. In other words, they all function as co-investigators. Second, they embark on multiple, successive cycles of research, action, and reflection. In the peace world, Alexandra and her colleagues decided, Participatory Action Research would entail empowering ordinary citizens to develop their own analyses of their communities' conflicts, agree on the most feasible answers, and implement those solutions. LPI would constantly monitor its actions, partners, and effects, so that it could benefit from the advice of local people, learn from them, and adapt its strategies whenever necessary.

The resulting process was messy, time-consuming, and unconventional. But it worked.

In fact, LPI met with striking success the first time it ever put these principles in practice. From 2005 to 2007, a remote rural area of South Kivu province faced a spike in massacres, murders, tortures, kidnappings, and rapes. The violence affected more than 100,000 people living in 52 villages, all clustered around the Nindja chiefdom and Kaniola sub-territory. Eastern Congo was a far cry from being a peaceful place at that time, but in Nindja and Kaniola the situation was so bad, and the violence so horrific, that foreign interveners finally started to pay attention.

In the minds of the diplomats and the United Nations staff I met during those years, the culprits obviously belonged to the Democratic Forces for the Liberation of Rwanda, a Rwandan rebel militia whose members survive by preying on the Congolese population. The area was so remote and difficult to access, and the insurgents hid in the surrounding jungle so well, that there was no consensus on how many Rwandan combatants were based around Nindja and Kaniola—estimates varied from 6,000 to 20,000. What we interveners knew is that they were formidable opponents: ruthless, disciplined, well-armed, and with nothing to lose. And their escalating violence threatened the social order. In a growing witch-hunt, communities condemned neighboring villages for collaborating with the attackers. These accusations raised threats of retaliation and resulted in even more bloodshed.

A political solution to the crisis was impossible, because the Rwandan government refused to even consider letting these Hutu rebels back onto its territory. From its point of view, the combatants were perpetrators of the 1994 genocide. They still posed a threat to the Tutsi minority, and thus they should all be killed—not repatriated or resettled somewhere else. A military solution seemed just as unfeasible. The Congolese army and the United Nations peacekeepers launched large operations, but they failed to disarm the rebels, who then retaliated with even more rapes, kidnappings, and murders. The situation appeared hopeless.

Enter the local farmers' association. The first step, the peasants' representatives thought, was to understand how the militiamen operated. Indeed, as Urbain Bisimwa, the general secretary—a towering man with a bald head and a mustache—recalled, it was clear that the perpetrators did not strike at random:

> For instance, they would know that there was a wedding, that so-and-so had received a $2,000 dowry, and they would come and ask for that exact amount. Or they would know that Didienne, a high school student, had come over to visit her grandfather, and she would be kidnapped the very evening of her arrival. Bizarre stuff. At the same time there were people who did their business in the forest [where the insurgents were hiding], and nothing happened to them.

Urbain and his colleagues asked LPI for support and, together, they spent a lot of time talking with the residents and the people who had been kidnapped. At first, they constantly heard that "the perpetrators were more than 10,000, maybe even 100,000." All of the victims held "the exact same discourse," with each citing similarly impressive estimates of the number of combatants. To Urbain and his colleagues, something felt fishy.

The researchers kept coming back, and they kept interacting with the community, which slowly started to trust them. Tongues loosened up. "Sometimes," Urbain remembered, "we would arrive in the evening, when there was a funeral wake, and people would start drinking and they would start talking more freely." Eventually, the victims told them the truth:

This discourse, that's what they [the perpetrators] told us to say. In fact, they are no more than 15 people, and they are not from the Democratic Forces for the Liberation of Rwanda, they are a dissident group called Rasta.

This was "the first revelation." "This kind of information," Urbain believed, "foreigners could never get": He and his colleagues did so only because they were "a peasant association from the area," with ties to the local people, rather than outsiders—and because they took the necessary time to deepen their relationships with the community.

Progressively, they also learned the names of these combatants. It turned out that the Rasta included two young guides from Kaniola, as well as a handful of people who had lived in the village and thus knew who owned cows, when soldiers slept, who the regular visitors were, and so on. The combatants also had local accomplices. Most important were the village chiefs who let the fighters come and buy products on their territories, enabling them to obtain whatever they needed to enjoy a comfortable life. Urbain was struck by the stories he heard and the photos he saw: "You wouldn't have imagined that they lived in the forest, because they had everything: generators for electricity, good food, creams to whiten their skin..."

Surprisingly, even some of the victims were sympathetic to their kidnappers. One of them, an 11-year-old girl who had been kidnapped, eventually came back to her village pregnant. But living with the Rasta was the life she knew, and she cried: "They are people like us! Yes, they are criminals, but I want to go back to them." The rebels also had hostages who acted under duress—"If you don't do what I want, I'll kill your entire family." They had no choice but to comply. "And that way," Urbain concluded, "the Rasta managed to control the entire area."

The peasant association tried to pass on the information to the Congolese army, but their efforts backfired. Not only did the local commandant not believe them, he also suspected them of being in league with the rebels. So they changed tactics: They went through LPI, and slowly, progressively, managed to convince the local head of the United Nations peacekeeping mission, who then persuaded the Congolese army commander to change his strategy. Once both of them understood that the perpetrators didn't belong to the Democratic Forces for the Liberation of Rwanda, and actually included Congolese people, it became clear that high-level negotiations with Rwandan elites were pointless. So were large military operations based on the assumption that the combatants were outsiders with no local information and little knowledge of the local terrain.

Using this new intelligence, the Congolese soldiers killed three Rasta and scared away the others, thus putting an end to the massacres. The peasant association then started the long process of social reconciliation. They organized a roundtable in which all of those involved told their own version of the story. They helped the inhabitants identify, arrest, and prosecute accomplices of the Rasta; they also clarified who had acted under duress, and thus whom should be left alone. Slowly they helped rebuild the communities and reestablish links among residents and between villages. And just like that, the Rasta problem became history.

To Urbain, LPI's support was crucial for three reasons. Firstly and most importantly, members of the peasant association learned the Participatory Action Research approach: spending a lot of time interacting with and listening to affected populations. All the while, Urbain, his colleagues, and LPI acted only to amplify local voices and ideas, not to direct them. Then there was the funding that covered transportation costs, paid the association's staff, etc., and which the group used incredibly efficiently: The whole initiative cost around $50,000 to $60,000—a stark contrast to the millions of dollars Peace, Inc.–type efforts typically require. And finally, LPI helped the peasants' representatives connect with the local heads of the state administration, the Congolese army, and the United Nations peacekeeping mission, and convince them to adopt a new strategy. Without LPI's endorsement, Urbain recalls, none of these powerful people would ever have taken his small rural organization seriously.

The Golden Years

The next country director, Pieter Vanholder (a Belgian native in his 30s), continued the transformation started by Alexandra. Participatory Action Research became LPI's core strategy, the methodology that all of the staff and local partners I met over the years kept proudly referencing.

The broad principles are simple: LPI bases its actions on in-depth local expertise and rejects universal approaches to peacebuilding. It relies on local employees supervised by a few foreigners, who often have extensive preexisting country knowledge. It does not implement programs directly; instead it works with and through a few handpicked local organizations, whose main role is to support people on the ground. In this model, it is not foreigners based in capitals and headquarters who conceive, design, and implement conflict-resolution initiatives. Instead, it is the intended beneficiaries and community members themselves—including ordinary people—who, with the help of LPI's local partners and Congolese staff members, are the arbiters of their own peace efforts.

To better understand how these principles work in practice, take how LPI approached the longstanding, deadly conflict in the Ruzizi Plain. It's a mountainous part of South Kivu province, near the border with Burundi—a green, fertile region, with sparsely populated hills covered by mist, cassava plants, and low-rising bushes. Most of us at the time analyzed the fighting there as a simple struggle between two ethnic groups and their foreign patrons: the Banyamulenge supported by Rwanda versus the Babembe allied with the Congolese government. In 2007, three Congolese organizations, Réseau d'Innovation Organisationnelle (Network for Organizational Innovation, the local branch of a Protestant church), Action pour le Développement et la Paix Endogène (Action for Development and Endogenous Peace, a grassroots nonprofit organization), and Arche

Cows rest in a field while Congolese soldiers and local villagers walk past. The misty hills in the distance, the tin- and straw-roofed houses, and the presence of soldiers make this scene typical of the seasonal migration of livestock in the Ruzizi Plain.
Photo credit: Life & Peace Institute, 2012

d'Alliance (Ark of the Covenant, a human rights association), decided to address these tensions with LPI's support.

From the start, conflict analysis—i.e., understanding who's fighting, why, and over what—became just as important as the design and implementation of solutions. LPI and its partners progressively realized that antagonisms between herders and farmers were in fact at the heart of the conflict. For years, all of the residents had fought over the seasonal movement of livestock in the area. Banyamulenge and Bafuliiru herders needed to move their cattle from the highlands to the lowlands in search of pasture. On the way, the cows would often eat or damage crops cultivated by Babembe and Bavira farmers, who responded by killing the animals and, at times, their herders. Not only did the tensions have local consequences—many people were murdered and injured in scuffles and retaliations—but they also took on a broader dimension as armed militias fought on behalf of each ethnic group. On top of that, the Babembe allied with the Congolese government and army, while the Banyamulenge joined efforts with Congolese rebel movements and, on occasion, Rwandan and Congolese military units.

So, although the conflict was fought along ethnic lines, it was not merely an ethnic dispute or a proxy-battle between Congo and Rwanda, as interveners believed. Rather, it was a complex disagreement between all residents over land rights, which was exacerbated by preexisting ethnic divisions and further strained by otherwise unrelated local, provincial, national, and international disputes between militias, rebel movements, and governments. If you feel like you have to read that again to understand it, that's precisely the point: These conflicts are complicated, and they can't be summarized in a sentence or two; you need a 50-page report—way too long to catch the interest of busy foreigners, to the despair of LPI staff.

Tobias Petrelius, one of the Swedish LPI staff members at the time, recalled that when he worked in Kosovo and Georgia with another organization, he used to see conflict analysis "as a dead space, something to be done before we acted." What he and his colleagues focused on was the product, the end result. By contrast, once he joined LPI, he discovered that "conflict analysis was key." What mattered was the process—the fact that they wanted to understand the local points of view, because that was "the vehicle for people starting to come together."

In the case of the Ruzizi Plain, this process took three years. "That conflict analysis was given time to mature," Tobias explained. "There was no hurry in trying to understand or coming up with what we would do," because they would not be the ones deciding on solutions; local people would direct LPI's actions. Of course, Tobias was stressed—after all, he "wanted a product"—but both Pieter (the country director during these years) and Loochi Muzaliwa (a key Congolese staff member of LPI at that point), kept reminding him to trust the process and be patient. "People will tell us what they want to do," they always said, "let them talk, give them time; we don't have to produce a report now."

"That was a tremendous realization for me," Tobias recalled: Conflict analysis "was not a dead space where everyone sat, but a very active, challenging process, with a lot of meetings, a lot of action going on."

LPI's innovation was also the conviction that this task should be completed by the very people involved in the fighting. As Loochi explained to me:

> Most peacebuilders don't have time to understand the conflict. They use standardized responses. Nowadays, a lot of people call themselves "experts," and so when there is a problem, they imagine that they already know the answer—they have their catalog of responses: This is issue X so this must be therapy Y.

In contrast, the LPI team believed that foreign interveners, consultants, experts, and even local partners should not try to understand the context in order to intervene as soon as possible. Instead, the role of outsiders is to help local people to better analyze their problems—by providing safe spaces for residents to share their perspectives and confront difficult questions, which helps them move from accusations to enquiry. And, as Pieter emphasized the first time I met him, "local people" means "everyone: civil society, politicians, army officers, soldiers, rebel leaders, ministers, farmers, women's groups, so that they are *all* on board." This includes not only village residents but also the individuals "who pull the ropes in [the capital] Kinshasa"—not only victims and peacemakers but also perpetrators. In Pieter's words, "We don't work with firemen only and leave pyromaniacs on the side."

In this new approach, the conflict analysis process is dynamic. It keeps evolving based on the peace initiatives implemented, the challenges faced, and the results achieved. In the case of the herder-farmer fighting in the Ruzizi Plain, LPI's initial plan was to analyze the context, organize a large meeting to ensure that all parties agreed with their findings, and then put in place inter-communal mediation structures. But the teams quickly real-ized that, contrary to what they thought, they weren't dealing with cohe-sive groups that were unified in their hatred of the other ethnicity and that squarely supported the militias fighting in their names. In fact, the very first action that local people requested was a dialogue to foster unity within each community. To them, this was an essential step to prepare the planned meeting with their opponents—and so LPI obliged.

It took two and a half years of intra-community dialogue, preparation, and shuttle diplomacy (with the three aforementioned Congolese organiza-tions going back and forth between the various ethnic groups) before local residents felt ready to meet with representatives from other groups. This time was far from wasted: As the dialogue progressed, it became clear that each ethnic group was divided internally. Members had a lot of different views of the "enemy." They also had misgivings about "their" militias, whose combatants committed rapes and extortion even amongst their own people.

Residents of Southern South Kivu (Congo) discuss the initial findings of the Participatory Action Research facilitated by Action pour le Développement et la Paix Endogène, Réseau d'Innovation Organisationnelle, and Arche d'Alliance with support from the Life & Peace Institute. Women were also involved in the process, but in this specific instance, they met separately.
Photo credit: Life & Peace Institute, 2009

Progressively, through the sharing of these stories, the various local armed groups lost some of their legitimacy. They stopped being able to claim that they protected community members, represented their beliefs, or fought on their behalf.

In March 2010, an inter-community roundtable finally took place among 60 representatives of the four ethnic groups. Four days of intense discussion, followed by additional meetings in 2010 and 2011, eventually resulted in farmers and herders coming to a series of comprehensive agreements, which were endorsed by all of the traditional chiefs and local administrators. The agreements were both creative and highly specific to the unique situation on the ground. They stipulated routes for moving cattle from the highlands to the lowlands with minimal disruption to farmers. They also mandated that pastoralists would pay taxes to traditional chiefs, who in exchange would allow them "customary passage" on their lands through specific trails and would ensure their security. Lastly, they established mediation committees in which representatives of both herders and farmers would smooth out any tensions that might arise.

One of the lessons Pieter learned that year was that his team had to increase its engagement with the ministers, rebel leaders, and business elite, among others, who lived in Kinshasa but nevertheless had a stake in the area—because of a piece of land they owned, or a herd of cattle they kept, or an uncle or cousin they supported. Some of them indeed tried to convince their kin and allies to stop participating in the roundtable, or to ignore the agreed-upon measures that jeopardized their own interests. One of the Congolese vice presidents even asked LPI's donors to cut off funds. So, from then on, LPI and its partners made sure to keep the relevant national elites informed at each step of the peacebuilding process, giving them ample opportunities to provide their input and voice their concerns. That way, capital-based elites progressively came on board, and they ended up supporting the peace efforts rather than trying to derail them. This part of LPI's work actually became so important that, in 2013, the organization set up a liaison office in Kinshasa and sent Zaurati Nasibu—a smart, dedicated woman, and a long-time Congolese staff member—to take charge.

Meanwhile, in the Ruzizi Plain, thanks to LPI's funding and logistical help, the local organizations marked paths alongside fields for herders to use with their livestock (complete with crosswalks marking the way for cattle), and they erected public signposts to clearly indicate the proper routes. Pastoralists started paying the required taxes, often in the form of a cow or a case of beer.

Primus, a locally-brewed Congolese lager, was often the currency of choice. (I don't like beer, and I find Primus too bitter, but I have to say, for currency it's pretty tasty!)

As for the mediation committees, again things did not go as initially planned—and yet, they eventually worked. Instead of immediately setting them up, as LPI originally intended, the participants of the inter-community roundtable opted for more preliminary dialogues within their communities. The residents eventually agreed on the new structures, but with a twist: These should not be tribunal-like arrangements, aimed at deciding who among the parties in conflict was right and who was wrong, but rather forums in which all could continue the dialogue. And again, LPI obliged.

In the following years, from 2011 to 2014, these grassroots committees (all staffed by volunteers that LPI and its affiliated local organizations trained and supported) arbitrated conflicts before they escalated into violence. For instance, when a cow owned by a Banyamulenge herder left the path, trespassed on a field cultivated by a Babembe farmer, and destroyed its crops, or when an influx of cattle from Rwanda threatened the area's fragile equilibrium, these committees would intervene and mediate a solution before things got out of hand. In 2014, local inhabitants also formed three new negotiating teams to convince combatants to demobilize.

Of course, all of these committees faced a myriad of issues. They were too few for the vast territory they had to cover, so they had trouble informing all of the inhabitants about the new agreements. They also did not find consensual solutions to every single conflict they mediated (close to 1,500 per year!). But they did learn, quickly, and their success rate in reaching an accord and resolving disputes jumped from 28 percent in 2013 to 68 percent in 2014. In addition, these local mediation units had two significant advantages over the state judicial system. They enabled impoverished people to seek redress without having to pay for lawyers and "buy" the support of the judges— a practice that regularly fuels tensions rather than dampening them, as the losing party often feels wronged and seeks revenge. Plus, the units' rulings focused not so much on punishing the offender, but on promoting mutual respect and finding solutions that worked for all involved.

The combined effects of the clearly marked paths, improved relations between ethnic communities, and troubleshooting work of the committees were tangible. For several years, the seasonal migration of cattle took place with little violence. Dozens of militiamen handed in their weapons. Ethnic groups that were accustomed to conflict slowly resumed the process of collaboration—sharing the same market, for instance. All in all, many residents saw their quality of life improve significantly.

Using the same approach and methodologies, LPI supported two other bottom-up initiatives in North and South Kivu during that same period. One of them centered on Déo's native territory of Kalehe—and, to manage this peacebuilding process, Déo left LPI and created a new Congolese association focused on resolving conflict through Participatory Action Research.

To make a long story short, the initial results were so promising that Congo eventually became LPI's largest program in the world. In addition, LPI's approach became a model for other peacebuilding agencies working in the region—not only Vijaya's Resolve Network, but also the stabilization unit of the United Nations peacekeeping mission.

At the time, LPI in Congo exemplified what I believe to be the ideal relationship between outsiders and insiders. The expatriates stayed for several years and focused on developing their knowledge of local conditions and their local networks. They viewed their roles as that of providing technical and financial support to the plans formulated by local stakeholders. They did their best to maintain a low profile and emphasize the work and achievements of grassroots communities first, and Congolese partners second, rather than broadcasting their own contributions.

Pieter himself struck me as a model foreign peacebuilder. I met him multiple times over the years, and he always appeared warm and friendly, respectful of all those around him, thoughtful, and passionate about his work. When I asked his colleagues to describe him, the recurring adjectives were "committed," "knowledgeable," "funny." Above all, they emphasized, "he loved Congo." Indeed, Pieter spent close to ten years there—the first three with the humanitarian agency Oxfam, and the rest with LPI. He married a Congolese woman and had two children with her. He learned local languages and studied local cultures and histories. He stayed away from other expatriates and instead tried to develop strong friendships with Congolese people. In short, he did his best to integrate into the surrounding community, to such a point that there was even an unfounded rumor that he had applied for Congolese citizenship. If you don't live in the aid world, Pieter's behavior may seem like common sense—after all, how could someone help build peace in a country whose language they don't speak and whose people they have no personal relationships with?—but, in fact, these attempts to integrate locally are very much the exception to the Peace, Inc. norm.

From my point of view, the work that LPI and its partners did over the years—and the impressive results they achieved—is also important because it challenges many assumptions that the proponents of Peace, Inc. hold dear. Peacebuilding does not need to come after the war is over. Conflict analysis is not a preliminary step that has to be completed as quickly as possible. Supporting grassroots efforts does not mean deciding what strategies local people should use or resolving conflict for them. It does not always require a lot of money. Furthermore, dialogue is not enough. You can't talk your way into peace; you need to act as well. It should not be a one-off event, and its outcome is not more important than the process itself. And we can't do all of that quickly.

Instead, peacebuilding can and should take place while fighting and massacres are still ongoing, precisely because it helps control violence. Conflict analysis is an integral part of the operation, and supporting grassroots efforts means letting intended beneficiaries—including ordinary people with no specific skills, education, or qualifications—decide how they want to address their own problems. Dialogue is an ongoing, long-term process, which is beneficial in and of itself, but needs to be complemented by concrete follow-up actions. All of this can be done on a limited budget (remember that approximately $50,000 was all it took for Urbain's local farmers' association to resolve the Rasta problem and bring peace back to more than 100,000 people), but it takes time, a lot of time. And the resulting peace is something that needs to be worked on and maintained afterward on an everyday basis.

The Fall and the Legacy

I found LPI's staff and approach so innovative that I mentioned them as *the* example to follow in a 2011 op-ed I published in the *International Herald Tribune* (the former name of the *Global New York Times*). The article brought a lot of attention to LPI, which became flooded with requests for meetings, briefings, advice, and partnerships from politicians, donors, diplomats, United Nations officials, and the employees of various nongovernmental organizations. This was perfect for visibility and fundraising, and great to help spread the idea of Participatory Action Research among other interveners, but it also added a lot of demands on the time and energy of the staff.

In hindsight, all of this attention may be one of the reasons for the subsequent downfall of LPI's programs in Congo. Well-meaning donors and foreign agencies tried to scale up LPI's achievements and reproduce them in various parts of the Kivus, but in most cases they based their action on a superficial understanding of the LPI model. To them, it simply meant rolling out as many programs as possible at the local level to address local conflicts, ideally through local structures that LPI had already set up or supported. They didn't realize how crucial it was for intended beneficiaries to design the whole program, and how much time and flexibility such an approach required. In short, they focused on quantity and speed, rather than quality.

LPI's local partners were, in Pieter's words, "bombarded with offers of funding"—but usually for projects based on donors' and foreign agencies' priorities and timelines. In the resource-strapped environment of eastern Congo, this financial bonanza was too good to pass up, so the Congolese organizations expanded their staff and activities to try to meet the demand— they, too, opted for quantity over quality. To make matters worse, the influx of money created perverse incentives: to participate in grassroots conflict resolution not because of a desire to build peace, but to access cash and other resources. As Tobias deplored, this phenomenon resulted in "a lot of incompetent people" starting to "mess with very sensitive issues" and eventually destroyed some of the local peace committees in the Ruzizi Plain. Members started fighting over who could control the funds available, excluding whomever they could from getting a piece of the pie, refusing to participate in meetings when they didn't receive a per diem, and so on. They eventually lost legitimacy in the eyes of their communities, and their effectiveness and influence crumbled.

Of course, Pieter was not perfect either, and he received his share of criticisms. Provincial authorities and United Nations officials complained that he met with them too rarely. His staff and local partners viewed him as "too rigorous" in terms of funds and time management and "too quick" to dismiss ideas that did not square with his views. His integration into Congolese society was also more difficult than one might expect: Apart from his close family, he never felt that the rest of his Congolese friends and colleagues fully accepted him. Even worse, in 2015, Pieter and his donors started suspecting that some of LPI's local staff and partners had embezzled funds. What Pieter viewed as "one of the best times of [his] life," "a dream" job, slowly became "an ordeal."

Pieter tried to make things work—investigating the corruption accusations, firing the people responsible, rebuilding trust with donors and partners. By that time, however, he was burned out. Above all, he felt betrayed. People he trusted, supported, mentored, even considered as friends, had taken advantage of him, and that sent him reeling—in his words, his "whole world exploded." Plus, he received messages threatening him and his family, some of them clear and open, others veiled and, actually, even more disquieting. Pieter sounded so depressed and hopeless when I met him in 2015 that, like many of his friends and colleagues, I started worrying about him. The following year, he broke down, gave up, and left Congo. Just like Hans ten years before him—and many other peacebuilders I've met throughout the years—the combination of overwork, death threats, suspicions, and betrayal eventually proved too much to bear.

Pieter's departure marked the beginning of a dark period for LPI. Although nobody conclusively proved that funds had been mishandled, its donors lost trust and abruptly cut funding. LPI's headquarters also decided to stop all of the Congo programs for a while, in order to clean up the administration and finances of the country office and reassess its involvement. As a result, it fired virtually its entire staff based there. As of the time of this writing in 2020, LPI still has only a small office in Congo, with a few staff members who look for funding and ways to resume larger initiatives. Their ethos and operating principles remain the same: They focus on bottom-up action, Participatory Action Research, and working *with* local people instead of on their behalf.

Deprived of financial support, LPI's partners, including Réseau d'Innovation Organisationnelle and Action pour le Développement et la Paix Endogène, in turn have had to close down some of their own projects. In certain cases, this happened before they managed to consolidate the achievements of their ongoing work and address the broader dimensions of the local conflicts. In 2015, for instance, the Congolese army mounted operations against Rwandan and Congolese rebel groups based in the southern part of South Kivu, and political tensions escalated in neighboring Burundi. The consequences in the Ruzizi Plain were dire. Local militiamen who had demobilized and were waiting to be reintegrated into civilian life took up arms again. The fighting also caused massive displacement, rendering the livestock routes obsolete and overwhelming the local committees with requests for mediation. Violence between herders and farmers picked up, leading to a familiar string of murders and retaliations. By 2020, at least

300 people had died, 300,000 were displaced, and more than 140 villages had been burned to the ground.

I used to feel guilty about writing the op-ed and contributing to the destruction of what I admired so much, until I asked Pieter about it years later, in 2018. He burst out laughing and told me that my article was the best thing that could have happened to LPI at the time, because it publicized their efforts in a way that he and his colleagues never had the time or the skills or the inclination to do. What transpired afterward was not my fault, he said—so I'm trying hard to believe him, and I'm hoping even harder that the same thing won't happen to any of the organizations I mention in this book.

When Pieter, Déo, Loochi, and their colleagues reflect on this sad turn of events, they often emphasize the lessons we can all learn from it. First, throwing money at problems does more harm than good: The fleeting flood of funds for grassroots conflict resolution in the Kivus distorted and destroyed local peace efforts rather than boosting them. Second, peacebuilders need better procedures to preempt the misuse of resources and deal with accusations thereof. After all, suspected embezzlement is hardly unique to LPI's partners or to Congo. Accusations of corruption abound in all kinds of organizations, from American investment firms (the Bernie Madoff Ponzi scheme) to global aid agencies (the millions of USAID dollars that went missing in Afghanistan) to Russian political parties (along with Austrian, Belgian, Brazilian, Chinese, French, Italian, Indian, Senegalese, and Spanish ones). Immediately shutting down every single activity might be the right thing to do for a bank or a hedge fund, but using this tactic on a peacebuilding project carries a tremendous cost—paid in human lives. Lastly, bottom-up initiatives need to be complemented by top-down efforts involving provincial, national, and international elites. Otherwise the hard work done at the grassroots can all too easily be jeopardized by tensions at the treetops, as happened in the Ruzizi Plain right after the 2010 round-table and then again when the Congolese army and Burundian rebel groups launched new operations in 2015.

As for Pieter's personal experience, it may have been awful—a failure, as he reportedly saw it at the time. However, his efforts to integrate locally gave him a much better understanding of the context and a legitimacy among Congolese people that no other expatriate had. All of this made him a better intervener.

And what's more, even if LPI had to virtually stop their Congo operations for a while, and even if the current office is a mere fraction of what it used to be, large parts of their intervention did last. To start, it is in part thanks to Pieter and his colleagues' tireless efforts that foreign peacebuilders started paying attention to grassroots conflicts in Congo. As I'll explain later, bottom-up peacebuilding still does not receive the support that it deserves, but enormous progress has nevertheless been made over the past ten years—at least now the followers of Peace, Inc. discuss the importance of local conflict resolution, rather than dismissing it out of hand. LPI was certainly instrumental in that.

In addition, all of LPI's former partners that I talked to afterward—Réseau d'Innovation Organisationnelle, Action pour le Développement et la Paix Endogène, Urbain's Union Paysanne pour le Développement Intégral, etc.—proudly mentioned how they still used the Participatory Action Research approach they first learned from LPI, and how it was the best possible way to address conflicts on the ground. So did the former Congolese staff members—people like Déo, whose peace association now operates in exactly the same way LPI did in the Ruzizi Plain, and Loochi, who has tried to spread the LPI gospel to every organization he subsequently worked for. And, just like it did with LPI, the approach works. The last few times I met with Déo, for instance, he couldn't stop talking about how land-related tensions and violence had decreased significantly in his territory of Kalehe. Both residents and outsiders credited his Association pour la Paix et la Concorde for a large part of this improvement.

The foreign staff also carried on LPI's legacy. A few of them went on to work for the Stabilization Support Unit of the United Nations peacekeeping mission, and some of its initiatives—like the multi-million-dollar, multi-donor, multi-organization strategy meant to stabilize the whole of eastern Congo (dubbed "I4S")—clearly reflected some of LPI's analyses and operating principles. Many other interveners I met also mentioned how influential LPI had been to their own thinking: people working for organizations as varied as Resolve, International Alert, and the United Nations. And LPI used the approach its staff had developed in Congo—and the lessons learned from both its successes and its challenges—to shape its programs in East Africa.

Not to mention that some of LPI's concrete achievements in Congo still live on. The peace committees put in place in the Ruzizi Plain continue to arbitrate disputes, promote better relationships between communities, and work to prevent conflicts from escalating into large-scale violence (although they, too, desperately look for funding in order to maintain and expand their operations). And many grassroots structures that LPI's partners helped create in other parts of the Kivus, like in Masisi and Kalehe, also continue to thrive. Above all, it's thanks to LPI that thousands of men, women, and children are still alive and still have hope for the future—and, in my book, that's what really matters.

Outside-the-Box Peacebuilding

LPI's experience in Congo was not a walk in the park. It did not end the war in the whole country, or even in one province or district. Its staff made mistakes and faced challenges. Something went wrong financially—either because funds were actually embezzled or, in the best-case scenario, because the money was properly managed but the reporting channels were not strong and transparent enough to convince donors.

However, these administrative problems should not distract from what LPI did accomplish. Over the years, its team helped decrease conflicts in several parts of the Kivu provinces. They devised a new approach to confronting violence, as well as concrete ways for foreign staff to help local people build peace from the ground up.

Rather than focusing on outsiders' knowledge and ideas, as the adepts of Peace, Inc. usually do, LPI builds on the expertise and insights of insiders. Its story shows that putting local people in the driver's seat is not a naïve and impractical idea, nor a bumper-car slogan useful for raising funds but devoid of applicability on the ground. Instead, it is a principle that leads to noteworthy achievements in addressing violence.

Alexandra, Déo, Hans, Loochi, Pieter, Urbain—these extraordinary yet ordinary people have developed one of the most effective peacebuilding strategies I have ever seen. Their experiences give us a sense of how Peacelanders can and should behave. They provide a model to follow, a way to avoid the usual, counterproductive relationships that take place so often between insiders and outsiders in conflict zones.

PART II
PEACE, INC.

3

Insiders and Outsiders

Before my first mission as an aid worker, in Kosovo, I naïvely expected my colleagues' attitudes, behaviors, and strategies to be as varied as the countries they came from and the organizations they represented. But instead, I quickly noticed striking similarities among foreign peacebuilders—whether they were peacekeepers, diplomats, donors, or the staff of international or nongovernmental organizations.

I wanted to fit in, and it wasn't hard. I attended coordination meetings, followed standard security procedures, threw going-away parties, and socialized primarily with other expatriates. Instead of learning the local language, I became fluent in the language of intervention, with its technical vocabulary and alphabet soup of acronyms. In brief, I became an ordinary resident of Peaceland (the world of aid workers who hop from conflict zone to conflict zone) and an adept at Peace, Inc. (the conventional but problematic way to end wars—a formulaic, top-down, outsider-led approach).

My next deployments—in Afghanistan and Congo—went smoothly. True, these countries have little in common in terms of geography, culture, language, people, or political dynamics. And yet, both times, I was in familiar territory. The way we foreigners related to each other and to the local population, the manner in which we organized our lives and went about our work—it was all very similar to what I had experienced in Kosovo. After learning the ropes once, I never again felt out of place when I arrived in a new war zone.

This way of living and working is so common that most interveners hardly notice it. But these habitual relationships between insiders (people living in conflict zones) and outsiders (the foreigners who come to help) seriously jeopardize the chances of attaining peace.

Peacelanders often assume that local people do not have what it takes to eliminate violence, but that outside experts do. This assumption lies at the core of the Peace, Inc. approach to wars, creating multiple challenges for both domestic and foreign peacebuilders. As a result, standard international strategies rarely work, and they are at times counterproductive. This is why it is so important that we learn from people like Leymah and her fellow women activists, Vijaya and Justine, Kaer and Livingston, Pieter and Déo, and shake up the routine.

Enduring Stereotypes

Michel Losembe is a Congolese businessman. He also happens to be the father of one of my all-time favorite students. When I met him, he told me how frustrating he found it that international interveners tended to talk down to their Congolese counterparts and dismiss local ideas out of hand. Losembe, who is of mixed African and European descent and has lighter skin than most Congolese people, once decided to conduct a social experiment. In a meeting abroad, he pretended to be Puerto Rican. The participants' attitude toward him was completely different from anything he had encountered before. Foreign aid workers spoke to him more respectfully, listened to him more attentively, and considered his ideas more seriously.

Losembe's experience is typical of the relationships between insiders and outsiders in Peaceland. Foreign peacebuilders widely believe that inhabitants of conflict zones lack the expertise, skills, qualities, and resources they need to resolve their own problems. In fact, Peacelanders often see local people as uneducated, lazy, self-centered, violent, and untrustworthy. When I was working in Congo in 2003, a Tunisian peacekeeper lectured me about the normalcy of the abuses I was witnessing:

> Do not come here with your European sensibilities and your European ideas. Violence and corporal punishment are a part of the life here. Congolese people are used to it. Whipping people is the way of Congo. The Congolese do not feel it the same way we do.

Another time, a European diplomat erroneously claimed that the Congolese approach to violence was essentially identical to that of European citizens in the Middle Ages; in both cases, he alleged, perpetrators and victims considered sexual abuse natural. A humanitarian donor similarly explained to me that "for generations, eight women out of ten have been raped by their father, their uncle, or a neighbor." Widespread violence, looting, entrenched corruption, complete disorganization: Many aid workers, including those from Africa, reacted to such events with a resigned "Congo is as Congo does."

As a Peacelander, I encountered these pejorative stereotypes everywhere: "Afghans are violent," "Albanians are mafiosi," "Burundians are hypocritical liars," "Israelis are rude," "Serbians are cruel," "Sudanese are inept and aggressive," "Timorese are backward," etc. In fact, during my first few years as an aid worker, I found myself inadvertently parroting many of these prejudices. Usually, I would just repeat what I had heard around me. And every time I paused to think about it, I would find fodder for these claims. A Congolese politician demanded a bribe in exchange for the landing permit I needed to send a plane full of medicine to my colleagues on the frontline—so, from that single incident, I assumed that all Congolese politicians were corrupt and oblivious to the needs of their fellow citizens. An Afghan warlord tortured and killed thousands of residents in the Hazarajat region where my Médicos Sin Fronteras team ran a hospital—so I began to believe that all Afghans were dangerous. One of my Kosovar colleagues had family ties with the local mafia. He embezzled some of our program funds, and when we caught and fired him, he told my boss that his "cousins" would come and kill us. So, I became adamant that we couldn't trust any of our local staff members, regardless of where in the world we were.

These stereotypes are so widespread and common that, during interviews, numerous foreign peacebuilders I spoke with emphasized how surprised they were when they met "good" local people: hardworking citizens, leaders with a vision for their countries, activists who managed to make a difference for the better, or authorities who did not abuse their positions of power.

Because I held negative views of local people, I tended to associate only with other foreigners. This lack of contact with host populations made it difficult for me to realize that the few "bad apples" I encountered did not represent all local residents. On occasion, I would realize how unfair it was for me to judge an entire group of people based on the actions of a handful of individuals, and I would feel ashamed of myself. And yet, I wished to fit in so badly that I didn't want to challenge those widespread stereotypes, embarrass my peers, or force awkward discussions. So I remained silent.

Of course, interveners like Vijaya, Pieter, Hans, Alexandra, and many others strive tirelessly to rein in these types of careless comments. They emphasize that few individuals back home would be able to endure the hardships that host populations face with such strength. They point to the numerous local residents they know who are competent, intelligent, selfless, reliable, honest, hardworking. However, at best, they are able to change a few people's opinions or prevent conversations from getting out of hand. They rarely manage to improve the overall image of local people.

Such negative beliefs cause a pervasive atmosphere of suspicion. During my first years working abroad, for instance, I was trained to be very careful when sharing security information or sensitive papers. I could pass them on to my foreign contacts, but not to local colleagues—because they might tell their friends (and these friends could be combatants, spies, warlords, corrupt governmental authorities, you name it), or because they might use it to harm us. The underlying, largely unfounded assumption was that our local associates, by nature of their being Afghan, Congolese, Kosovar, etc., were part and parcel of the broken system that we outsiders were trying to fix, and thus they could not be trusted.

Entrenched stereotypes also influence numerous programs. Take, for instance, all of the trainings on sexual violence that peacebuilders organize for army and police officers in war zones—places as culturally varied as Colombia and South Sudan. Sexual abuse by law enforcement and military is a problem everywhere in the world, including in ostensibly peaceful countries, and well-designed violence prevention courses can have real results. But too often, in conflict zones, the instruction focuses on delivering the simplistic message that raping women, and sexual abuse in general, is bad and usually illegal. As if the reason why combatants raped and tortured was because they didn't know it was wrong! This is, in the officers' words, demeaning, humiliating, and *very* frustrating. A better approach would be to understand why combatants rape *despite* knowing that it's wrong and illegal (they may follow direct orders from their commanders, or try to assert their masculinity, or take revenge for perceived humiliations, or a myriad of other reasons), and then adjust the intervention to tackle the root causes of this behavior.

Furthermore, these biases often lead outsiders to overlook valuable peacebuilding resources, such as existing local organizations already working to resolve conflicts, and the local people themselves, whose knowledge and capacity for forgiveness can make all the difference between success and failure—as you've seen in Idjwi and the Ruzizi Plain.

"Outsiders Know Best"

The widespread belief that residents of conflict zones need foreign expertise to solve their own problems is also due to the hierarchy of knowledge that exists in Peaceland. In the eyes of most interveners, what makes a good peacebuilder is education and work experience in specialized topics, like election organization or cross-cultural conflict resolution.

The job postings that foreign ministries, peacebuilding agencies, donors, and other interveners publish for positions in conflict zones usually call for specialists in gender, rule of law, disarmament and demobilization, elections implementation, environmental protection, and so on. The desired skills typically include a graduate degree and several years of experience in the field. Country expertise and knowledge of local languages are not required—or, when they are, they usually appear last on the list. In the words of James Scambary, a long-time aid worker from Australia, because of this "tenacious belief that to teach people to grow carrots you have to have a degree in growing carrots," it's too often "curriculum idiots" who get jobs on the ground: well-educated experts with little to no local experience.

When I started my career in the aid world, I viewed this baffling practice as perfectly logical and legitimate—just like most interveners do. Peacebuilding organizations are global in scope, so they need staff who can be deployed at a moment's notice regardless of where the next crisis breaks out. Plus, as I'll explain later, their favorite strategy is to resolve conflicts from the top down through interactions with national and international elites, most of whom speak at least some English. It therefore makes sense to hire a generalist rather than, say, someone fluent in Wolof and familiar with West African histories, societies, and cultures, because the latter can only work in a few countries, while the former can operate everywhere.

What's more, my colleagues and I proudly viewed our work as a highly professional endeavor for which experts were needed. From this perspective, war and poverty are universal issues, rooted in human nature, which is the same everywhere. They are technical problems, too, which can be solved using technocratic solutions based on best practices and a large body of universal, time-tested ideas. These solutions can often be standardized into templates that help cut down the time and energy needed to respond to crises, and thus save lives on the ground. That's why foreigners trained in general peacebuilding techniques, with extensive experience in a variety of conflict situations, enjoy the most clout.

Certainly, knowledge of local languages or cultures would be nice—it would make our lives on the ground a bit easier, and more fun. But this is seen as a luxury, not a necessity. Like many of my colleagues, I once firmly believed that a few books were enough to learn the basic features of the local histories and societies, and along with a few key phrases in the local language, I would have everything I needed to perform my best on the ground. So, in my graduate studies, I focused on acquiring the kind of general skills that would boost my chances of getting a job upon graduation. In other words, I tried my hardest to become one of James Scambary's "curriculum idiots."

I was not alone. In Cyprus and South Sudan, I found only a handful of foreign peacebuilders who spoke Greek or Turkish, or Arabic or Nuer. Of the 1,700 police officers stationed with the United Nations in Haiti in 2005, only 100 could communicate in French or Creole. Some 140 diplomats worked at the United Kingdom embassy in Afghanistan in 2010, and only three of them were proficient in an Afghan language. The first time I attended a management meeting for the peacekeeping operation in Congo, I was stunned to see that participants literally couldn't understand each other: Some of them had no command of French, others no knowledge of English, and yet others could only communicate in Spanish.

Unsurprisingly, not speaking the local language makes it very difficult for interveners to interact with residents and thus understand the conflicts they seek to address. One day, I accompanied a patrol of United Nations peacekeepers from India to a remote Congolese village called Kaseguru. Fighting between government and rebel soldiers during the night had left several people dead, so the peacekeepers went in to investigate. Unfortunately, none of the officers or soldiers spoke a word of French or Swahili. During the whole time we spent in the village they stood on guard near their pickup trucks while their translator—an energetic man in his 30s—went farther down the road to speak with local leaders and residents. We left as soon as he was done. It wasn't until we were in the car, on the long drive back to the base, that the translator told the peacekeepers what kind of information he had received. I had spent some time with him in the village and, as a French speaker, I had understood part of the discussion, so I knew that he forgot quite a few important points and misrepresented several others. No wonder the United Nations had a hard time grasping the already complex situation on the ground!

United Nations peacekeepers in full protective gear keep watch in Kaseguru (Congo), while their translator investigates recent fighting between rebels and the Congolese army there. The soldiers spend less than 20 minutes in the village; they never leave the main road, and they don't interact with anybody.
Photo credit: Philippe Rosen, 2011

Throughout my time in conflict zones, I've met very few foreign aid workers who possessed deep preexisting knowledge of their countries of deployment. Instead, most were specialized experts who had done the same technical jobs in other war situations—as soldiers, lawyers, doctors, diplomats, accountants, social workers, or professional managers of aid projects, for instance.

As far as promotions go, most peacebuilding agencies reward the number of missions completed in different countries rather than the amount of time spent in a particular area. In fact, I have often heard interveners discredit foreigners who stay too long in a specific place (like Hans and Pieter) as having "gone native"—implying that they are too immersed in the local culture, and too close to host populations, to effectively carry out their mission.

As a result, peacebuilding organizations experience high turnover among expatriates. Diplomats usually move every two to three years; nongovernmental organization staff stay six months to three years (with an average of a year in a mission); peacekeeping contingents rotate every six months to a year, and United Nations civilian employees have six-month contracts that they usually renew a few times. Even development practitioners, who pride themselves on working for the long term, change countries on average every two years. At this pace, foreign peacebuilders simply aren't able to develop an in-depth understanding of the local situations that they want to change. Instead, they hop from conflict zone to conflict zone and continent to continent, at times serving multiple tours a year. In the wry words of a peacebuilder in Timor-Leste, some of her colleagues end up bragging that they "have 'created peace' for 20 countries by the time they are 30!"

When peacebuilding organizations do hire people with language skills and knowledge of local conditions, they routinely send these staff members outside their area of expertise. When I was looking for a job after finishing my PhD, I applied to both academic and nonacademic positions, including one as political affairs officer with the United Nations mission in Congo. I had already worked in the country for more than a year and had written a 600-page dissertation on its conflict and local politics. Naturally, I thought I might be a good fit. I never heard back from the recruiters—not unexpected, given that they must have sorted through thousands of applications for the job. What did surprise me, however, was the phone call I received telling me that I was short-listed for a position as economic advisor with the peacekeeping mission in Burundi.

Every time I tell this anecdote to friends who work in Peaceland, they all have their own version of that same story to share with me. One of them, for instance, is a historian who specializes in the politics of Congo's Katanga province. He accepted a position with the United Nations peacekeeping mission in Congo in 2010, and did everything he could to be deployed to Katanga. It never worked. He was first sent to the Oriental Province, a thousand miles away, where he had no contacts and little knowledge of the local situation. After more than a year of lobbying, he eventually managed to get transferred to another part of the country—but ended up in the capital, Kinshasa.

Who's the Boss?

For me, the focus on education and specialization in aid organizations meant that my career as an intervener got off to a great start. At the age of 23, my very first job out of graduate school was as the assistant country director in Kosovo for Médecins du Monde (the French branch of Doctors of the World). Did I speak Albanian or Serbo-Croatian? Not a word. Did I know Kosovo well and have an extensive local network? I had been there once, for a week, as part of an internship. Was I an expert on Kosovar history, culture, and politics? I started reading my first book about the Balkans on the flight there—and I never finished it. So, you might wonder how on earth I got the position. It's simple: I had a solid training in political analysis, a good command of English, two fancy master's degrees, and some field experience in other postwar places and developing countries. That was enough for me to get a position as protection officer (the person in charge of our program to help Kosovar minorities) and to be promoted to assistant country director within a couple of months.

I was incredibly proud and excited at the time. I felt important, glamorous, courageous. I tried to do my absolute best, so I worked 12 hours a day, seven days a week. When I received a promotion, I thought I deserved it because I was doing such a great job. But looking back, I feel terrible about this period of my professional life. I wasted a lot of people's time and energy. I spent hours trying to "help" and "coordinate" the work of an independent local doctor. Dr. Sonja was the only person providing medical care to residents stuck in the Serbian enclaves of a territory controlled by Kosovo Albanians. In six months, I achieved absolutely nothing. I couldn't provide what she really needed: more cars and doctors, and more safety for her patients. And she didn't care about what I had to offer: a rational, organized, routine way for her to make her rounds—which I had painstakingly designed, after lots and lots of meetings, and which I now realize was utterly unnecessary.

I'm also quite ashamed when I think about my assistant, Nerim. I was tasked with analyzing Kosovo's political and security situation, and writing reports for my supervisors, but it was *he* who had the expertise and the training that I lacked. He had 20 years of experience investigating political issues, a tremendous knowledge of the Balkans' history, politics, and culture, and he had lived in Kosovo all his life. He was also older and wiser than I was. But I was the foreigner, so I was in charge. I had never managed anyone in my life before, and I had no idea how to deal with him. I eventually found a way to keep him occupied: I asked him to compile, translate, and summarize clippings from the local press. He religiously posted his work on our bulletin board every morning, and none of my colleagues ever read it. Even I often failed to find the time to do so. It was such a waste of time, energy, and talent.

Then Médicos Sin Fronteras (the Spanish branch of Doctors Without Borders) sent me to Congo as its head of finance and administration. I was thrilled to have this amazing opportunity: This was a management position with even more prestige and responsibility. At 24, I was the mission's third in command. In addition, I would discover a country I knew nothing about. And I would learn a lot: I had absolutely no background in any of the things I would do—no financial skills, no administrative knowledge, no experience supervising human resources—so I received a week of training at the Médicos Sin Fronteras headquarters, and then the assumption was that I would learn on the job.

Again, I worked as hard as I possibly could. And again, my bosses were happy: I received praise, and I was offered the opportunity for further deployment at the end of my mission. But in hindsight, I'm mortified when I think about my Congolese assistants, Christine and Olivier. *They* had university degrees in finance, administration, and accounting, as well as years of experience working for various international agencies. Much like Nerim, they could have easily done the job without me. And yet, I was the foreigner. I had the degrees from prestigious Western universities. I had worked in other conflict zones. So naturally, I was the boss. And not a very good boss at that: I was in way over my head, and so stressed that I ended up devoid of empathy, patience, and several other important human qualities.

Sadly, my experience is nothing out of the ordinary for peacebuilders in conflict zones. In sharp contrast to the LPI model, virtually all aid and peacebuilding organizations place foreigners in management and local people in the lower-level positions. Very few local people make it into leadership roles in international agencies in their countries of origin. To move up the organizational ladder, they have to go abroad and become expatriates.

Most foreign peacebuilders now pay lip service to the idea that "local ownership" is essential for successful interventions. However, very few interveners practice what they preach the way LPI and Vijaya's Resolve Network do. They rarely solicit local input when strategizing. When they meet with local populations and authorities, it is to flesh out pre-established project proposals rather than to question whether the programs themselves are appropriate. In their jargon, the main goal is usually either "sensitization" (convincing authorities and populations that the program is good for them) or "mobilization" (getting local support for the implementation of the initiative). Not to mention that, if anyone is consulted, it is usually the national or local elites—rarely the ordinary citizens who are meant to benefit from the international initiative. Likewise, local partners may participate in the validation of previously designed projects, the process of follow-up, and the evaluation of impact, but not in the actual conception of the intervention. In most cases, the crucial design phase instead takes place far away from on-the-ground realities: in headquarters and capital cities, among high-ranking interveners, based on information gathered from other outsiders, with foreign donors signing off on the results.

In fact, if you travel throughout conflict zones, you can't help but realize that foreigners actually "own" the aid and peace projects: Their logos are plastered everywhere. It is common to see, for instance, a police station with an insignia indicating that the building was funded by the United States Agency for International Development and constructed by the United Nations Office for Project Services, while nearby billboards emphasize that a road was rehabilitated by the International Rescue Committee, thanks to a grant from the European Union. This could be next to a hospital whose entrance bears the emblem of Doctors of the World and its donor, the French government.

This all results in a massive power imbalance. In Haiti, for instance, local residents call their country "the Republic of the NGOs." After the 2010 earthquake, a journalist asked the interior minister what he would do. His answer: "You should ask the NGOs."

This hierarchy of outsiders over insiders is so ingrained that it is extremely hard to correct, even for those who want to. My husband Philippe used to work for the humanitarian organization Action Against Hunger and visited his Africa-based colleagues regularly. During one of his trips to Kenya, he raved about how progressive the team there was. Admittedly, the management staff included only foreigners, but they did try to promote local leadership. Kenyan employees chaired the bi-weekly coordination meetings on a rotating basis, and even the lowest-ranking members got their turn.

As the days passed, Philippe became less enthusiastic. Despite all of the efforts by the international supervisors, the Kenyan staff still felt powerless. They believed they couldn't say no to any of the expatriates' requests, regardless of what it cost them. For example, when one of the foreigners would ask a Kenyan colleague to run an errand, the Kenyan employee felt he had to comply, even if it meant forfeiting his lunch break.

Philippe spent a lot of his time there trying to address this issue, but even he did not appreciate just how insidious it was. One morning, he entered the office's kitchen, saw that there was no coffee left, and started grumbling. The woman cleaning the kitchen became so scared at the idea that an expatriate—especially someone sent by the headquarters—might be upset with her that she dropped everything she was doing and ran to buy coffee. Within ten minutes, Philippe got a cup. "And yet," he told me sheepishly, "I had not requested anything. I had just showed that I was annoyed."

Tense Relationships

The power imbalances, interveners' negative stereotypes of local people, their failure to consider local ideas, and their assumption that foreign solutions are better than local ones inevitably generate resentment among host populations. Michel Losembe, the businessman who realized that he was taken more seriously when he pretended to be Puerto Rican, described how he and other Congolese elites felt during meetings with Peacelanders:

> We are imprisoned in a sort of cliché that makes us feel uncomfortable: "You are incompetent, corrupt, inefficient, and you cannot work in a group." When you are a Congolese today, and you arrive in a meeting, you have to overcome this conception and make an effort to tell yourself "I am not incompetent, I am not corrupt, I am not inadequate" even before you can start talking.

A Congolese military officer similarly complained that he was "treated like a kid." A Cameroonian lawyer recalled being "very ill at ease" when he was attending informal gatherings of interveners, and "very frustrated" by what he heard, wondering: "Who are these people to talk about my country in this manner?" A Sri Lankan friend had the exact same reaction while attending foreigners' parties in her country and in the United States. Even local people valued by Peacelanders resent these blanket stereotypes. One morning in Goma, I interviewed Vianney Bisimwa, a conflict-resolution expert, who ranted:

> They [foreigners] have the nerve to tell people: "You are among the rare brilliant Congolese individuals that I've met in peacebuilding" . . . I hear that *all the time*. It really annoys me . . . It's not a compliment! There are many Congolese people who have fantastic ideas about peacebuilding.

Sadly, the standard narrative is so pervasive that numerous local inhabitants buy into the idea that foreigners know best. My friend Christiane Kayser, a German aid worker, regretted that "often Congolese people ask me to do things that I know the guy who's sitting next to me and who's from the area knows how to do better." But she also added, on a hopeful note, that "this is changing with the new generation ... The fact that they don't automatically think: 'She's white, she must know better; she's white, she must be the one to ask,' is progress."

If you are like many of my readers, Christiane's last comment may make you wonder how much the legacy of colonialism affects relationships between foreign peacebuilders and residents. It's a fair point. Colonization too relied on the idea that African, Asian, and Latin American people were barbaric and their societies backward. White people believed that they were smarter, less corrupt, and less violent, so they had a duty to "civilize" other parts of the world—a "civilizing mission" that conveniently helped advance Western political and economic interests across the globe. Europeans and North Americans knew little about the societies they were trying to fix, and yet, because of the entrenched perception that outsiders knew best and local knowledge was primitive, they always put themselves in the leadership ranks.

Most colonies gained their independence between the end of World War II and the 1970s, but European and North American states, companies, and citizens have continued to dominate the globe economically, politically, and culturally. In other words, the legacy of colonial power relations is ever-present. Today, interventions often target places that bore the brunt of colonization, and the persisting assumed superiority of outsiders over citizens of the Global South helps perpetuate Peace, Inc.

Imagine if I were to tell you that the United Nations had tasked a conflict-resolution expert from, say, Kazakhstan with ending gun violence in Baltimore, but that neither this expert nor any of her bosses were familiar with American racial politics, police-community relationships in the United States' inner cities, debates over the right to bear arms, or even spoke English—you would think this is absurd, wouldn't you? The very idea of sending foreigners to a country they have never visited or studied so they can help people they know nothing about makes sense only in a world where individuals and institutions place the highest value on outside expertise and deem local input unnecessary. So, in places as varied as Congo, the Palestinian territories, and Timor-Leste, certain local intellectuals have told me that the interveners' behaviors reminded them of what their parents or grandparents said colonialism felt like: demeaning, dehumanizing, and infuriating.

Across many conflict zones, I've heard local people complain that many foreign peacebuilders are "arrogant," "condescending," "bossy," and "preachy," and that they provide aid in a "humiliating" manner. My friend Onesphore Sematumba, a political analyst based in Goma, even remarked that "with all their self-confidence, [interveners] think that they can construct Congo without the Congolese."

In many cases, local partners actively reject any sort of foreign imposition, regardless of whether or not they support the strategies and the values of the international programs in question. At times they simply drag their feet— they arrive late to meetings, "lose" papers, or pretend to misunderstand. On occasion they actively embezzle funds. Sometimes they outright refuse to participate in international projects, eventually causing them to fail. (As you can imagine, interveners see all of these behaviors as further evidence that their negative views are well founded.)

Mean jokes about peacekeepers also abound. In the beautiful Mediterranean island of Cyprus, residents mock them for doing "beach keeping" rather than peacekeeping. Throughout Central and South America annoyed inhabitants refer to the Naciones Unidas (the Spanish translation of United Nations) as "Vacaciones Unidas" (United Vacations). People in Côte d'Ivoire jest that although peacekeepers are expected to monitor breaches of the ceasefires, in fact they "n'y voient rien" (French for "They see nothing," which sounds identical to the name "Ivoirians"). Other types of agencies are also the butt of jokes. Residents of countries where English is the vehicular language—like Kenya, for instance—often joke that "NGO" stands for "Nothing Going On."

Thus, host populations share some responsibility for the divide that exists between them and the interveners. They often make it difficult for international peacebuilders to integrate into their surrounding communities, as you remember from Pieter's experience trying to develop strong friendships with Congolese people. In addition, in many settings, local residents also treat all foreigners as if they were the same. When, as a Peacelander, you take a stroll in a provincial town or a rural village in Congo, South Sudan, or Rwanda, for instance, chances are that you'll have an identical experience whether you are a diplomat or a volunteer, African-American or Caucasian. Children follow you everywhere, dare one another to touch you, mimic the way you walk and talk, sometimes make faces or throw rocks, other times they jostle to hold your hand or ask you to take a photo. Adults rarely rein them in. Often, they stare themselves, and sometimes, they participate in the catcalling and mimicry. The first time you experience this, you'll likely find it cute. The tenth time, you'll find it a bit tiring. The thousandth time, chances are that, like me and most of the people I know, it will get on your nerves so thoroughly that you'll dream of the day you're back home and can walk down a street anonymously. This may seem like just a minor annoyance, but this kind of everyday interaction further widens the gap between foreign peacebuilders and host populations.

My students often ask me whether race, gender, or ethnicity might attenuate this divide. They hope that ethnic or religious similarities might help them connect with local populations. This would be great, given how diverse aid workers are in any given location; they usually come from all over the world, profess all kinds of religious beliefs, and comprise people of all genders, ethnicities, and sexualities. So, chances are that any host population might find a bunch of foreign peacebuilders who share their continental origin, spiritual orientation, or physical appearance. Unfortunately, however, residents of conflict zones see little difference between outsiders who may be from their own continent, religion, or racial and ethnic groups, and those who share none of these similarities.

Everywhere I've worked, local people have reminded me that "a foreigner is a foreigner." Regardless of our skin color, language, ethnicity, religion, or anything else, they can spot us easily. Our body language—our way of speaking, walking, dressing, smiling, talking—is different. In fact, to many residents of remote areas, we interveners literally all appear identical. A case in point: In South Sudan, a colleague once confused me with my friend Shirley, who had worked there for several years. The Sudanese man claimed that she and I "look exactly the same." Granted, we're both women, with skin lighter than most African people. But Shirley is Chinese-American with beautiful, deep brown eyes and black hair. I've got blond-ish hair, blue eyes, and freckles—and I'm taller! In Congo, I've also been confused with a lot of my Asian, Caucasian, Latin, and African-American colleagues—both men and women.

Even worse, no matter where we come from, what we look like, what we believe in, or how intimately we've experienced war and intervention, we Peacelanders share the same internal culture and daily routines that separate us from local populations and compound the tensions between insiders and outsiders.

Peace, From Afar

Headquarters require foreign peacebuilders to adhere to strict security procedures—which I've always had a hard time respecting—such as living in a fortified compound surrounded by high walls and barbed wire, driving with the doors locked and windows closed, never giving a lift to people outside your organization, and staying in the rich parts of town at night. These standard practices are perfectly reasonable ways to deal with danger, but at the same time they further divide foreigners from local populations. As one Kenyan peacebuilder I interviewed put it, they transform expatriates into "other kinds of human beings"—superior, detached, and alien. Personally, I felt so selfish every time I was in one of my fancy, air-conditioned cars, and on the side of the road I saw women walking with huge loads on their heads or a sick child in their arms. They would seem downtrodden, exhausted; they might see my car and light up, look at me with hope, a smile,

A United Nations soldier stands guard while Congolese men and women press along a barbed-wired fence at the South African base of Mushake (Congo). The villagers are watching the peacekeepers celebrate their Heritage Day with their guests: other foreign peacebuilders and select local elite, notably police and military officers.

Photo credit: Philippe Rosen, 2011

a gesture, but I knew that I was forbidden from giving them a ride, so we always passed by, remote, inaccessible, with our doors locked and our windows up.

These security rules also make it much more difficult for peacebuilders to collect and analyze information, and thus to understand the conflicts that they mean to address. For instance, when I was working for aid organizations, my bosses often told me that I couldn't speak to certain warlords, because they were "too dangerous." However, doing so was the *only* way to get specifics on the location, timing, and reasons for the fighting—details that my team absolutely needed in order to gain access to people who were dying by the hundreds. While such procedural precautions ensured our safety, they severely inhibited our ability to do our job well.

What's more, foreign peacebuilders operate on what they see as a moral high ground: Their primary goal is to "help others," and they identify local populations and authorities as "beneficiaries." There was a saying that came up constantly in my discussions in Central Africa: "The hand that gives is always higher than the hand that receives."

To top it all off, interveners share a similar, insulated lifestyle in conflict zones. These experiences go beyond obvious, superficial commonalities like driving in big SUVs, frequenting favorite bars, and engaging in inside jokes. On a deeper level, they include the feeling of belonging to a specific group—a sense rooted primarily in the reality of being an outsider living and working far from family, in constant fear, and confronting a lack of basic facilities while performing a job that is emotionally draining. So after work, when foreign peacebuilders want to unwind or just relax, most of them end up reaching out to people like them—people who share their experiences in a tiring and often frightening environment.

Many conflict hotspots feature weekly social gatherings where nongovernmental organization staff members, United Nations officials, and diplomats mingle. When I was in Kabul in 2002, my social life revolved around Thursday evening drinks in the compound of the World Food Program. There was even alcohol at these parties, although it was illegal in Afghanistan at the time, so I got to enjoy terrible Pakistani whiskey and awful Tajik vodka. In Juba (South Sudan) in 2011, the places to be were the headquarters of the International Committee of the Red Cross on Wednesday evenings and the main compound of the United Nations peacekeeping mission on Saturdays. In Goma (Congo), it was usually the Wednesday happy hour at the upscale restaurant Le Chalet and, on weekends, it all depended on which hotel had the best chef at the time. Always fancy, beautiful, and very expensive, these venues were well beyond the means of ordinary citizens.

After several years of hopping from one country at war to another, chances are that you'll know others like you wherever you end up in the world—as long as it's a conflict zone. My husband and I have such a wide network all over the planet that whenever I decide to research a new conflict, I just need to put a note on Facebook and, within a few hours, I have a list of individuals to contact when I arrive. This social network does wonders to ease peacebuilders' deployments in new foreign postings and fulfill their desire for community. We often meet people we know from previous missions and slip right back into the way we lived, worked, and socialized when we were in that other country. These kinds of links also make the weekly expat parties that much more attractive, because they're where you're likely to meet people you know from other places or organizations— and having friends on arrival further decreases the incentive to socialize with host populations.

Relationships between local people and expats become even more fraught when safety conditions deteriorate—situations in which foreigners are typically more dispersed, isolated, and frightened. To my friend Christiane, who has decades of experience, life as an international peacebuilder is like "dancing on a volcano." The whirlwind of difficult living conditions, stressful work assignments, and much-needed revelry often results in a "work hard, play hard" mentality. It also produces tight bonds between foreigners, along with significant and intense feelings of camaraderie. My status as an intervener was frequently enough to garner invitations to dinners, parties, and meetings, or to gain access to confidential information and documents. Unsurprisingly, "family" has become the word of choice for many seasoned expatriates when describing their fellow foreign peacebuilders, people who become islands of comfort amidst a sea of the unknown.

This all makes perfect sense from an individual point of view. But at the end of the day, it leads interveners to live in a sort of bubble, where they interact mostly with other outsiders and lack contact with host populations. During my first few months in Peaceland, I recall feeling surprised that my Kosovar colleagues were rarely included in the many late-night get-togethers that foreign aid workers organized. In my organization, on the other hand, we threw a party each month, invited our international friends and all of our local staff, and danced with them to the tune of local music, a custom which

I later learned other interveners viewed as weird: They got bored with the music, at times felt uncomfortable with the local staff being there, and considered our close relationships with them promiscuous.

One event I attended in Congo illustrates vividly the divide between the two groups. A friend of mine who worked for a United Nations agency had invited about 50 people to his farewell party, including all of his Congolese and foreign colleagues, plus a few expatriates who worked for non-governmental organizations. When I arrived at the restaurant, I saw all of the seats occupied by Congolese guests, and at the back of the room were all of the foreigners—and only foreigners—crammed around one table. The party lasted for hours, and the two groups never mixed. A year later, while visiting another friend in Timor-Leste, I observed a similar split: The United Nations compound in Dili had two cafes, with the expatriate employees frequenting one, and the Timorese staff frequenting the other.

White container offices mark the perimeter of a United Nations military base located next to a camp for displaced people in Nyanzale (Congo). Despite the physical proximity, the Indian peacekeepers living here have virtually no interactions with their Congolese neighbors.
Photo credit: Philippe Rosen, 2011

There are many daily routines that I learned during my first few months as an international aid worker, and which my colleagues and I faithfully reproduced across the world. And they all have similar consequences. We foreign peacebuilders spend an incredible amount of time and energy writing reports, hunting for quantifiable ways to prove that we've made a difference, and advertising our achievements. These professional routines are so banal, so quotidian, that most of the time on-the-ground interveners and their higher-ups dismiss them as unimportant. Yet, these habitual ways of working reinforce an image of the foreigners' superiority over host populations, thus antagonizing local counterparts and leading them to further resist international programs. They also perpetuate the separation between interveners and local people, which decreases the effectiveness of international peace efforts.

A Comedy of Errors

Lack of local knowledge and networks means that peacebuilders are often out of their element when they arrive on the ground. My husband and I had similar disorienting experiences—he in Burundi, and I in Afghanistan. We kept seeing men holding hands in public, walking with their arms around each other, hugging each other, and we both thought that, for all of the stereotypes of these two countries as conservative and intolerant, they were actually quite the pioneers in terms of gay rights—until we realized that these were absolutely not manifestations of LGBT+ pride, but a different conception of politeness: Physical contact is how you show that you're paying attention to the person you're talking to. And gender norms make it perfectly fine for men to touch other men, but certainly not women.

These kinds of cultural misunderstandings regularly result in aid programs that completely miss the mark. My favorite such story involves the use of condoms, which humanitarian organizations often distribute as part of HIV prevention efforts. Large numbers of people often show up to get the healthcare items, making the donors happy at how effective their programs are. Local populations are thrilled too: The adults get free, durable plastic pouches in which to transport their tobacco crops in South Sudan, or store water in Burundi, and the kids get new balloons to play with.

Another classic story has to do with disarmament projects that monetarily reward combatants who hand over their weapons. In Congo, for example, one could get $100 for handing over a gun. So people would bring in their most beat-up rifle, then go out and buy two new ones ($40 apiece on the black market) and still have money left over for beer.

I also found the way United Nations peacekeepers tried to protect civilians in Congo in 2010 particularly absurd. They distributed cell phones to point persons in unstable villages. On paper, it was a beautiful idea: The villagers could call the nearest peacekeepers if they were attacked. In practice, the mission distributed cell phones in villages where there was neither mobile coverage nor electricity to charge the phones.

Foreign aid workers' lack of familiarity with local culture, coupled with their speedy rotation, explains why they often replicate programs from previous deployments as if they should have the same effect in their new posting. Peacelanders regularly acknowledge that one-size-fits-all templates are ineffective, and that adapting programs to each individual context is crucial, but their tendency to use blueprints and models impedes both the general approach and the completion of daily tasks.

There's one anecdote in particular that periodically makes the rounds in Peaceland. As the story goes, the United Nations published a report on its action in Kosovo, but, surprisingly enough, entire sections of this document focused on Liberia. The organization launched an internal inquiry to determine the reasons behind this puzzling discrepancy. It was discovered that the staff member who had prepared the report had just been redeployed from Liberia to Kosovo. Upon arriving in his new position, he implemented the exact same strategies in the exact same way as he had done in his previous posting. And when the time came to prepare his report, he took his template document, hit "search and find," and replaced "Liberia" with "Kosovo." This time, he unfortunately missed a few occurrences. (I can only imagine the grade my students would receive if they dared to try such a stunt!)

Depending on whether I was in Kosovo, Congo, or Afghanistan, I heard different versions of this anecdote ascribed to various international organizations. While amusing and perhaps apocryphal, it encapsulates a complaint I keep hearing when I am in conflict zones: Many peacebuilders use the same strategy, write the same reports, and organize their lives similarly, regardless of where they are in the world.

When Disaster Strikes

Professional habits and misunderstandings can lead to analytical mistakes—which are often dangerous, and even deadly. I realized this early in my research, when I was in Bukavu (Congo) in May 2004. Every week, I attended a coordination meeting where diplomats, donors, peacekeepers, and other aid workers discussed the humanitarian and security situations in the area. After a month of reports and conversations, our consensus was that the province was calm, and that Bukavu itself was perfectly safe. A few hours after our late May meeting, large-scale fighting broke out in town. I spent the next two days stuck in the United Nations compound, in the company of those same diplomats, donors, and peacekeepers, with rifles firing all around us and bombs exploding in the streets.

Rebels eventually took over the city, and they went on a looting, raping, and killing spree. At one point, a boy and his mother saw several soldiers enter the house next to theirs. They heard screams and shouts—it was obvious that their neighbor was about to be raped. The boy ran to seek help at the nearby United Nations base. Unfortunately, the sentry on duty was a Uruguayan soldier who spoke neither Swahili nor French. The boy did his best to communicate what was happening, but it seemed he just couldn't get the peacekeeper to comprehend. Finally, the soldier broke into a large smile and signaled that he understood. He went inside the camp and came back a few minutes later with a pack of cookies, which he proudly handed to the boy.

This appalling episode, which a furious and ashamed United Nations colonel recounted to me a few years later, points to more than just a language problem. In the midst of fighting, bombing, raping, and killing, it would appear rather obvious that, when a boy tries to attract the attention of a peacekeeper—whose job literally requires protecting neighboring residents—there is a good chance that the boy is asking for help. However, in this case, the soldier's ingrained perception of what Congolese children want (cookies or money, which they often request from foreigners) overcame his common sense.

I experienced and heard countless similar stories during my years in conflict zones. I once went patrolling in Congo with South African peacekeeping troops, and the officer-in-charge spent most of his time shouting greetings in Kinyarwanda to every resident he met. On the one hand, I was impressed: He had made the laudable effort to learn a local language, and he was being very friendly. On the other hand, I felt awkward: In a place where ethnic tensions between Kinyarwanda-speakers and other Congolese had caused tens of thousands of deaths over the past 15 years, greeting people in the tongue of their arch-enemy was probably not the best idea.

Even worse, these mistakes often result in country-wide disasters. It is the insider-outsider divide, along with the dominance of foreigners, the disregard of local residents, and the premium placed on the interveners' knowledge, that makes possible and perpetuates the top-down, formulaic approach to peace that we see in use all over the world. In Afghanistan, Congo, Colombia, Israel, the Palestinian territories, Somalia, and many other places, Peace, Inc. has routinely failed to help local populations—and at worst, it has actually hurt them. But before I tell you these stories, let me be clear—not all is lost.

Give Up or Fight Back?

Given all these challenges, it is easy to believe that the system cannot work, and many aid workers fall prey to a kind of hope burnout. A friend of mine, Carla*, was struggling with this when I saw her at a Christmas party in 2010 in Congo. It was a warm and sunny day, and everyone was in a festive mood, except for Carla. During cocktails, she took me aside and started ranting about how she could not stand Congolese people anymore; she went on and on about all of the problems she had with her local colleagues. After a while, she paused, became very glum, and remarked on how she had changed since she had arrived in Africa. She used to believe in equality, respect, and fairness; that's why she came to work for the United Nations. But her experiences had transformed her into the kind of person she used to hate. She had to leave Peaceland, she told me, so that she could finally get back to normal.

Thankfully, Carla was wrong. Though she did leave Congo, she didn't quit peacebuilding work, and after taking some time off, she went back to conflict zones. She initially returned to Africa, but then the United Nations sent her to another continent. For the first time in her career, Carla served as a peacebuilder in a country whose residents spoke her native language. She was based in a small town that hosted few other international aid workers, so her social life started to include local people in addition to foreigners. She became fascinated by this new place and took to reading everything she could about its history, politics, and culture. She decided to stay there as long as possible.

When I went to visit her, she kept telling me how smart, courageous, and committed the inhabitants were, how privileged she was to interact with them, how captivating she found the area—and then she would go on and on about obscure events that happened 50 years ago, and cultural norms that her foreign colleagues and I had never heard of, but which she said shaped the entire trajectory of the conflict. Finally, I thought, Carla had returned to her usual self. She was friendly and courteous with local residents; she paid attention to their ideas; she was devoted to her work; she was passionate, committed, and above all, effective.

Like Carla in her United Nations missions, Vijaya with Resolve, and Pieter with LPI, any of us can help change the habitual patterns of relationships between outsiders and insiders in order to both challenge enduring stereotypes and boost the chances of peacebuilding success. It's not easy, and it takes time, but it is possible.

4

Designed Intervention

Every month, the French ambassador to the United Nations used to invite a select group of people who worked on Congo for lunch at his New York residence. In November 2009, I made the cut. It was a posh affair: cocktails in a room twice the size of my entire apartment, with sofas too stylish to sit on and fancy paintings on the wall, followed by a meal with a lot of different plates, glasses, and cutlery, but little food.

At first, I felt intimidated, and it wasn't just because of my surroundings: In attendance were some of the most eminent figures in the field I study. Then, as the lunch progressed, I became utterly confused. The Congolese ambassador to the United Nations, who was sitting next to me, kept telling us how well things were going in his country—even describing the situation as "peaceful" and "democratic." The big shots from the United Nations seated on the other side of the table (the head of political affairs, the director of the Africa division, and the deputy chief of peacekeeping) agreed, and boasted about their organization's role in helping Congo achieve stability. I expected the French ambassador or one of his other guests—visitors from the defense and foreign affairs ministries in Paris—to challenge these statements. But no, they just kept nodding and smiling.

I didn't dare say anything, and I probably wouldn't have, if the French ambassador hadn't turned to me and asked me to give them my opinion with "all of the cheek" and "brutal honesty" he expected from academics. So I told them that, by my standards, Congo was still in the midst of a civil and international war, and the United Nations peacekeepers were doing a terrible job. I gave evidence, statistics, data—as any good researcher would. I emphasized that hundreds of people were dying every month and dozens of armed groups remained active on Congolese territory. After I stopped talking there was a silence, a few embarrassed chuckles, and the lunch ended shortly afterward. I was never re-invited.

Granted, I lack diplomatic skills and tend to be too blunt (even for an academic). But that's beside the point. To me, this story illustrates what the decision makers around the table viewed as the proper way to build peace and the results they aim for, as well as the problems inherent to their Peace, Inc. approach.

Trickle-Down Peace

You remember that the inhabitants of Peaceland—outsiders such as United Nations peacekeepers, foreign diplomats, and the staff of many non-governmental organizations involved in conflict resolution—share a specific way of seeing the world. I was one of these people, and I lived in this culture, so I know all too well how powerful it is.

Like most foreign peacebuilders, I was trained to see elites as the cause of conflicts, outside intervention as the best hope to stymie the violence, and diplomatic peace processes as the only relevant method. Accordingly, during my first few missions, I viewed violence as a top-down problem, where fighting and massacres primarily result from national and international disputes. In Kosovo, I focused on how rebel-leaders-turned-politicians competed for power. In Afghanistan, I obsessed about the conflict between the government, supported by the United States and its allies, and the Taliban and their foreign backers. Most interveners similarly believe that tensions involving elites (for instance, the president and various rebel groups in Colombia), governments (such as the Israeli administration and the Palestinian Authority), or countries (like Russia and Ukraine) are always the root causes of violence.

If this is what you genuinely think, then the solution is clear: To build peace in war and postwar zones, you have to help reconcile the leaders of various countries and armed groups. Only *they* can make the all-important decisions that can end violence, like telling their followers to stop fighting, deploying troops and police officers to places plagued by rebels or criminals, or changing discriminatory laws that trigger resistance. Ideally, you also need to bolster state structures, so that governments have the tools they need to control their territories. As the accepted dogma goes, once the elites stop fighting and the state bureaucracy is working properly, peace will trickle down to the entire country. So, you set up your base in capital cities, you seek out national and international counterparts, and you focus all of your energy on high-level negotiations.

United Nations peacekeepers watch over the demilitarized zone separating the Turkish-Cypriot from Greek-Cypriot residents of Nicosia. Although Cyprus is a rich, safe, touristic place, peacekeeping bases there look the same as in Afghanistan or South Sudan—and so do the intervention strategies that peacebuilders use.
Photo credit: Michelle K. Farley, 2011

You don't work on grassroots tensions because you view them as unimportant and undeserving of your attention: a waste of time, energy, and resources. You also genuinely believe that supporting the efforts of ordinary people is pointless. Common citizens usually can't do much to reconcile national and international leaders like presidents and rebel commanders—just like you and I would be pretty powerless to reconcile Trump with Kim Jong-un. In your view, top-down approaches that rely on powerful outsiders can get the job done. You can even point to one of several successful experiences to support your case: El Salvador, Namibia, Northern Ireland, and Eastern Slavonia in Croatia, where the elite-focused, top-down interventions throughout the late 1980s and the 1990s ended bloody wars and ushered in decades of peace.

By way of illustration, let's look at how you would portray the end of the civil war known as "The Troubles" in Northern Ireland. At first glance, if you're a follower of Peace, Inc., this is a perfect success story. In the 1990s, after three decades of violence and 3,500 casualties, the British and Irish governments, with support from the United States and the European Union, convinced the leaders of local armed groups to negotiate and sign a peace deal. The Good Friday Agreement set up a new governing structure and state institutions that placated all warring parties, including Unionist (mainly Protestant) and Republican (mainly Catholic) militants. Northern Ireland remained part of the United Kingdom but received its own parliament and government as well as an open border with Ireland, and its residents were offered Irish citizenship in addition to (or instead of) their British citizenship. The legislators also reformed the local police (until then a tool of oppression at the hands of Protestants), and invested massively in jobs, housing, infrastructure, and health services for disadvantaged Catholic communities. And they convinced their followers to continue their fight through peaceful political engagement rather than violent action. Eventually, most militias disbanded, the number of conflict-related deaths per year dropped to less than half a dozen, and the British army withdrew from the territory in 2007.

It's true that the political, economic, and security situation in Northern Ireland is far better today than it was in the 1980s or 1990s, and elite-focused, state-centric strategies have largely driven this improvement. But there is a caveat: This top-down peacebuilding is far from an unmitigated success, as the residents, activists, and former combatants I talked to in 2020 emphasized again and again. Many sources of tension, notably resentment for past atrocities and social and economic inequalities between Catholic and Protestant communities, still exist. Unionist and Republican residents still live in mostly segregated neighborhoods, often in fear of one another. Armed groups still control parts of the main cities like Belfast and Derry. And Brexit is jeopardizing some of the key achievements of the peace process, like the open border and the possibility of dual citizenship. So, from 2018 onward, violence has picked up again. All in all, as of today, the Northern Ireland conflict is frozen rather than resolved.

My students often ask me why it's necessary to keep using top-down approaches at all. The case of Northern Ireland provides a clear answer: Thanks to a series of international agreements and national reforms, its leaders have ended decades of fighting and built a strong democracy with inclusive political representation. So elite-focused strategies can indeed help—but they also fall short in many ways.

Regardless of these limitations, if you're a typical intervener, like I was, there is another assumption that you hold dear: All good things come together. In your view, elections, good governance, human rights, separation of powers, free press, education, gender equality, and so on reinforce each other and promote peace. So you implement them as a package deal for conflict zones. You're especially keen on organizing general elections because you view them as a sort of cure-all. After all, aren't they the most crucial mechanism for democratization and state reconstruction? So you spend a lot of money on this—the United States, for instance, devotes more than $2.4 billion per year to democracy promotion, including electoral assistance efforts.

Academics call this approach the "liberal peace" agenda, and critics denounce it as an attempt to impose Western institutions, policies, and values on war-torn places. It's an agenda shared by numerous countries such as France, South Africa, and the United States, as well as institutions as diverse as the African Union, the United Nations, the World Bank, and various non-governmental organizations.

Now you see what the ambassador's guests had in mind. Like most politicians, peacebuilders, and ordinary observers, they genuinely believed that agreements between world leaders and elites, along with national elections, were the best way to end violence in Congo. And, in late 2009, they thought they had done their job.

There has been massive outside involvement to end the Congolese wars, which started in the mid-1990s and caused the deaths of more than five million people. Foreign diplomats, peacekeepers, and the staff of countless international and non-governmental organizations have organized numerous big-budget conferences to reconcile presidents, rebel chiefs, and opposition leaders—in Lusaka in 1999 ($3 million), Sun City in 2002 ($4 million), Goma in 2008 ($2 million), Addis Ababa in 2013, and so on. At the end of each of these meetings, the Congolese, Rwandan, and Ugandan governments, along with Congo's main rebel chiefs, signed multiple agreements. Throughout this entire period, interveners also focused on organizing general elections.

For a while—from 2003 to 2007—this approach seemed to work quite well. Most foreign armies left Congo. The country became one unified territory again under the (nominal) control of the Congolese government, instead of a patchwork of areas controlled by competing armed groups. Deputies and senators passed new pieces of legislation, and they wrote a new constitution—all very liberal and democratic.

In 2006, when Congo held its first free national elections since 1960, many observers thought that an end to violence in the region had finally come.

Foreign journalists, activists, and politicians lauded the successful organization of these elections as an example of effective international intervention.

By the time the ambassador's lunch took place in 2009, interveners had implemented the main elements of their standard package deal—elite agreements and general elections. Therefore, the ambassador's guests trusted that violence on the ground would eventually die down.

It did not.

Throughout the 2010s, Congo faced massive population displacement and horrific human rights violations. Fighting in the eastern provinces repeatedly reignited full-scale civil and international wars. Basically, every time foreign peacebuilders felt that they were on the brink of peace, the conflict exploded again.

As Congo prepared for new rounds of general elections in 2011 and then from 2016 to 2018, heads of state, journalists, activists, and foreign diplomats focused mostly on the drama surrounding President Joseph Kabila's attempts to cling to power (which he had held since 2001). In their view, violence continued because of the electoral tensions, and it would stop once the vote had taken place. And again, this didn't happen.

By 2017, Congo was home to 4.5 million internally displaced people—the largest such population in all of Africa. In 2018 and 2019, it reported the highest levels of sexual violence in the world. In 2020, there were an estimated 15.6 million individuals in need of humanitarian assistance. The number of internally displaced people had grown to 5.5 million, and approximately 922,000 sought asylum in neighboring countries.

Cutting Corners

To understand how we could arrive at this kind of situation, let's see how Peacelanders usually decide on strategies. As you remember, they lack the in-depth knowledge of local situations that could enable them to design programs tailored to the specifics of each conflict. To make matters worse, they are always pressed for time: Their superiors, donors, and colleagues expect them to act quickly—after all, if they don't, people will continue to die.

Take the story of Erik*, a Swedish peacebuilder who had read my book *The Trouble with the Congo* and told me he agreed with a lot of the points. When he was put in charge of his agency's programs in Congo, he decided to take time to analyze the situation he confronted and involve local people. And then his bosses criticized him for thinking too much and asking too many questions. They expected him to act by implementing projects, rather than to spend time considering how his work would actually improve the situation on the ground.

Countless Peacelanders from all over the world have told me similar stories. Due to the incredibly difficult circumstances in which they work (tight deadlines, political pressure, lack of proper country knowledge, etc.), instead of developing an in-depth analysis of each specific problem and evaluating the best way to respond, peacebuilders have to use shortcuts: ideas born of habits, donor demands, trends that sell, and inner organizational logics. In some cases, these ideas are formalized into what peacebuilders call "theories of change"—hypotheses regarding how and why a specific action (e.g., organizing elections) will help reach an intended goal (e.g., peace). One of Erik's colleagues summed it up: "We use assumptions all the time. We don't even think about it. We just act."

The problem with all of these beliefs and theories of change is that they are often unrealistic or reductive. I have frequently heard peacebuilders and their donors explain that a six-month or year-long project focused on organizing a series of workshops will produce democracy or peace—both of which in fact take decades to develop, and require a little more than just a few workshops.

Even worse, many peacebuilders assume that their initiatives will influence war and peace outcomes, but they often do not have evidence to support this belief. A couple of years ago, the Evidence for Peace project reviewed all available impact evaluations of peacebuilding initiatives. It found that interveners use surveys and interviews to measure how their efforts affect targeted individuals, societies, or organizations. Unfortunately, they virtually never assess whether they influence "actual peace and violence outcomes" such as displacement, repatriation, crime, gang violence, intergroup or interpersonal conflicts, and perceptions of safety.

Part of the problem is that peacebuilders and their donors view quantifiable results as the gold standard—such data is objective, concrete, and it can be produced with minimal involvement from local populations. However, not everything can be measured in numbers. For example, in the early 2010s, the United Nations peacekeeping mission in Burundi wanted to assess the success of its Disarmament, Demobilization, and Reintegration program. A useful evaluation would have studied whether armed violence had decreased in Burundi, but isolating the program's contribution to such a macro outcome was impossible. Alternatively, the peacekeepers could have assessed whether Burundians wanted to use arms and still viewed violence as an acceptable political strategy. However, "Nobody knows how to measure that," the staff told me. So, they counted the number of arms that they had collected—an irrelevant indicator in a country where most people own guns, weapon caches abound, and borders are so porous that it is easy to import more.

There is a way to go about this differently: one that fully involves local people in the design and implementation of peacebuilding evaluations, so that *they* can decide what kind of indicators are relevant and what kind of results *they* are looking for. It means acknowledging, like Vijaya did, that a project is successful when, for instance, a former child soldier like Luca starts speaking in the future tense, or when his mother Justine sees him wanting to "hold a pencil instead of a gun." In fact, my colleague Pamina Firchow has written a whole book on the methodology of such an approach (using focus groups with affected populations to design quantitative inquiries) and has conducted several pilot projects to show its benefits. So far, however, she hasn't convinced many interveners to follow her advice.

Peacebuilders often define success by whether or not they have carried out the actions they had planned—like the number of workshops held, or the number of people trained—rather than by their actual impact. Take the meetings I held in Timor-Leste with the staff of Ba'Futuro, an organization that many local and foreign contacts had mentioned as an excellent peacebuilding agency. After working through the grapevine, I eventually interviewed Julio*, who, I'd been told by his boss, could speak in-depth about the group's effectiveness. Unfortunately, no matter how many questions I asked Julio, and regardless of how I phrased my questions, he only gave me stories of people saying that they had enjoyed the training in conflict resolution that his organization provided. I tried for more than half an hour; Julio even looked at the extensive notes he had on his computer and at the monitoring and evaluations that Ba'Futuro had conducted. At the end of our meeting, he had found only one example of someone using her newly acquired skills to actually resolve a conflict.

I had the same frustrating experience throughout conflict zones. Most of the peacebuilders I talked to described their projects at great length—radio programs, mediations, meetings, etc.— but they remained vague or failed to answer when I asked about the actual impact of these actions.

It's not just me. Milt Lauenstein is a successful businessman from the United States, who, upon retiring, found an all-consuming passion—a "second career," as he told me—to which he has devoted a lot of his financial resources: building peace. In 2003, Milt established a prize to reward research on what he calls "results-oriented peacebuilding." He received more than 80 papers, but even among the top eight, only one looked at outcomes on the ground. In 2016, he convened peacebuilders from Europe and North America to brainstorm the most cost-effective approaches for post-conflict environments. Again, the discussions yielded virtually nothing on the actual results of peace interventions.

All in all, an alarming number of interveners rely on flawed notions about what works rather than actual evidence when they design their programs. You have probably already spotted many such misconceptions as you have been reading this book: the ideas that

- specialists' knowledge is better than local expertise
- outsiders know best
- local people are untrustworthy and incompetent
- it's a good idea to use templates
- only top-down action is needed
- grassroots peacebuilding cannot take place while violence is ongoing
- dialogue is enough and can be a one-off event
- the outcome is more important than the process
- peacebuilding is very costly
- more money for a program is always a good thing
- international efforts should be visible
- and peacebuilding can succeed rapidly (in a few months or years).

In addition, let's look at the widespread idea that "good things"—like democracy and peace—go together.

The Elections Fetish

It is true that democratic countries are on average more peaceful than authoritarian ones—there is an enormous body of research on this matter. In fact, no two mature democracies have ever gone to war with each other. Democracies also experience relatively few civil wars because they have institutions in place to peacefully address their citizens' grievances.

Logically, it would make sense to promote democracy as a way to build peace. But this would mean overlooking an important caveat: The countries most likely to engage in wars are those undergoing a transition from

dictatorship to democracy. And, in fact, the larger the magnitude of the regime change, the more aggressive states in transition are likely to become.
In other words, the places most at risk of violence are precisely those that
organize free and fair elections for the first time and try to implement a free
press, good governance, etc.—as the interveners' package deal prescribes.

A case in point is the peace agreement that was supposed to mark the end
of the civil war in Rwanda, but in fact served as a catalyst for the genocide.
When the Hutu government and the Tutsi rebel group negotiated a peace
deal (in Arusha in 1993), their foreign backers (Belgium, France, Germany,
the United States, etc.) managed to impose elections and power sharing. To
them, this was the perfect way to resolve Rwanda's conflict. Unfortunately,
the Hutu leaders did not want to relinquish their absolute control of the
country. So they rounded up the army, set up youth militias, and stoked
ethnic antagonisms so as not to lose power. These tensions quickly escalated into the 1994 genocide, which left an estimated 800,000 to one million
people dead.

This is also how the democratization process sparked civil wars in Angola,
Congo, and the former Yugoslavia in the early 1990s, and how it fueled violence in many countries that tried to recover from conflict, including Bosnia,
Cambodia, the Central African Republic, and El Salvador. The problem was
not the idea of democratization, but the way in which interveners forced the
process: by focusing first and foremost on organizing rapid elections and
overlooking the necessary conditions that make such an exercise safe and
meaningful. Indeed, once a dictatorship starts breaking up, myriads of social groups begin competing for power. Unfortunately, in many cases, transi-
tional democracies lack state institutions that are strong and coherent enough
to effectively regulate this mass political competition. It becomes a problem
when (as often happens) the elite mobilize followers by running electoral
campaigns on identity lines; appeals to nationalism unite all of the citizens
against a neighboring country, while calls to religion or ethnicity mobilize
some groups against others within the same territory. And, unless freedom
of speech, assembly, and campaigning are already the norm, incumbents
are highly likely to use the army and the police to repress opponents and increase their chances of victory. All of this regularly escalates into generalized
fighting.

Contrary to the conventional wisdom, democratization is not an antidote
to violence, but rather the opposite: It doubles the risk of civil war resump-
tion. In countries emerging from conflicts, the chance of renewed violence

jumps from 21 percent (without democratization) to 39 percent (with democratization). Time helps—the chance of war recurrence decreases by 31 percent when leaders wait five years instead of one to hold an election. But, in recent years, they've been waiting less and less—on average 2.7 years, which is half the time they used to wait prior to 1989.

What's more, academic colleagues have found that holding elections decreases the chances of economic recovery in countries emerging from wars. And to top it all off, terrorism is more likely in regimes that are neither fully autocratic nor fully democratic—like the many postwar states undergoing democratization.

In brief, the various components of the "package deal" that peacebuilders offer are often in tension with one another. In the short term, there is often a trade-off between democracy and peace (or economic prosperity) in societies emerging from war. Elections can be organized quickly, but doing so may fuel violence. Alternatively, the time, resources, and efforts required to organize elections could be used instead to address the root causes of the conflict. In Congo, for instance, it is not elections that are likely to lead to peace; it is addressing the poverty, inequality, and unemployment, as well as the discrimination and poor access to land and justice that are at the root of the long-standing conflict. The same is the case for many developing countries.

The problem is similar with other essential elements of the package deal, like education and state reconstruction: They can and regularly do fuel violence instead of promoting peace.

For instance, interveners generally view education as a force for good. To them, higher rates of education lead to less violent societies, so they use school projects as the backbone of many peace initiatives. Unfortunately, although certain educational programs help decrease tensions and promote reconciliation, others end up actively feeding conflict. We've seen that for centuries. Just think about how teachers depicted Jews to their students in Nazi Germany: the eternal saboteur striving to bring down the strong and powerful Germans, the vermin that any upstanding citizen should help eliminate. In the 1970s, the Sri Lankan government took a page from the Nazis. They depicted Sinhalese Buddhists (the ethnic majority) as heroes who had vanquished their nemeses, the Tamil minority. This twisted version of history played no small part in fueling hatred between the two groups during the 26-year-long, bloody ethnic war that followed. Along the same lines, educational programs promoted intolerance, stereotyping, and ethnic antagonisms in Rwanda before, during, and after the 1994 genocide. And in

Afghanistan, even schools funded by international donors as a way to help build peace ended up reinforcing violence.

Likewise, statebuilding does not always contribute to peacebuilding. Of course, in an ideal world states would undertake, coordinate, or support all of the peace efforts in their territory as they do in Iceland and New Zealand, for example. This would make grassroots conflict-resolution initiatives more sustainable, and it would help link them to top-down developments.

But, unfortunately, we don't live in an ideal world. In places like Somalia and South Sudan, the state is unable to carry out its most basic responsibilities, like providing safety or building infrastructure. The proponents of Peace, Inc. argue that this is precisely why we need to "build" or "rebuild" states. But in most war zones, from Afghanistan to Colombia, the people who control the local and national bureaucracies are integral parties to the conflict. In all of these cases, rebuilding state institutions enables the local and national governments to be more effective at oppressing their fellow citizens.

In Congo, as you may remember, a stronger state hasn't promoted social peace; instead it has enabled the Congolese government to jail, torture, and kill residents more easily. Extending state authority to Congolese mining towns has replaced one kind of perpetrators (rebel groups) with another (the army) and expanded the pool of combatants, as vulnerable populations have lost their livelihood and many of the newly unemployed young men have joined militias as a way to get by.

The situation has been even worse in Iraq, where statebuilding efforts led by outsiders have fueled massive violence and sectarian conflict. After toppling Saddam Hussein's regime in 2003, the United States and its allies disbanded the existing Iraqi army and dismissed the civil servants affiliated with the Ba'ath party. Approximately 300,000 trained combatants, along with tens of thousands of civilians, ended up deprived of their livelihood, alienated, and resentful, and as a result many decided to join resistance movements. The new Iraqi government and its foreign sponsors had to find a way to maintain order across the country and promote some kind of representation in the new state. So, they rapidly rebuilt police and army forces, but with little screening of the recruits' political alliances. They also relied on local militias as well as traditional community and tribal leaders. These two measures empowered radical religious movements and ethnic nationalistic groups. All in all, instead of promoting peace and reconciliation, the state-rebuilding efforts triggered power struggles, reinforced social divisions, and caused an increase in attacks against minority groups.

Once again, the problem is not the idea of statebuilding per se—after all, while I dread filing taxes and renewing my ID cards with every iota of my being, I sure am glad I can rely on bureaucracies and institutions when I'm home in France or the United States. The issue lies with the automatic, thoughtless use of templated, technocratic, top-down measures and the failure to acknowledge that, in certain circumstances, such tactics can actually worsen the situation. Sadly, all good things do *not* come together.

The Missing Part of the Picture

Two other problematic notions shape most intervention strategies. The first is the idea that local tensions mirror national and international ones. For instance, if two politicians are competing for control of a country, Peacelanders assume that violence on the ground is likely the result of this political competition. The second is the belief that peace achieved on the national or international stage tends to trickle down to the local sphere. In other words, if these two politicians sign a peace agreement, interveners trust that the deal will also bring peace to the entire country.

In fact, local conflicts are often distinct from national and international ones, even if they are linked to them—as you may remember from the stories of the Rastas hiding in the jungle and the conflicts over livestock routes in the Ruzizi Plains. As a result, national and international reconciliation does not necessarily translate to peace on the ground. This is not merely my opinion, nor is it a Congo-specific issue. A team of leading experts recently assessed how frequently elite bargains end wars. After years of work, and in-depth analyses of 21 recent conflicts on different continents, the researchers reached a disheartening conclusion: There is not a single clear-cut example where deals among elites have actually ended violence. Trickle-down peace, it turns out, is just as fraught an ideology as trickle-down economics.

What really brought this home to me was when I met Isabelle*, a Congolese woman who was my age, in Nyunzu in 2003. A couple of years before, during a particularly violent episode of the conflict between Bantus and Pygmies, local militias had attacked Isabelle's village. They had killed many residents, raped many others, and stolen everything. Isabelle and her fellow villagers fled to the bush, but local militias soon found their hiding place. "They were coming almost every week," Isabelle recalled, "even two to three times a week, to loot our properties, beat us, leave people naked, and make forced love [rape] to the women." One day, they tried to kidnap Isabelle, but her husband stepped in, and he said: "No, please, don't take Isabelle, take me instead." So he went to the forest with the militias, and Isabelle had not seen him since.

Isabelle was so proud—and so in love. She was also clearly in need: The reason we met is that she had brought her malnourished toddler to the local nutritional center that my Médicos Sin Fronteras colleagues supported. She told me how she struggled to find food, every morning hoping that this would be the day her husband would come back. And yet, she held her head up. She met my eyes, talking clearly and softly.

She explained at length the reasons for the recurrent attacks on her village. It was not because of anything related to national and international tensions, like the war between Congo and Rwanda. Instead, it was because the rebels wanted to take the land that the villagers needed to cultivate food and to survive. And when I asked her why she did not flee once again or try to find a new hiding place, she told me, in a matter-of-fact voice: "We are used to it. We are near our land. We do not want to leave it."

Isabelle's story has stayed in my mind all these years, not only because I saw myself in her—in another universe, she and I could have been friends— but also because it embodies the awful consequences of local conflicts that foreign peacebuilders so often ignore.

What's more, after years of research, I saw that Isabelle's experience was unfortunately typical. Contrary to what the French ambassador's guests believed (and what I used to think), in Congo, it is not only international and national issues that cause violence. Longstanding, bottom-up tensions do too. The main instigators are villagers, traditional chiefs, or community authorities. Many conflicts revolve around political, social, and economic stakes that are distinctively local. And when I say local, I really mean at the level of the individual, the family, the clan, the village, or the district.

For instance, there is a lot of competition over who will be chief of the village or the territory according to traditional law—that means being the highest-ranked individual in the area, akin to a mini-king, complete with a court of trusted (and, often, sycophantic) advisors, a lot of prestige, respect from all those who live on your territory, and the authority to distribute land to the subjects you choose. People also vie for administrative power, as being mayor, governor, or police chief brings significant revenue and standing.

In addition, individuals compete over who can control specific plots or estates. Too often, given the high poverty rates in rural Congo, your ability to cultivate land is the difference between life and death. It means being able to grow crops that will feed your family, and maybe, if you're lucky, getting a bit of extra money so that you can send your children to school and buy them clothes. In Congo's culture, being a landowner also improves your social status and gives you a voice in the affairs of your community. Not to mention that some pieces of land have mining resources on them—diamonds, gold, copper, etc.—so their exploitation can make you rich.

This competition often results in localized fighting, say in one village or territory, and it quite frequently escalates into generalized hostilities, across a whole province and even at times into neighboring countries. Take the conflict that you're most likely to be familiar with if you've ever read about Congo outside of this book: that between Congolese of Rwandan descent and the so-called "indigenous communities" of the Kivu provinces. The tensions started in the 1930s, during Belgian colonization, when both communities competed over access to land and local power. Animosity between these groups escalated after Congo's independence in 1960, because each camp allied with national politicians in order to secure the control of various villages and advance their claims to specific plots of land or estates. And at the time of the 1994 genocide in Rwanda, all of these people allied with Congolese and Rwandan armed groups in order to further promote their own local agendas in the Kivus. Since then, these local disputes over land and power have continued to fuel violence from the bottom up, and they have regularly jeopardized the international and national peace settlements.

This is not just a Congo story. Personal feuds and a range of local conflicts (over land, water, livestock, status, power, resources, etc.) fuel violence in many war and postwar contexts. Throughout the world, they cause unspeakable anguish, like what Isabelle experienced. And, just like in Congo, they regularly endanger the results achieved by the conventional approach to building peace.

A case in point is Timor-Leste, a Pacific island whose one million inhabitants won independence from Indonesia in 1999, after 24 years of occupation. The ongoing violence there is as much a result of disputes over land, family antagonisms, and traditions of retribution as it is of ethnic enmity, rivalries between national political elites, and the conflict with Indonesia. Unfortunately, most international peacebuilders have ignored these bottom-up drivers of tension, focusing instead on reconciling people from the eastern and western parts of the island, assuaging frictions between the police and the army, and supporting the Timorese state. But as a consequence of ignoring grassroots issues, extensive violence has persisted. In 2006, local conflicts even escalated into massive riots that caused the entire peace process to collapse.

Likewise, Peacelanders and politicians usually emphasize the national and international dimensions of Afghanistan's wars: the rebellions triggered by the communist coup of 1978, the Soviet and American invasions (respectively from 1979 to 1989 and since 2001), and the current struggle between the government and its Western allies versus the Taliban and its international network. It's true that all of these conflicts have caused extensive bloodshed for over 40 years. But so have a range of other issues that Afghan people mention whenever researchers take the time to talk to them: quarrels over local power, land, water, debts, marriage, divorce, and other personal and financial matters. These tensions fuel—and are fueled by—the elite struggles that outsiders keep talking about. The result of these overlapping conflicts? More than one and a half million deaths, and the displacement of five million civilians. So far.

In South Sudan (where an ongoing civil war has led to 400,000 casualties since 2013), it is not only tensions between President Salva Kiir and Vice-President Riek Machar that fuel fighting; it is also countless spats between herders and farmers, cattle raids, and clan rivalries. In Bougainville, the destructive violence that raged from 1988 to 1997 was as much due to the conflict between Papua New Guinea and the island's separatist movement as to land disputes, accusations of sorcery, and grabs for local political power. In Nigeria in 2018, clashes between herders and farmers killed *more* people than the Islamist extremist group Boko Haram, which consistently made the headlines. Burundi, Indonesia, Nepal, Mali, Somalia, Sudan: The list of places where local antagonisms motivate significant violence goes on.

This dilemma is something my friend Kenny Gluck experienced constantly as he spent years supporting efforts to broker an agreement between warring parties in Darfur (Sudan). Time and again, he would voice the same frustration. The African Union and the United Nations, both of which he represented, as well as the key diplomats involved in the process, assumed that militia chiefs controlled their soldiers. So, Kenny's job was to help mediate between government and rebel leaders, get them to sign a ceasefire and a comprehensive agreement, and then wait for the violence to stop. But every time militia commanders made concessions and eventually signed a peace deal, large groups of local combatants would object to the compromises, defect, and keep fighting. The problem, Kenny and some of his colleagues realized, was that the troops' motivations were different from those of their top leaders, and the latter had little actual control over the former.

Kenny was eventually reassigned to the mediation team for the war in Yemen; then he went on to work in the Central African Republic, and in both places, he faced the exact same problem. "We still train mediators and design [peace] processes as if we were dealing with conflicts between the Swiss and the German governments," he complained. The United Nations and the African Union organize negotiations as if they include "groups of well-disciplined lawyers" for whom "the text is everything." While in fact, in the Central African Republic and Yemen, just like in Sudan, there is little cohesion within armed groups, the chain of command is weak, and rank-and-file combatants often pursue agendas at odds with those of their leaders—so the international peace efforts fail repeatedly.

Kenny's predicament is unfortunately common. According to the International Committee of the Red Cross, 44 percent of today's conflicts involve three to nine different forces, and 22 percent include more than ten. Some have hundreds (like in Congo and Libya) or even over 1,000 (in Syria). In all of these places, armed groups keep fragmenting, so the Peace, Inc. efforts that gather a handful of top leaders in foreign capitals are bound to have little impact on the ground.

Bringing attention to bottom-up causes of war does not mean ignoring the impact that elites have on conflict and peace. In many cases, it is because of a combination of local, national, and international issues that violence starts, becomes pervasive, and continues during peace processes and after the signing of peace agreements. National and international leaders often instigate fighting as a way to pursue their own agendas. They manipulate armed groups. They fuel hatred among ordinary people. They launch large-scale attacks that harm thousands of civilians. Thus, the top-down approach that aims to reconcile these elites remains crucial.

However, we have to revise these top-down strategies to eliminate the problems inherent to Peace, Inc. And we shouldn't stop there. Because local causes of conflicts are often different from national and international ones, establishing peace at the top does not necessarily end tensions on the ground. If we want to understand and address violence in war and postwar contexts, we have to look beyond elites, governments, and rebel leaders, so that we also take into account provincial, local, and individual motivations. Conflicts must be resolved from the tree-tops and the grassroots.

Fortunately—and contrary to what the cogs of Peace, Inc. often assume—supporting local efforts doesn't need to be very costly. People have asked me countless times for $20 or $50 so that they could organize an initiative that they knew would help bring peace to their villages—a trip to talk with the leader of a neighboring militia, a meeting between two groups in conflict, etc. And you remember how Urbain Bisimwa and LPI helped resolve the Rasta crisis in Congo: With less than $60,000, they successfully reestablished peace throughout 52 villages with a combined population of more than 100,000 residents. Vijaya's pilot project for Resolve—the one that transformed the lives of Justine, Luca, and their entire village in eastern Congo—cost less than $5,000. Contrast this with the millions of dollars that diplomats spend on international plane tickets, luxury hotel rooms, generous daily stipends, and fancy meeting venues in order to support negotiations among elites—only to reach agreements that fall apart in a matter of days or weeks. For instance, the 2008 Goma conference to "end" the war in eastern Congo cost more than $2 million, and violence continued right through it. Same for the 2012 Arab League summit to tackle the war in Syria ($500 million), and the 2018 Trump-Kim meeting to bring stability to the Korean peninsula ($12 million).

Even when local recruits and partners receive a salary equivalent to that of comparably-skilled interveners, as they should, relying on them is usually much cheaper than employing foreign peacebuilders. With national staff, there is no need to cover the expensive insurance plans, plane tickets, bunker-like accommodations, bonuses paid to reward placement in dangerous areas, or other benefits that expatriates often require.

Ruffled Feathers

If you're like most of my readers, what you probably want to know now is why so many interveners are still holding on to their flawed view of the best way to build peace after war. Personally, I've often been surprised by how virulent my critics are—and you may have been similarly shocked when you read the harsh criticisms of Hans and Pieter (the LPI country directors). After all, the ideas that elections are not the silver bullet solution, that local issues also fuel violence, that target populations should be involved in the design of peacebuilding initiatives, and that ending wars requires both top-down and bottom-up work are quite commonsense. And yet, time and again, I've had the same experience: I present my research at a conference or meeting, and at least one person in the audience, sometimes more, goes on an angry rant along the lines of "How dare you say that?"—or, "As a white woman, you can't possibly understand what's going on!" in whatever country we are discussing.

I know now that this is not personal. Instead, all of these angry reactions reflect how deeply attached policymakers and practitioners are to the common approach to building peace. They reveal the profound challenge posed by the notions of putting insiders in charge and addressing violence from the bottom-up, and thus how threatened those experts of Peace, Inc. feel when confronted with such suggestions.

There are a few ideas that interveners hold so dear that questioning them is bound to trigger emotional reactions. One of them is, as we saw, the deep-seated belief that organizing elections is the best way to reduce war and violence. Whenever I dare question it, I'm asked: "Don't you think Afghans (or Congolese, or Timorese) deserve democracy?!" Another is the norm of non-intervention in a state's domestic affairs. I'm often told, "You're such a colonialist" (or an imperialist), when I say we should support local conflict resolution or deal directly with ordinary citizens. Personally, I find this accusation pretty ironic, given the Peacelanders' mantra that only outsiders can help inhabitants of conflict zones recover from war. It's as if Peace, Inc. was respectful of state sovereignty merely because it prioritizes interactions with national elites!

In fact, this last stance is so entrenched that it shapes the very structure and identity of international organizations and foreign ministries. They focus on diplomatic, inter-governmental, inter-state relations, and they lack the employees, units, procedures, and funding patterns necessary for local action. As a long-time employee of the U.S. Department of State retorted after hearing me brief his colleagues on the importance of bottom-up peacebuilding, "But, Séverine, we are *State*. We get states. We're not set up to work at the local level." Likewise, United Nations employees always remind me that, for any major initiative, their organization needs both the approval of the 15 countries that make up the Security Council and that of the host government. For all of these high-level peacebuilders, their work is and should be inherently state-centric.

Challenging these core beliefs naturally generates a lot of defensiveness. Imagine you're a typical intervener: Like most foreign peacebuilders, you've built your career on the assumption that your external action can make a difference. You've spent years, sometimes decades, acquiring the skills you need to better help the inhabitants of conflict zones. You've learned the diplomatic codes and language. You've become an expert in high-level negotiations, adept at resolving national and international issues, experienced in talking with world leaders and other kinds of elite—or you're on your way to finally possessing all of these abilities. And then someone arrives and throws all of that into question. You hear that the work to which you have dedicated your life may actually not matter as much as you had thought, and that you may, in some cases, have actually caused harm.

You may see some logical value in the argument that local conflict resolution matters and that ordinary people should have a say in their own future, but this does not make you feel any better. If you're smart, discerning, and well-intentioned—like most peacebuilders are—you start wondering what you could have done differently. You ponder whether you should leave the industry, or "go native," or do nothing—or maybe you could try to change the system? Unfortunately, you're likely to feel trapped: All of my friends and colleagues who work for the United Nations, or a foreign ministry, or some kind of large peace organization, believe that they have no power to change the overall goals and structures of their employers, because these bureaucracies are massive, complicated, and notoriously resistant to change and new ideas. In these circumstances, wouldn't you too become distraught when you hear my arguments?

Besides, it's much nicer to work on national or international peace processes than on local ones. When I do, I spend most of my time in capital cities, with their fancy hotels, pleasant restaurants, and reliable supply of water and electricity. I interact with elites, to whom I can easily relate—it's not only that they have mastered French or English, but also that we have many cultural references in common like movies, books, and music. Sometimes we've even been to the same universities, lived in the same cities, or run in the same social circles. And I get to meet with ministers, governors, generals, presidents—people who are way out of my league in my home country.

I still remember how weird I felt after interviewing the leader, the deputy, and the president of the three most important rebel groups active on Congolese territory during my doctoral research. Going into our meetings, I suspected that they were responsible, directly or indirectly, for countless killings, rapes, tortures—as a friend put it, they had blood "up to their elbows." (One of them was eventually imprisoned for war crimes, which included ordering the killing of more than 200 people.) But in these meetings, I fell under their spell. The leader treated me like an equal; he was thoughtful, polite, interested in my research—even flirty. The deputy acted as if I was his friend. He joked, marveled at the technology I used to take notes (an electronic agenda with a keyboard—quite nifty at the time), mentioned common acquaintances; we compared notes on life in Belgium, where we had family. The president answered all of my questions gently, kindly, patiently, and openly, giving me tons of useful information and advice for my research. In all three cases, I felt I was interacting with people who were similar to me and understood me. And then I left our meetings feeling disgusted with myself—how could I possibly like such monsters?

When I managed to overcome the shame and share this story with colleagues, I realized that many peacebuilders and researchers have had the same experience. Rebel leaders and dictators may be responsible for horrible human rights abuses, but they are also often charismatic, intelligent, or articulate enough that talking to them is pleasurable for interveners. Plus hanging out with them makes you feel important and, when you're back home, glamorous and exciting—my students think I'm a total badass when I tell them these kinds of stories.

Compare that with working on local conflict resolution and involving ordinary citizens in peace efforts. When I participate in these kinds of initiatives, I end up spending most of my time in rural towns and villages. I stay in hotels or guesthouses with basic (and often run-down) furniture, little or no electricity, rarely any running water, and usually no Internet. I eat local food that I don't necessarily like—and that regularly disagrees with my stomach. I interact with people who have little in common with me and often consider me an oddity or a walking moneybag. At times they view me as such an important person that they stutter when they talk to me—once one of them even kneeled (it was terribly, terribly embarrassing). My alternative peacebuilding strategy may be the most logical way to proceed, but it's not always fun.

Many interveners would lose their status, their comfort, at times their jobs if they had to move away from the current approach to building peace. My suggested approach also challenges their worldviews and identities. So, of course, they put up a fight when someone like me dares to suggest that outside expertise and top-down action are not nearly enough. Wouldn't you?

The Top-Down Tyranny

The Swedish diplomat Lena Sundh paid a heavy price in this fight, and she also happens to be one of my heroes. Not only because she is a woman who made it in a male-dominated world—she has been ambassador to Angola, second-in-command of the United Nations peacekeeping mission in Congo, and Sweden's Special Envoy for the African Great Lakes. Not only because she is kind, funny, and approachable—she was one of the few people who treated me like an intellectual equal, and not a student to be lectured, when I interviewed her for my doctoral research. But also because she was one of the first outsiders to realize the importance of local conflict resolution in Congo, and she has spent most of the past 20 years advocating for a reform to the Peace, Inc. approach in the region.

When Sundh was deputy special representative of the United Nations secretary-general in Congo (2002–2004), she set up a unit with a few trusted collaborators and, together, they advocated for a new approach to the on-going violence: managing the conflict from the bottom up until the time was ripe for top-down action. They felt they had much more influence with local and provincial leaders than with national and international ones, so working with the former would be a better use of their time and energy.

As Sundh recalled, this was such a new and controversial idea that her team first had to write a policy document to explain that addressing grass-roots tensions was indeed part of the United Nations peacekeepers' jobs. Sundh also realized that, if she wanted her colleagues to pay attention to local conflicts, her best bet was to argue that local problems threatened national reconciliation.

The headquarters endorsed her new strategy in mid-2003, but apart from a few analyses of violence in various eastern provinces, a couple of action plans for approaching these conflicts, some training sessions, and a handful of negotiations toward ceasefires between select villages, nothing much materialized. Indeed, Sundh did not benefit from the credibility, power, and influence usually attached to her rank. She and her collaborators faced tre-mendous resistance whenever they tried to implement their ideas. Some of their peacekeeping colleagues launched a smear campaign, criticizing them as "authoritarian" and "arrogant," deriding them as having slept their way to the top, and ridiculing them through countless creepy jokes. Sundh herself was rumored to be a lesbian—a libelous accusation meant to undermine her in the eyes of her many sexist and conservative colleagues. And unfortu-nately, it worked. Sundh was hurt, deeply, and she and her team never man-aged to put her alternative strategy in practice.

Another local peacebuilding advocate, François Grignon, tried to keep the initiative going after Sundh left the mission in 2004, but again without much success. Within a few years, Sundh's idea became a guarded secret. Only a few United Nations staff members agreed to talk to me about it, only under conditions of strict confidentiality, and only after I had gained their trust through repeated meetings. During our conversations on the topic, they reacted as if we were discussing something shameful.

It was also very hard to get a copy of the documents Sundh's team wrote between 2002 and 2004, even though they had been discarded and never implemented, and even when I promised to keep these papers for my eyes only. Interestingly, confidentiality conditions did not motivate the reluctance to share the documents—most people said that the papers did not include any restricted information, and those who finally did give them to me did not ask me to keep them private. Rather, my contacts gave me trivial pretexts, claiming they had "lost" the documents or they had "put them in their country house and could not dig them up." William Swing, the head of the peacekeeping mission at that time, even told me that he "had to ask" if he could give me these records. Since he was the highest-ranking official on site, I wondered whose permission he had to seek. At the end of the day, I felt that Sundh's bottom-up peacebuilding strategy had become a dirty secret that nobody within the mission wanted me to investigate.

There were a few other attempts to get United Nations peacekeepers to rethink their approach to local conflicts. The most sustained one took place in the mid-2010s, by members of the newly created Stabilization Support Unit. They too developed extensive analyses of various Congolese provinces, showed that local agendas fueled the ongoing violence, tried to get their colleagues to complement their top-down approach with an increased attention to local issues, and ended up derided and ignored. When the Department of Peacekeeping Operations asked me and two other researchers to present on "Tensions Between Local and National Dynamics: Dilemmas for International Interventions in the Democratic Republic of Congo" at the New York headquarters in May 2017, they invited all of the United Nations staff who could be interested—all except those most concerned by the debate: the members of the stabilization unit. I asked why they were not included, when they spent all of their time and energy working on precisely this topic, and my host told me that nobody had thought to involve them. They were too marginalized within the mission, and viewed as too irrelevant.

In the meantime, Sundh continued to advocate for a better approach to peace. When I met her in 2017, she was Sweden's Special Envoy to the African Great Lakes. Despite her new position, despite 15 years of advocacy to get the

United Nations to finally address local conflicts, she felt that not much had changed. The overall focus was still on elections, high-level negotiations, and meetings with elites. Admittedly, there was now some attention paid to local conflict resolution, and Sweden had allocated some funding to grassroots peacebuilding programs. Nevertheless, she thought the Peace, Inc. approach still ruled the day.

Sundh was unfortunately correct. That same year, when I published an essay in *Foreign Affairs* arguing that presidential elections would not end violence in Congo, four researchers immediately wrote back to explain that elections, state reconstruction, and institution building were the only relevant solutions to the ongoing crisis, and that local conflict resolution was inadequate and unnecessary. I saw two of these researchers shortly afterward, at a breakfast meeting with a high-ranking Belgian diplomat, who told me bluntly that he agreed with them: Resolving the struggle for power in Kinshasa, the capital city, would end violence throughout the country. (He must have felt that something was not quite right, though, as he immediately told me not to quote him on that.) The United States Congress organized a hearing on Congo a few months later, and again our discussion focused on how to set up elections and convince the president to leave power—despite my efforts to bring other issues into the debate.

True to form, peacekeepers remained obsessed with elections. In 2017, a senior adviser for the mission complained to me that his colleagues mentioned "holding elections all the time" as if it was "the only thing" that mattered. They even wrote a 16-page conflict analysis document, 12 pages of which were about elections.

Admittedly, things have improved over the past 20 years. When I first started researching local peacebuilding in the early 2000s, most of my contacts did not understand what I was getting at—they often thought I was working on sexual violence (I'm still not sure why). When they did catch on, they frequently became defensive, and at times rude. A diplomat who had been polite and respectful during most of our meeting started acting increasingly bored when I began asking follow-up questions about his embassy's actions on grassroots tensions. Several others started laughing. In many cases, diplomats and United Nations officials who had been friendly eventually became annoyed when I enquired about local efforts. The few people I knew at the time who also tried to raise the same issue with interveners—like Lena Sundh and her team, and like LPI's country director Hans Romkema—encountered similar reactions.

In contrast, today, even important leaders mention the role of local tensions in fueling violence, whether in Afghanistan, Congo, Iraq, or South Sudan. Mandates for United Nations peacekeeping missions occasionally include a note encouraging the resolution of grassroots conflicts. Donors like the United States Agency for International Development (USAID) and its British and Swedish equivalents have dedicated funding for local peace work. An increasing number of international non-governmental organizations specialize in grassroots conflict resolution, implementing programs all over the world, from Syria to the Philippines.

Nevertheless, politicians, diplomats, peacekeepers, and other aid workers still spend most of their time and resources on national and international issues, as do journalists, and even some academics.

Take the international approach to the war in South Sudan, as analyzed by Stephanie Schwartz, a peacebuilder with a lot of experience in that country (and one of my former doctoral students). There have been "hundreds of pages of analysis of local conflicts," and journalists increasingly cover local issues as well. And yet, the patrons of the peace process—Norway, the United Kingdom, and the United States—keep insisting on high-level negotiations and organizing large elite conferences in neighboring countries like Ethiopia or Kenya. "That's where all the money goes," Stephanie deplored. And a lot of the funds end up in the pockets of the negotiation teams for the president and the main rebel leader, notably through large daily allowances and accommodation in fancy hotels.

Admittedly, there have been attempts to "involve the grassroots." However, they involve selecting a few activists, flying them to Addis Ababa or Nairobi, and telling them to represent their fellow citizens at the elite conferences. This is certainly not what the proponents of local conflict resolution have in mind when they advocate for a bottom-up approach.

It's not just an African problem. An important Timorese politician I interviewed in 2016, José Teixeira, spent our entire meeting trying to convince me that local issues are unimportant: What matters is the national leadership, notably relationships between the government and opposition leaders. A top-ranking United States government official I met that same year described peacebuilding work by his colleagues as "high-level peace negotiations" meant to "broker a deal between major powers." "All of the other elements are secondary to that," he explained, and "grassroots peacebuilding is often seen as a sideshow." When I met Jean-Pierre Lacroix, the big boss of United Nations peacekeeping (the under-secretary-general), in April 2018, he told me bluntly that his subordinates' job was not to support local conflict resolution; instead, they have to focus all of their efforts on national political processes. Like him, many peacebuilders continue to argue that any intervention not explicitly linked to national or international dynamics is a waste of energy.

"You've Had Your Moment!"

A colleague once jokingly complained that he can't teach my books at the beginning of the academic semester, because once his students read my work, they get so excited about bottom-up peacebuilding that they don't want to talk about the standard conflict-resolution approach anymore. They become "little Autesserre clones" and keep criticizing the usual strategies that focus on elections, governments, institutions, negotiations between national elites, etc.

One of the researchers who participated in the May 2017 meeting at the United Nations Department of Peacekeeping Operations voiced similar concerns. During her presentation, she grumbled that local conflict resolution is now the hot, fashionable topic of the day; it's what everyone is talking about, at the expense of the very important top-down work. This is why, to her, we have to go back to basics: elections, high-level negotiations, and so on.

I wish my alternative peacebuilding strategy was indeed at the top of everyone's agenda today. Bottom-up peace initiatives can address many of the issues inherent to our standard top-down efforts—just like top-down efforts can address the drawbacks of grassroot strategies. By the same token, foreign and local peacebuilders make the greatest contributions to peace when they work together, because each compensates for the limitations of the other. So our goal should not be to eliminate international or top-down involvement, but to rethink it.

Ordinary residents, grassroots non-governmental organizations, community authorities, and civil-society representatives should be the main actors in the bottom-up process. Only they have the knowledge, networks, and legitimacy to address grassroots issues.

Of course, there are obstacles. Ordinary people and local elites often lack the money, transportation, venues, and sometimes specific skills to implement effective peacebuilding programs. Therefore, international interveners should expand the financial, logistical, and technical support available for local conflict resolution.

As you'll remember, in the Congolese region of the Kivus, the Life & Peace Institute and its Congolese partners have set up intercommunity forums to discuss the specifics of local conflicts over land, and these forums have found solutions to manage the violence. That's the kind of program that is sorely needed throughout eastern Congo—the kind that directly helps people like Justine, Luca, Kaer, Isabelle, and her husband. No, these approaches will not magically improve things overnight. Yet, because they take deeply rooted causes of the conflict into account, they could be game-changers—not just in Congo, but in conflict zones around the world.

However, we need a change of mentality for this revised strategy to work. Supporting bottom-up initiatives is not as simple as just talking to local people or giving them money. We have to also overcome Peace, Inc.'s inherent culture of fraught relationships between insiders and outsiders, and we have to abandon our assumptions about what peace requires. Unfortunately, so far, most interveners are talking the talk, but not walking the walk. The Peace, Inc. approach is still alive and thriving. Fortunately, there is a better way forward, and there are models that we can follow.

PART III
THE NEW PEACE MANIFESTO

5

Peace by Piece

Proponents of Peace, Inc. tend to ask the same questions when they hear the story of Idjwi. "Isn't this island an exception?" they usually wonder. "Are there other pockets of peace like this one?" "Can we generalize?" "Maybe we can't have Idjwi elsewhere..."

No, Idjwi is no exception. There are similar success stories all around the world. And it's not just a few isolated instances. They exist in Afghanistan, Colombia, Iraq, Israel, Kosovo, the Philippines, and several other countries. Among these cases, Somaliland is particularly noteworthy. Against enormous odds, its inhabitants have managed to control violence in a relatively large territory for an extended period of time by using techniques similar to those employed on a smaller scale in Idjwi.

The residents of Somaliland, Colombia, Israel and the Palestinian territories, and other places have incredible stories to share—and we have much to learn from them if we want to build peace successfully, both at home and abroad.

Somaliland and Somalia

I've long been fascinated by Somaliland—an arid territory on the eastern horn of Africa—because it's the largest case of effective bottom-up peacebuilding that I've found in the entire world. For years, though, I couldn't get over my fear of going there. Every time I thought of it, I remembered that, officially, the Republic of Somaliland does not exist: It's in the northwest part of the Federal Republic of Somalia.

Somalia's reputation certainly scared me: decades of fighting, bombings, and terror attacks, no functioning state, extreme poverty, and so on. And yet the situation there is not so different from what I found in Afghanistan, Congo, and South Sudan. The real reason I was terrified of going to Somaliland is because my good friend Randal Rhoade was kidnapped in Northern Kenya and held hostage in Somalia.

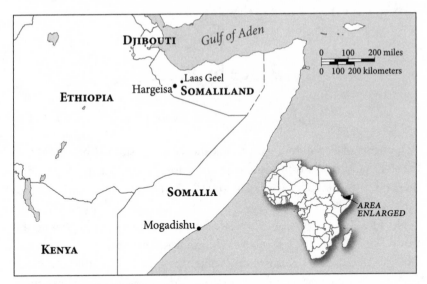

Map of Somaliland in the Horn of Africa

It was an evening like any other—Randal was making a routine visit to the border town of Mandera to see his team—when men heavily armed and clad in military uniforms stormed his compound, taking him and two other aid workers. It would be months before anyone saw them again.

My husband Philippe was the human resources director for Randal's humanitarian organization at the time, so the kidnappers decided to use him as one of their contacts. During those long months, we slept with Philippe's cell phone on his nightstand, waiting for the abductors to call. When they did not, the lack of news was agonizing (*Is Randal okay? Does silence mean he's dead? Is he being tortured right now? Starving?*). It was even more excruciating when they did. I vividly recall these phone calls: the ring in the middle of the night, my husband rushing to pick up, me, half asleep, hoping that we would finally get good news, and the kidnappers yelling, so loudly that I could hear them from across the room: "WE'RE GONNA KILL HIM! Give us the money, or we're gonna kill him!" Try falling asleep again after receiving a call like that in the middle of the night...

It took 79 days for Randal to be released. I'm still amazed at how quickly he recovered from the whole ordeal. After a few months, he was back on a humanitarian mission in South Sudan. He has remained his usual self: thoughtful, funny, and friendly. The main change since his release from captivity is that he has become a black belt in karate.

Although I was only involved from afar, it still took me eight years to face my fears and do what was best for my research. But I progressively realized that my apprehension was misplaced—and quite literally so. To start, Randal was kidnapped in Kenya and held hostage in the south of Somalia, while Somaliland lies in the north of the country. Like most outsiders, I had made the common mistake of applying one local incident to an entire country— ironic, given that my whole career is built on studying subnational variations. And most importantly, Somaliland is completely different from Somalia, in almost every way.

In Somalia, the government and its army hold sway over the capital city Mogadishu, and little else. The rest of the country is either disputed territory or under the control of one of the many local armed groups. Of these, the most powerful ones are the al-Shabaab militia (allied with al-Qaeda) and the Islamic State (the jihadist network from Iraq and Syria). Battles and blood-shed happen every day. Attacks against the government and its foreign allies are a weekly occurrence. If this isn't enough to make would-be visitors ap-prehensive, Somalia has also achieved some of the highest rankings in the world's least desirable categories: most corrupt country, second most fragile state, third highest rate of brain drain, fourth highest rate of economic de-cline and poverty, and so on.

Somaliland's secessionist movement had two main motivations: to escape persistent discriminations and abuses by Somali elites and to abandon the sinking ship that was the Somali state. And it worked. Since the Republic of Somaliland declared its independence in 1991, local people have built functioning state institutions, including an effective administration, a de-cent army and police force, and competent intelligence services. They hold relatively democratic elections to select their president, parliament, and district leaders, and the losers concede without violence. This was the case for one presidential candidate, who lost by an 80-vote margin, and another one who suspected his opponent of corruption and vote-buying. This quasi-state effectively rules most of Somaliland's territory, in large part thanks to alliances with local elders.

I was tipped off on how exceptional Somaliland was even before I set foot there. When I travel to conflict zones, I usually take a whole collection of external batteries with me—and usually end up well over the 50-pound limit on the plane. Somehow, a lot of my anxieties about my upcoming trips tend to focus on all of these extra devices. Did I take the right cable? Do I have enough batteries? Should I take my surge protector? In my mind, the extra care I have to take when I'm packing symbolizes that I'm going to an unstable and violent place, where a power cut can easily mean a new armed group has just taken control and is trying to thwart resistance. In con-trast, before I left for Somaliland, I was told that residents don't even need generators. This may seem like a minor detail, but to me it's a pretty telling one. It indicates that there is a reliable electricity supply. This means that Somaliland is safe, stable, and wealthy enough to maintain a good power grid. Going to conduct field research without all of the usual paraphernalia felt like a luxury.

There are a lot of tensions between clans, sub-clans, sub-sub-clans, sub-sub-sub-clans, and families in Somaliland, but these conflicts erupt in violence far less frequently than in Somalia. And, when they do, they rarely escalate into large-scale fighting. Between 2000 and 2018, 21,645 people died due to conflict in Somalia, compared to 357 in Somaliland. That's 60 times more casualties in Somalia, while its population is only three times greater than that of Somaliland (11 million in the former versus four million in the latter). Plus, Somaliland's last terror attack took place in October 2008. The last time a foreigner was kidnapped was just as long ago, in February 2008—and, within 12 hours, the local army had caught the abductors and freed the hostage.

I felt perfectly safe when I spent time in Somaliland in late 2017. As long as I stayed clear of the area around the eastern border—a swath of territory over

Night falls on a residential neighborhood of Hargeisa. About 90 percent of the city was destroyed in the "independence" war of the 1980s, but today Somaliland's capital boasts safe streets, large houses, and a well-functioning electricity grid.
Photo credit: Séverine Autesserre, 2017

which Somaliland and Puntland (another breakaway region of Somalia) keep fighting—it seemed that I was in a peaceful country, with sleepy rural villages and a bustling capital city, complete with a great nightlife and terrible traffic jams. Even as someone who very much looked like an outsider, I could walk to my meetings in the capital city Hargeisa, something that would have been way too dangerous in Somalia. I went out at night—traveling only by car, and never alone, but still I was not locked up in a secure compound like I was in Afghanistan. I visited Somaliland's main tourist attraction, the 7,750-year-old cave paintings in Laas Geel, and hiked back with a friend (and the mandatory armed guard that the government assigns to all foreigners who leave Hargeisa) to the nearest village through the rock-strewn landscape. I later strolled alone on the beach in Berbera while my friend went swimming. And many of the ordinary people I interviewed in rural villages outside of Hargeisa brought up the same example when I asked them whether there was peace in their village: They all said that even I, a foreigner and a woman, could spend the night there, even sleep outside or walk around—by myself—and I would be just fine.

Laas Geel's prehistoric painted caves offer stunning views of Somaliland's semi-desert. Because of climate change, droughts and floods have become increasingly frequent, jeopardizing people's livelihoods and fueling conflicts over land, water, and livestock.

Photo credit: Séverine Autesserre, 2017

Of course, Somaliland is not a paradise—no more so than Idjwi. Being a woman there is enormously challenging. Although women face few legal restrictions, in practice they are treated like second-class citizens. They have no political power, and have little access to education, stable employment, or business opportunities. Female genital mutilation is the norm, with virtually all adult women having undergone "cutting." Child brides are also common. Even everyday activities are limited; women cannot go to the gym or the main room of certain restaurants, for instance, because they are reserved for men.

It's not only women who suffer. About 65 percent of the population is unemployed—many of them young people with college degrees, some of whom end up in gang-like bands that fight against other clans' youths. Rural areas are much poorer than the main cities and enjoy less access to public services like electricity, education, and health. There is constant low-level fighting among sub-clans. Minor clans face discrimination when seeking access to power, wealth, and employment. Citizens complain of growing corruption among their political leaders and state administrators. And everybody I talked to demanded international recognition of their independence from Somalia, because not being a sovereign state means missing many opportunities for development, business, foreign aid, and political influence. All in all, Somaliland has many issues. Nevertheless, it is vastly more peaceful and prosperous than the rest of Somalia.

Bottom-Up Peace versus Peace, Inc.

Understanding the reasons for Somaliland's extraordinary peace would require a full-length book, but even a brief analysis yields an important insight: Like Idjwi, Somaliland benefited from sustained grassroots peacebuilding initiatives, while the Peace, Inc. approach prevailed and failed in the rest of Somalia.

Haroon Yusuf, an intellectual who participated in the conflict-resolution efforts from the 1980s onward and currently works as the director of a local research institute, told me how "in South and Central Somalia, the international community's approach of bringing the warlords to Mogadishu, to Nairobi, to make peace [was] completely detached from the population, without real involvement of the grassroots," which led to distrust among the public.

Foreign donors spend more than $1.5 billion a year on peacebuilding in Somalia. They focus on top-down strategies and interactions with "warlords," meaning militia commanders—often clan strongmen or political faction leaders—who, like the feudal lords of old, use military force to control a territory, exploit its population, and extract resources. Diplomats and United Nations officials keep trying to build a state similar to those we see in the West, with modern bureaucratic institutions led by an elected government. They regularly invite rebel leaders and government elites abroad for large peace summits (24 in the past 30 years!), during which they insist on using foreign-designed templates and timelines. And they celebrate cease-fire agreements and power-sharing deals that signatory parties routinely break almost immediately. This approach has not only failed to decrease violence, but it has also created a massive dependence on international aid— foreign funding has accounted for 45 percent of Somalia's annual budget in recent years.

By contrast, Yusuf emphasized, "In Somaliland, the traditional system [of governance] was stronger, peace was built from the grassroots, and people trusted the traditional leaders, as compared to the warlords."

Differing colonial and post-colonial histories explain why Somaliland's traditional leaders still command the power and respect they need to maintain peace on a daily basis, while their counterparts in the rest of Somalia do not. When the Italians colonized Somalia in the late 19th and early 20th century, they hoped to establish a modern version of the Roman Empire, complete with full control of the territory, its resources, and its population. To do so, they became heavily and directly involved in their Somali colony, destroying existing power structures and relegating indigenous elites to an ornamental status. The British, on the other hand, didn't have to meddle in Somaliland's internal affairs in order to achieve their main goal: protecting their global trade routes. They therefore ruled through existing leaders, and in doing so they preserved some of the social and political structures of their protectorate and reinforced the influence of its traditional elites.

When colonization ended in 1960, both territories merged into a unified Somalia, whose government tried to replace clan practices with modern state institutions. But Somalilanders soon became discontent with the new regime. The Southerners who controlled it were corrupt and they failed to provide essential public services like security and development. The military dictatorship that took over in 1969 further discriminated against Northerners, eventually repressing them bloodily. In 1981, Somalilanders rebelled. The insurgents first wanted to overthrow the central government, but then opted for secession—which they declared in 1991. All throughout, they placed the clan system at the heart of their political program, and they relied on elders to mobilize and control combatants.

Somaliland experienced widespread violence during the last decade of its union with Somalia, as well as in the immediate post-independence period. The Southern-led government killed more than 50,000 inhabitants between 1987 and 1989 alone (a massacre that the United Nations later classified as a genocide), and half of the population had to flee. Upon their return in the early 1990s, Somalilanders found mass graves, wrecked cities, and a country in shambles. Clans fought against clans and sub-clans against sub-clans—over livestock, pastoral land, food aid, ports, airports, roads, trade, and the control of the central government.

The Hargeisa War Memorial, located in the city center, includes an actual downed fighter jet atop murals that depict violence and destruction. Officially, the monument commemorates Somaliland's struggle for independence, but certain residents prefer to see it as a symbol of humanity across enemy lines: They told me that, at the last minute, the pilot of this specific plane refused to carry orders and drop bombs, thus saving thousands of lives.

Photo credit: Séverine Autesserre, 2017

So, of their own initiative, local elders organized peace conferences—39 in total. Local communities, notably those of Somaliland's main towns (Boroma, Hargeisa, Berbera), hosted and fed the participants. Local businessmen financed the gatherings, as well as the freshly established security apparatus, the printing of new banknotes (a task typically reserved for the federal government), and more. Religious and social elites from the region helped guerilla leaders reach agreements. Even members of the diaspora provided funds and mediated between combatants.

All of these people talked endlessly, often for months, sometimes longer. Eventually the fighters would agree to a ceasefire, a code of conduct, a way forward—forgiving and forgetting the killings that took place and compensating those who had lost their buildings, cattle, and other property. And then clan elders, armed only with the immense respect they commanded, compelled combatants to hand over their weapons. They didn't use force, but instead drew on their moral influence: their image as neutral parties whose extensive knowledge of Islamic religious law and Xeer customary law (Somalia's traditional legal system) best enables them to uphold peace. As one of the officers told me, the reverence toward these traditional chiefs was such that he and his men didn't even think about disobeying.

In parallel, local residents both organized their own grassroots reconciliation meetings and helped implement the decisions the elites reached. For instance, when young men proved recalcitrant to disarm, fathers and uncles took away their guns—by force if necessary. By 1997, Somaliland was at peace, and it has remained so for the past 23 years.

As Yusuf emphasized, while foreign diplomats and United Nations officials led the peace efforts in Somalia, international involvement remained limited in Somaliland (just like in Idjwi). I wouldn't go so far as to say—like virtually all of the people I met there did—that Somalilanders built peace without any outside support, because there has been some international help. Nevertheless, with the notable exception of a bottom-up conflict-resolution initiative led by LPI's Horn of Africa program, the aid has centered mainly on responding to humanitarian crises (delivering food, providing water, repatriating refugees, clearing landmines), promoting economic development (constructing roads, power grids, schools, and so on) and, in recent years, coordinating anti-terrorism efforts, rather than on building and maintaining peace.

The fact that no country or international organization recognizes Somaliland's independence largely explains the lack of external involvement in its peace process. Every day, the authorities in Hargeisa run the show for all of Somaliland's residents. They build public infrastructure—schools, hospitals, roads, and ports—and maintain the remarkable power grid. They collect taxes, issue banknotes, and manage the economy. They direct the police officers and army units so that residents remain free from violence and terrorism. Working in tandem with traditional local leaders, they resolve small and large conflicts, from livestock disputes to clan infighting. Elites and elected officials in Somalia's capital Mogadishu have little to do with what happens in Somaliland most days. However, foreign powers fear that recognizing Somaliland as an independent state would open the door to more secessionist movements throughout Africa and jeopardize the peace process in Southern and Central Somalia. And, as you may remember, standard practices dictate that international peacebuilders should interact mostly with national leaders. So, in typical Peace, Inc. fashion, most donors, United Nations agencies, and other international organizations work with the central Somali government, which theoretically holds sovereign rule over Somaliland, rather than with the Hargeisa-based authorities, who control the territory in practice.

In addition, outsiders often view Somaliland as peripheral and unimportant, not the kind of place that is worth investing in or fighting for. Plus, like with Idjwi, international peacebuilders know that the territory is already relatively stable and peaceful, so why would they spend their limited time and resources there, when they could devote them to addressing the catastrophic situation in South and Central Somalia?

This lack of international support has deprived Somalilanders of much-needed resources and of the sovereignty they so desperately want. But, paradoxically, this may not be such a bad thing. To start, the fight for recognition helps promote cohesion and peace. Many inhabitants explained to me that they make sacrifices and do their best to smooth out tensions because it may help them achieve their long-term goal: independence and sovereignty at last.

Even more importantly, the lack of foreign funding is precisely what has made the locally-driven peace possible, as Yusuf hinted at and as many other local intellectuals and foreign scholars have emphasized. It forced politicians and guerilla leaders to rely on the local communities, business elite, and diaspora for funding and logistics. This produced increased government accountability toward citizens. In addition, because Somaliland's peace process was internally driven and funded, it moved at its own pace, with conferences lasting for months at a time and the entire process taking years. The negotiations relied on customary mediation practices, and they were tailored to the local context. They produced a unique social, political, and economic system that relies on Somaliland's clans and on its own version of Islamic laws and values. It's the mirror opposite of the detrimental Peace, Inc. approach that prevailed in Somalia.

I'm not saying that it's entirely the fault of the international peacebuilders that Somalia is still at war while Somaliland is not. To start, outsiders *are* present in Somaliland and they *do* support the peace process there. They just don't act in typical Peace, Inc. fashion. Because most countries and international organizations don't recognize the territory as an independent state, their staff doesn't have to work through Somaliland's government representatives. Instead, foreign interveners tend to interact with a wide range of grassroots elites. They also have to remain low-profile, and they can't impose their usual agenda. As a result, Somaliland's peace is locally-designed, locally-managed, locally-paid, and locally-owned, to use the words that the residents I met, from ministers to peasants to businesspeople, kept repeating throughout our discussions—mantras that encapsulate what I read in policy and scholarly articles.

Everyday Peace

There are other striking similarities between Idjwi and Somaliland, despite their very different histories, cultures, and geographic locations.

Just like in the case of Idjwi, foreign analysts kept telling me that there is a simple explanation for Somaliland's peace: Somalilanders are all from the same clan, so they have no reason to engage in the many ethnic conflicts that affect their southern neighbors. But this is not quite true. Although there is indeed one dominant clan in Somaliland (Isaaq people), a minority of the population comes from other clans (such as the Gadabursi and the Warsengeli). Even more importantly, clan infighting (between sub-clans, families, and lineages) is an enormous source of tension both in Somaliland and in Somalia, and in the latter, it does lead to extensive violence. Therefore, attributing Somaliland's relative peace to ethnic homogeneity is no more accurate than it was in Idjwi.

That said, Somalilanders of all clans do share underlying socio-cultural values (like the protection of women and children during war) and economic interests (like investments in local towns). Even more importantly, as with the residents of Idjwi, all Somalilanders pride themselves on—in their words—their "peaceful identity," their "peace-loving society," and their "community norms and values that have always supported peace." The title of their national anthem is "Long Life with Peace." Granted, there is more everyday violence in Somaliland than in Idjwi, but the whole time I was there I kept hearing "We are peace, we are a peaceful people—not like our Somali neighbors!"

A family gathers wood next to their dwelling—a large, portable, traditional tent made of desert materials—near Laas Geel. Like them, more than half of Somaliland's population lives a nomadic existence.
Photo credit: Séverine Autesserre, 2017

In addition, like in Idjwi, traditional leaders, local elites, and ordinary citizens actively work to maintain the peace.

The top clan leaders sit in the *Guurti*, the parliament's House of Elders, which Somalilanders and outsiders alike credit for effectively mediating many large-scale conflicts that have arisen since independence. For instance, shortly before I visited Somaliland, two sub-clans started fighting because members of one of them had taken their cattle to graze on the other's land. 22 people died, 99 were wounded, and the conflict was escalating. So the *Guurti* stepped in. It sent a delegation, which decided that the government owned the land at the heart of the conflict. Even more importantly, to promote long-term stability, the commission told the combatants to sit and talk about what to do regarding each person who had died during the hostilities. Eventually, the two sides reached a compromise: They would pay 100 camels for every man killed, and 50 for every woman. (I found the gender discrepancy infuriating, but that is a separate issue.) The members of the *Guurti* proudly told me that both sides followed through. Indeed, in Somaliland, once the combatants reach an agreement—in this case, regarding a ceasefire, a code of conduct, and compensations for victims—it is the elders at all levels (local, provincial, and national) who make sure that the deal is implemented faithfully.

Of course, just like in Idjwi, these traditional chiefs attract their share of criticism and accusations: of corruption, resistance to change, aloofness, and monopolizing power. Thankfully, just like in Idjwi, ordinary people step in whenever necessary.

Dr. Hussein Bulhan, the president of one of Hargeisa's many universities, explained to me: "If you want to study what keeps the peace, it's not the stories of leaders alone, but the story of common people." He regretted that this tale hasn't been told yet, because analysts always focus on "power structures, leaders, elites," and proceeded to tell me the story of the individuals and communities at the grassroots level organizing for peace:

> It's not because somebody is giving them funding, but just out of this neighborhood they say: "We have had enough problems, there have been victims here and there, let's do something." . . . They have this feeling: "I lay down my gun, you lay down your gun."

In this story, "it's not the Somaliland government that keeps the peace," nor is it armed soldiers. It's not outsiders either—"Forget the foreigners," Bulhan said. Instead, it's ordinary residents.

All Somalilanders keep an eye out for signs of trouble. On my first day there, my research assistant Aamiina* briefed me:

> If you suspect anyone, or if anyone is acting strange, most people report it to the police station. Also, if some people or two parties fight, immediately people interfere and ask to keep the peace. As the fight comes out we immediately shut it down.

Whenever there is a problem that could escalate into bloodshed, such as a land dispute, a debt unpaid, a person killed in a personal feud or car accident, a dowry issue, etc., Somalilanders reach out to the sultans (the clan chiefs) and sheikhs (high-ranking religious men)—or, when necessary, units of the state bureaucracy, police, and army. And the local leaders work to reconcile the parties in conflict and their associated families and sub-clans straightaway, before the tensions spiral into mass fighting. In Bulhan's words, it is "the collective eyes and ears of people" that helps control violence—reminding me strongly of what I had observed in Idjwi.

It's not only *who* works to keep the peace that is noteworthy in Somaliland, it's also *how* they do it. Unlike in Idjwi, where government services are largely absent, Somalilanders rely on state institutions in addition to a range of traditional authorities. This is possible precisely because the residents themselves have built these structures from the bottom up rather than from the top down. In doing so, they have ensured that the Somaliland state, including its government, army, and police, is accountable to its citizens, responsive to their needs, and formed around their culture and traditions.

If you live in Europe or North America, the idea of keeping watch on your neighbors and relatives might seem strange and even reprehensible, given how much we frown upon snooping and "snitching." It would also probably not occur to members of disenfranchised communities to report suspicious activities to the police—more privileged citizens would do so, but they may not consider reaching out to local strongmen as an alternative. In brief, what we see in Somaliland is not the kind of peacebuilding tactics that most Westerners and many interveners would think about. But there, like in Idjwi, because those driving the peace process are members of the local communities, they devise norms and strategies that work for them—just like First Nations people have done in Canada, and inhabitants of impoverished areas in the United States.

Like in Idjwi, everyday involvement of ordinary citizens works wonders to prevent minor tensions from escalating into major violence. It even enables residents to thwart the notorious al-Shabaab militias—al-Qaeda's ruthless allies in the region who, in the past five years alone, were responsible for the deaths of more than 20,000 people in Somalia and Kenya. In the early 2000s, al-Shabaab combatants tried to destabilize Somaliland the same way they had weakened—and continue to weaken—South and Central Somalia. They failed. A local businessman, Ahmed Mohamed Omar, remembers why:

One time they kidnapped a German guy. The people living in one village heard the car on the way, they blocked it, and they caught them. The society caught them—without the support of the police and military.

Then they [al-Shabaab] organized a big operation in Hargeisa, and the people, the neighbors, informed on them: "There are people we don't know; we don't know what they are doing; these are not people we knew before." So the police went and caught them. And they found a huge stock of explosives and ammunitions and lots of things.

The Somaliland government eventually formalized this approach into an official community policing system: All throughout the territory, every 50 to 70 households establish committees of residents, whose representatives work hand in hand with local police stations to monitor potential terrorists and maintain their own security.

There are countless differences between Idjwi and Somaliland in terms of size, geography, culture, history, politics, economy, and so on. Regardless, we can still glean crucial insights from the experiences of both places: It *is* possible to build peace from the bottom up; foreign support is *not* indispensable; strong beliefs around "who we are as a people" are very important; and local leaders and ordinary citizens can play a crucial role in preventing violence.

Zones of Peace

What's more, Idjwi and Somaliland are not isolated cases. We can find similar areas of remarkable peace throughout the world—with the most numerous, most institutionalized, and perhaps best-known examples being in Colombia.

Colombia has experienced nearly a dozen civil wars since its independence from Spain in 1819. From the 1960s onward, the main conflict has been between leftist guerillas and the central government—supported by paramilitary groups since the 1980s. Violence revolves around economic interests (access to land, in particular), political ideologies (most prominently communism versus capitalism), and social concerns (notably marginalization of peasant populations). Most of the pro- and anti-government militias finance their war efforts through kidnapping, drug trafficking, and extortion. An estimated 260,000 people have died over the past 60 years, more than eight million have been displaced, primarily in rural areas, and more than 15,000 sexually assaulted.

In true Peace, Inc. fashion, American diplomats and United Nations officials have focused on brokering peace deals between government and rebel leaders and on extending state presence throughout the territory. And they have spent a tremendous amount of money doing so: more than $10 billion since 2000. Despite various agreements signed in 1992, 2006, and 2016—the first two of which were successfully implemented—many insurgent groups are still active today, government and paramilitary forces still commit numerous human rights abuses, and many rural areas still experience extensive violence.

This sad story of failed top-down intervention efforts probably sounds familiar to you by now. What's more novel—and more uplifting—is that for decades, all throughout the country, dozens of different communities have found ways to stay out of the conflict.

I've been invited to Colombia for conferences on peacebuilding twice in recent years, and both times I stayed a little bit longer so that I could meet with the members of one such community. I decided to focus on San José de Apartadó because this village is located in the Urabá region, one of the country's most violent areas.

Getting there is no walk in the park. You have to go to Medellín, the bustling, congested, but very green regional capital—Colombians rightfully call it the "city of flowers" and the "city of eternal spring." From there you take a small plane to a tiny airport next to Apartadó, a poor, gray town in a district so remote, and so well protected by mountains and jungles, that the Colombian government—just like the Spanish colonizers of centuries past—has always had trouble controlling it. (These days, paramilitary groups and drug trafficking gangs dominate the region.) From Apartadó, you drive on a run-down dirt road that most normal cars can't handle. After an hour going up the mountain, surrounded by banana plantations, dense foliage, and sleeping hamlets, you see a fenced-off area that marks the territory of the peace zone. And if you're like me, the first time, you won't get in.

This came as a surprise, given how friendly and hospitable Colombians had been until then. People constantly went out of their way to help me out when I appeared lost or confused, invited me to their place, introduced me to their friends. Even the poorest citizens I met—those who live near San José de Apartadó—made a point of offering me coffee, juice, fruit, cake, whatever they had. And yet, it took me two trips, more than three months of discussion, dozens of introductions (by colleagues, friends, friends of friends, friends of colleagues), until I could finally enter the peace zone. Indeed, its members are so suspicious of outsiders that they all had to meet as a group, discuss, review my credentials (a presentation of my research, a copy of my passport, etc.), and vote on whether or not they would allow me to talk with them. Thankfully, I have a bit of a character flaw that just so happens to be perfect in instances like this: I'm very stubborn—a peacebuilder friend once nicknamed me "PerSeverine."

Upon finally gaining entrance, I was disconcerted—at first sight, there is nothing special about the peace zone. It's just a bunch of small houses, some made of wood and others of concrete, nestled in lush, green vegetation, much like the surrounding villages. The whole area was very quiet when I visited. It was the middle of the day, so everyone was out tending their cocoa crops, and the only thing I heard was the laughter of little kids playing while trying to keep roosters from eating the rice their parents had put out to dry.

But then two things stood out to me. The first was a large green meadow encircled by what appeared to be wooden pigeonholes. Within this space were a number of white, head-sized stones arranged in an intricate pattern—more than 300 stones in total, each bearing the name of a member of the peace zone murdered during the peak of the violence (in the late 1990s and the 2000s). The wooden structures around it bear the remains and photos of some of these members, such as the former leaders and their families—including an 18-month-old toddler—that the Colombian army and the paramilitaries assassinated in 2005.

This memorial honoring more than 300 people stood in a community that, on the day of my visit, counted approximately 300 residents (600 if you include the inhabitants of the neighboring peace zones). The survivors told me that the desire of local businesses to take over the villagers' land instigated the murders. The region is incredibly fertile, making it a prime spot to grow any kind of crop, from cacao to coca. The farming plots around the peace zone are a tremendously valuable natural resource and thus, like in Congo and so many other parts of the world, they generate a lot of competition. So, businessmen asked politicians and armed groups to clear the residents from the area. And because both the government and its enemies maintain that anybody who's not with them is against them, they happily obliged.

The other thing that stands out when you visit the enclosure is the billboard nailed to a tree trunk just behind the entrance. It proudly broadcasts the central principles of the community, the principles that every member has pledged to respect, the principles that are so fundamental that breaking them will get you expelled from the peace zone—the principles that are the key to the relative safety its inhabitants now enjoy:

Members freely commit to:
- participate in community works
- not tolerate injustice nor impunity for [those who commit] crimes
- not accept individual reparations for victims
- not plant any illegal crops
- not handle or submit information to any of the parties in conflict
- not carry arms
- not drink alcohol
- not participate in the war directly or indirectly

A billboard tells all passersby the rules that govern life in San José de Apartadó's peace zone (Colombia). These eight ideas are the basis of the community's identity and security.

Photo credit: Séverine Autesserre, 2017

Admittedly, these principles don't make the residents of the peace zone particularly popular. Surrounding villagers find them "a bit stuck up," and the armed groups roaming the countryside absolutely hate it that a bunch of peasants dare stand up to them—the other local citizens give them information, harbor and feed combatants, and pay protection money. But in terms of providing peace and security, the principles work—not perfectly, but well enough.

It was not the formal representatives of the peace zone who best explained the ins and outs of these principles to me, but Antonia and Luis, two leaders of the local farmers' association from a nearby village (a sort of leftist union that fights for development and human rights). I met them, along with a bunch of their colleagues, during my first trip to the area. They were all relatively young (in their 20s or 30s, maybe early 40s), and represented a diverse palette of skin tones—you could see a beautiful mix of African, European, and Indigenous ancestries. They sported old t-shirts and muddy boots, having taken a break from cultivating their fields to come and talk with me, but the passion with which they spoke, the sophistication of their ideas, their commitment, their enthusiasm, their persuasiveness, reminded me of the most compelling politicians I had seen in France and the United States.

They all explained to me that the main function of the peace zone is to protect its members. To do so, the residents don't cooperate with the parties in conflict—not even to sell them sodas or other goods. They don't grow coca—a common crop on the paramilitary-controlled land around them, as it is used to produce cocaine—and they don't allow the army or rebel groups to stay on their territories. Inhabitants of the peace community remain neutral and unarmed. When combatants try to extract information from them, they play dumb and pretend not to know anything. When rebels or paramilitaries get angry and start threatening people in the community, they make sure never to leave the targeted individuals alone. Large groups work alongside them in the fields; sometimes foreigners also accompany them in order to (hopefully) make the soldiers think twice before attacking.

The members of this peace community have also learned the hard way that they have to refrain from participating in political debates. In the past, they used to denounce problems publicly, but, Luis explained, "Every time they did that, someone was killed." Hence the memorial garden with its 300 white stones. Worse, the government kept mishandling the murders and reported abuses, so the community grew frustrated and now refuses any kind of engagement with or services from state institutions. They even have their own school, with its own curriculum, in which they teach the kids the central principles of the peace zone, like solidarity, along with love of its land, and love of its members.

They still believe in Colombia as a country, and proudly fly its flag in the middle of their enclosure, just next to the flag of their community. But, as they told me, they don't believe in their country's government or institutions. Instead, they've built peace outside the state—and despite its constant opposition (a stark contrast from Somaliland).

Even with these initiatives, violence never completely stopped in this area, and the residents still fear for their lives—they told me they receive death threats virtually every week. But the number of killings and armed incursions has decreased since the establishment of the peace zone and the expansion of its core principles, and today the inhabitants feel much safer there than they ever would outside. And while many lost their entire families to the violence that has marred Colombia for decades, they have found new "brothers" within the community—people they care about, who care about them, and who'll help them whenever they need it.

It's not only the members who benefit from the existence of the peace zone. The inhabitants of the nearby village have also found refuge in the enclosure when armed groups are fighting amongst themselves and civilians need a place to hide. Antonia actually told me that if the peace community had not existed, combatants "would have killed everyone." Even if her assessment is not entirely correct, her statement still shows what a positive difference the peace zone has made in the lives of both its residents and their neighbors.

Oasis of Peace

Another fascinating place resides halfway across the world, in the Middle East. Peace efforts there often make the headlines, so you're probably more familiar with them than with those in Somalia or Colombia. Iconic photos of men in suits may even come to your mind: Israeli prime minister Menachem Begin shaking hands with Egyptian president Anwar Sadat accompanied by a beaming United States president Jimmy Carter in the background (1978 Camp David Accords), or Israeli prime minister Yitzhak Rabin shaking hands with Palestinian leader Yasser Arafat under the benevolent gaze of United States president Bill Clinton (1993 Oslo Accords).

At this point, you may be realizing that the moments you have in mind are all elite-focused initiatives—and, as such, they perfectly illustrate the benefits and limitations of the top-down approach. On the one hand, these Peace, Inc. efforts have helped reconcile Israel with some of its neighbors, like Egypt and Jordan (although certainly not Iran, Lebanon, or Syria). On the other hand, they have done little to ease tensions between Israeli and Palestinian people. Cue other iconic photos of the region, with young Arab men throwing stones (these are the marks of Palestinian uprisings), Israeli soldiers in full body armor facing crowds of unarmed civilians, Palestinian suicide bombers killing scores of Israeli citizens, or the 300-mile wall that now divides Israeli lands from Palestinian ones.

There have been 12 formal attempts by world leaders to reconcile Israelis and Palestinians since 1967, all to no avail. In the past twelve years alone, the conflict has claimed the lives of close to 4,000 people, 95 percent of them Palestinian.

Against this depressing backdrop, let me tell you the story of Wahat al-Salam – Neve Shalom (respectively the Arabic and Hebrew translations of "Oasis of Peace"). It's the only village in the world founded for the express purpose of demonstrating that two enemy groups can live together. Binational, bilingual, and bicultural, it is located halfway between Jerusalem and Tel-Aviv, on the Green Line (the former border, established in 1949, that used to demarcate the outer limits of Israeli territory), on top of a hill surrounded by fertile fields of grapevines and olive trees. Despite constant opposition from the state of Israel, Wahat al-Salam – Neve Shalom has prospered in the 48 years since its creation and, by the time I visited in 2018, it was home to more than 300 inhabitants—half of them Israeli Jews, the other half Muslim and Christian Palestinians.

One of them, Samah Salaime, was born in a Palestinian refugee family and grew up with no contact with Jewish people. Although she learned Hebrew at school, she didn't speak it well, so she had a hard time communicating with her peers during her university studies in Jerusalem—not to mention that, as an Arab, she felt ostracized. She hated all of the tensions that surrounded her in the city. (Arabs don't feel safe walking in the Jewish part of town, and vice versa.) Samah wanted something different for her sons, but she couldn't find any place that taught both Arabic and Hebrew, as well as the histories of the two people. Upon her husband's suggestion, she visited the school at Wahat al-Salam – Neve Shalom, and there, she saw "small Arab and Jewish kids playing together, shouting with each other, Arab and Jewish teachers speaking Arabic and Hebrew." As she recalled with a wistful smile on her face, "I was fascinated by this very simple idea that peace is possible." So she told her husband, "Honey, we are not applying to this school, we are applying to this village!" They moved in five days before the start of the second Intifada—the period of intensified Israeli-Palestinian violence that lasted from 2000 to 2005—and raised their three boys in peace.

Today, it's not only the primary school that draws people in to Wahat al-Salam – Neve Shalom. The swimming pool too has become a favorite spot for Israeli Jews and Palestinians who want to relax without worrying that they speak the "wrong" language or look like the enemy. Religious groups from the region regularly use the spiritual center to conduct their ceremonies—whether Jewish, Muslim, Catholic, Orthodox, Buddhist, you name it. More than 70,000 adults have participated in the School for Peace, whose programs teach how to counter violence and promote equality in the region. And the village is so tranquil and pretty, the inhabitants seem so happy and matter-of-fact about their way of life, that the waitlist to join the community now numbers in the hundreds.

There are tensions, of course, around the management of the village, the ongoing process of gentrification, and so on. But they don't divide residents along the fault line of the surrounding conflict; rather, it's usually a matter of social class, or newcomers versus old-timers. Above all, these conflicts never escalate into violence. All are resolved through talking, arguing, debating, compromising, or voting. In a country that many of its inhabitants have likened to an apartheid state, where fear and hatred of the other group continually fuel violence, the people of Wahat al-Salam – Neve Shalom show that Israeli Jews and Palestinians can actually thrive together.

Picking Peace

We can find these kinds of peace zones across the planet, from Afghanistan to Bosnia, Fiji, Indonesia, Mozambique, Northern Ireland, and the Philippines. And their main characteristics are reminiscent of what we saw in Idjwi, San José de Apartadó, Somaliland, and Wahat al-Salam – Neve Shalom. The residents all embrace an identity that is localized, historically relevant, and fundamentally different from those of their neighbors at war. Rather than hold strongly to the belief that they are Muslim instead of Christian, or Croat instead of Serbian, or Catholic instead of Protestant, members of the community rally around the idea that it is in everyone's best interest to avoid violence. They rely on local input and codes of conduct to manage internal tensions, and they provide their members with services that are lacking in neighboring conflict zones.

These local successes are not limited to small villages. The entire provinces of Balkh in Afghanistan and Kurdistan in Iraq have remained demonstrably less violent than their surroundings. So did the town of Gity during the 1994 Rwandan genocide, and the cities of Anefis in Mali and Beckon and Tuzla in Bosnia during the wars there.

In fact, in every country where I have conducted research, I have found examples of ordinary citizens and local elite using their personal connections to convince the leaders of surrounding armed groups to come and negotiate. Fathers, mothers, uncles, brothers, sisters, and cousins reached out to their family members who were fighting. Teachers went to meet their former students who had become militia leaders. Priests, pastors, imams, sheikhs and rabbis rallied their flocks, and village leaders and traditional chiefs talked to their communities, so that all would come together and support an end to the violence.

In each case, committed individuals worked with combatants for months, sometimes years, until they found solutions that satisfied all of those involved. They ensured that agreements were implemented and continued to monitor the situation, tapping into their personal and community networks whenever they needed to address emerging issues. Their efforts paid off: They succeeded in containing fighting around their villages and promoting common interests across ethnic, political, social, or religious lines, at least for a time.

Other researchers have made the same observation in their studies of Bougainville, Burundi, Cambodia, Colombia, Congo, Indonesia, Iraq, Israel and the Palestinian territories, Kosovo, Lebanon, Myanmar, Nepal, Nigeria, Northern Ireland, Sierra Leone, the Solomon Islands, South Africa, South Sudan, Sri Lanka, Timor-Leste, and Ukraine. The international charity Peace Direct has identified more than 1,800 grassroots conflict-resolution organizations located in 20 different war and postwar zones. Everywhere that there is violence, there are also ordinary yet extraordinary people fighting it. They are not, in the words of peacebuilding scholar-practitioner Zachary Metz, "foolish dreamers singing 'Give Peace a Chance,' hugging trees, and living in the clouds." Instead they are courageous, smart, innovative citizens taking risks for what they believe in. They are people who understand the ins and outs of violence in their village or neighborhood—and find ways to confront it. Throughout the world, countless peace efforts occur far from capital cities, often below the radars of national leaders and international peacebuilders. And, remarkably, these solutions work.

These initiatives need not even be formal to make a difference. It's not only the residents of Idjwi and Somaliland monitoring potential troublemakers. It's also inhabitants of Northern Ireland being deliberately polite to members of other groups and avoiding contentious conversation topics so as not to fuel tensions. It's Israelis and Palestinians holding a ceremony to mourn all of the victims of the conflict, instead of only those from their own side. It's Bosnians of all ethnicities participating in chess clubs, hunting associations, and trade unions together. It's daughters playing soccer with the children of the rival group, sons marrying outsiders, aunts trading with longstanding enemies, and individuals of all backgrounds sharing a market, hospital, school, or art center with the people they've been told to hate. In their day-to-day lives, ordinary people often engage in actions that observers view as banal and un-important, when in fact these everyday acts help establish relationships that can prevent local outbreaks of violence and, at times, serve as the basis to deal with conflict.

Why Care?

An observer may feel the cases I've detailed here are meaningless, too spe-cific to be of value in the bigger question of how to build peace. But to me, Somaliland, San José de Apartadó, Wahat al-Salam – Neve Shalom, and the various other places I've just told you about matter a lot, because their successes help answer the questions I'm always asked when the proponents of Peace, Inc. hear my story of Idjwi.

"Can local peace extend to more than a small village or island?" conflict-resolution experts often challenge. Yes, which is why Somaliland is so im-portant: It demonstrates that pockets of peace can "scale up" to include a 53,127-square-mile territory (137,600 square kilometers)—an area compa-rable to the size of countries like Greece, Nicaragua, North Korea, and Syria, and much larger than places like Haiti or Israel and the Palestinian territories. With a population between 3.5 and 4 million people, Somaliland has more residents than Uruguay, Bosnia, Moldova, or Georgia.

"But aren't the factors that led to peace in Idjwi (the blood pacts, its reputation as the island of the sorcerers) or Somaliland (the clan structure, the respect for traditional chiefs) so unique that they can't be replicated elsewhere?" the proponents of Peace, Inc. often retort. Indeed, very specific factors are at play in each of these places. I'm not arguing that we can take the exact model of Idjwi, or Somaliland, or San José de Apartadó, and replicate it elsewhere. I'm simply arguing that ordinary people and local elites *can* build peace and that bottom-up initiatives *can* be effective.

At this point in the discussion, I usually have to address the anthropologists in the room, who say that I'm guilty of idealizing community-level work and believing that all local people are the same and agree with one another. I do acknowledge that local does not equal beautiful and unified; ordinary people are not saints, and their grassroots traditions are not inherently flawless either. In Idjwi, for instance, they perpetuate discrimination against Pygmies—and in Somaliland, against women. What's more, there is a lot of disagreement and division within each village, locality, district, and so on, such as the antagonisms between sub-clans and sub-sub-clans in Somaliland, or the tensions between Havus and Pygmies in Idjwi. That's precisely my point: We have to tackle these tensions just like we tackle the broader conflicts. Otherwise, they will not only cause a lot of people misery, but they can also escalate and threaten progress toward national or international reconciliation. And, of course, local leaders and ordinary citizens are not by definition more peaceful or less corrupt than national or international powerbrokers. But they *are* better placed to address grassroots issues, because only they know the ins and outs of the specific challenges within their local communities.

"Fine, but is this peace sustainable?" my critics often ask me. "What is the hope for peace at the bottom if we do not have peace from the top?" Or, the more loaded version of this question: "Isn't this peace fragile, as any army or rebel group can easily spoil it?" My answer: While the hard-won local peace that people enjoy in places like Idjwi and San José de Apartadó is indeed at the mercy of any neighboring armed group, the Somalilanders' experience shows that there are ways to make bottom-up peace robust and sustainable. For the past 23 years, Somalia has attacked their borders and questioned

their country's right to existence, the al-Shabaab militias have tried to destabilize them from the inside, and yet no mass violence has erupted, their state
has continued to function, and so has their democracy.

Still unsatisfied, the followers of Peace Inc. will argue that localized peace
is futile without national peace, often pointing to pockets of stability like
Idjwi in other countries that were peaceful for a few years, but then imploded
due to higher-level violence. "So the few years of peace don't matter, given
that everything was undone in just a few days, right?"

Admittedly, it would be ideal for national, international, and global peace
to last until the end of time. But what really matters is making sure that
we prevent death and suffering wherever and whenever we can. Bottom-
up peace may not be the answer to all of the world's problems, but it can
save lives. It can spare women like Justine and Isabelle, men like Kaer and
Livingston, and children like Luca from suffering, allow them to heal and
thrive, build community relationships, and possibly gain enough strength
and resilience to survive the next bout of conflict. So yes, it's worth looking
more closely at what these various places can teach us about how to control
violence.

Learning from Local Successes

We can draw important conclusions from these stories. First, local people
have the skills and knowledge necessary to promote peace and uphold
the mechanisms, structures, and networks that help to perpetuate it. The
resulting "peaceful" societies may not be paradises; conflict is inherent
to social life. I don't know any place where everybody holds hands, gets
along every moment of every day, and sings Kumbaya—not even at hippy
cooperatives, nuns' convents, or Tibetan monasteries. However, it is remarkable that thanks to the efforts of local people there are areas in the middle of
war zones that see little to no organized violence, places where inhabitants
have somehow managed to find ways to prevent conflicts from escalating
into mass fighting.

Second, bottom-up processes can be at least as effective as—and possibly
more effective than—top-down approaches. These locally-led initiatives
make a huge difference in the safety of the residents' lives, and, at times, this
security can even extend into the surrounding villages.

The involvement of government elites or state officials is not always required to control violence. It is precisely by staying away from central state authorities that the residents of Idjwi, San José de Apartadó, and Wahat al-Salam – Neve Shalom have managed to create pockets of peace. As for Somalilanders, they have taught us a key lesson: Statebuilding, as peacebuilding, may help achieve lasting stability, but only when it proceeds from both the treetops and the grassroots.

The stories of Afghanistan, Congo, Somalia, South Sudan, Timor-Leste, etc., show that an exclusively top-down strategy leads to disaster. By the same token, an exclusively bottom-up strategy can only produce a very fragile and temporary easement of violence, because manipulation by national leaders, or interference by neighboring armed groups, can jeopardize virtually any local peace. Furthermore, civilians cannot defeat armed groups single-handedly. Nor do ordinary people have the networks necessary to build peace over an entire country. Isolated local successes do not automatically translate into national peace: Certain villages, towns, or regions (like San José de Apartadó, Idjwi, and Somaliland) may be peaceful for years while the neighboring areas, and the country itself, remain at war.

It is not that national and international tensions don't matter—they do—or that national and international peacebuilding is unnecessary—it is. We need to convince the heads of states and rebellions to stop encouraging physical combat and fueling local tensions. We also have to address national and global issues that perpetuate war: discriminatory laws and institutions, arms trade and other economic interests, power struggles on the world stage, etc. In addition to any local initiative, top-down approaches are still very much needed to confront violence.

This leads to the third main insight: We should not abandon Peace, Inc. entirely, but revise it so as to change the relationships between insiders and outsiders, eliminate counterproductive assumptions, and get rid of harmful habits and routines. And we should merge it with more local peacebuilding efforts. As the consensus goes among all of the researchers who work on local conflict resolution, and as you've seen through LPI's work in the Ruzizi Plain and through Leymah Gbowee's improbable story of success in Liberia, only a combination of macro-level and micro-level initiatives can build a sustainable peace. Supporting bottom-up work should not take place at the expense of top-down efforts; instead we need both types of approaches, precisely because they complement each other.

The weight we give to each approach and our methods of implementation should depend on the specific conditions on the ground, so naturally they will vary widely across time and place—that's why an in-depth understanding of each conflict is so essential. Nevertheless, we can follow a few rules of thumb.

6

Recasting Roles

In 2003, the United Nations sent James Scambary, an Australian citizen, to neighboring Timor-Leste. James's job was to help develop and professionalize local media as a way to support the post-independence peace process. Inconveniently for him (but conveniently for our story), he did not have a car, so he could not join the other interveners on the beach or in the countryside during weekends. Instead, he told me, he spent his time off chatting in his neighbors' backyards.

The years passed, and James became part of the local fabric. He made Timorese friends who, eventually, started speaking in his presence in a way that they never did in front of other foreigners. They mentioned hopes and fears that they usually hid from interveners. "Wait until the United Nations leave," they said, "and then we'll get even"—referring to both the citizens who had taken their land during the Indonesian occupation of their country (1975–1999) and the current government that they thought was mishandling the country's resources. They also talked about underlying local tensions that the followers of Peace, Inc. couldn't have cared less about, such as the constant conflicts around water tanks and garbage disposal. They worried about endemic communal violence in rural areas that otherwise went unreported.

Riots erupted in 2006, and almost derailed Timor-Leste's entire peace process. They took virtually all interveners by surprise, but not James. He was one of the few outsiders who had predicted that the situation would deteriorate and had tried to convince his colleagues to help prevent the looming crisis.

James was able to foresee the conflict not because he was smarter or better trained than other foreign peacebuilders, but because he had talked to local people and developed strong personal relationships. These backyard discussions had provided him with a different and much more accurate perception of the issues and tensions on the ground.

It sounds obvious—talking to residents to gain an understanding of their culture and the challenges they face—yet few people do it. James's story illustrates a striking lesson, relevant both for top-down and bottom-up action. Many solutions to fix international efforts come from what seem like the most trivial aspects of peacebuilding, such as whom interveners have a drink with after work, how they talk to local people, and so on. And James wasn't the only one to figure it out.

A New Cast

When I ask both host populations and foreign interveners about the differences between the standard, often counterproductive "support" that Peacelanders give to conflict-resolution initiatives and the actions that actually manage to promote peace, people point to individuals like James Scambary, Urbain Bisimwa who worked on the Rasta crisis, and the LPI country directors Alexandra Bilak and Pieter Vanholder. Eirini Diamantopoulou, a long-time intervener who has worked with multiple aid agencies, and who eventually specialized in monitoring and evaluation, explained:

> It's not at the level of organizations or projects or donors. It's one or two individuals within a program, a project, an organization, who have a bit of a different vision [for their respective agencies], and who push things in that direction. Someone who has an iron will, who does not give up, because there is a lot of bureaucratic resistance . . . These kinds of individuals really make a difference—and they are rare.

After years of research, I began to develop a profile of these kinds of model interveners: a composite of their common characteristics, no matter where they work in the world.

Though none of these remarkable individuals are perfect, they all have several distinguishing features, which anyone can learn from—and apply both at the treetops and at the grassroots.

To start, they are humble. They don't believe that, as outsiders, they know better, have the right theories, skills, and expertise, or bring the ideal solution to people's problems. Instead, they respect local residents.

My friend Onesphore Sematumba, a Congolese political analyst, emphasized: "All of those who have succeeded are those who listened first and foremost." They understood that "people at the grassroots are not idiots or just receptacles for aid," but instead individuals who "have the right to give

A Model Intervener
Credit: Stick Figure by Nicole Malaise, 2019

their opinion regarding their own issues." "If you forget about listening," Onesphore said, "if you arrive as an expert who knows what's right, it's all over. Your work will always be something distant, an imposition." Adérito de Jesus Soares, a kind, thoughtful, and passionate Timorese student activist turned politician and then anti-corruption official, agreed: What makes the difference is humility; it is when someone has "the capacity to listen to local people—not only the elite, but also the women, the veterans, the widows' groups."

This kind of attitude doesn't require you to be a saint. Indeed, it can be quite basic. When I asked Kaer, my research assistant in Idjwi—the one who helped organize a soccer club and fishing project when the local boys were acting unruly—what he meant when he said "good peacebuilders should be unassuming and respectful," he referenced our visit to Livingston's Pygmy community a few years prior. "They brought you this small, wooden, rickety chair," Kaer reminded me, "and you sat down as if it was perfectly natural." (I actually remember feeling quite honored on that day, because, apart from Livingston and Kaer, everyone else had to stand or sit on the floor.) "It was a very poor village, reduced to a very basic level of living, and you met them at their level without complaint," Kaer continued. "You listened—we had planned one hour for the meeting, and you actually spent three hours there." Kaer got antsy after a while, because we were late for another appointment, but he remembers that whenever one of the villagers wanted to talk, I kept telling him "Kaer, it's important, we have to listen!" Although I hardly felt like a hero on that day (there was so little I could do to help this profoundly mistreated community), somehow my behavior struck the right chord. "It honored the Pygmies," Kaer concluded. "It made them feel valuable."

In the same vein, model interveners often challenge the enduring stereotypes about local people. They point to authorities who have the expertise, competence, motivation, and work ethic essential to peacebuilding, and to ordinary citizens who are intelligent, selfless, and trustworthy. They emphasize that host populations have far more relevant knowledge, contacts, and means to resolve their own predicaments than interveners usually believe. They maintain that, to be effective, peace efforts must involve both insiders and outsiders. That way, in Adérito's experience, "instead of preaching and coming with a blueprint—which is a recipe for disaster—they develop ideas together."

These individuals are prepared to acknowledge that their definition of justice, peace, democracy, development, and the like is not the only valid one. This is important to ensure that projects actually address residents' concerns. For instance, most interveners—and, I assume, most of you—define peace by the number of people killed, raped, or injured, the frequency and intensity of combat, and the presence or absence of armed groups. Ordinary citizens at times use these criteria, but they also have other indicators that are more immediate, more concrete, and often very specific to their lives.

Do you remember how Justine, the mother of Luca and a participant in one of Vijaya's projects, "knew" that the peacebuilding efforts were succeeding? It was when her son started speaking in the future tense. Likewise, a Colombian high-level negotiator told me how he once apologized to the inhabitants of a remote rural area: Despite his best efforts, the deal he had helped broker with the main rebel movement had failed to promote peace. One of his interlocutors, a middle-aged peasant woman, forcefully disagreed. For the first time in 20 years, she could sleep in her pajamas and turn off the light. Before, she had to sleep fully dressed, with her boots at the side of her bed, so that she could run out at a moment's notice when she heard gunfire. That, to her, was a better sign of improvement than any of the macro-criteria the negotiations focused on.

Along the same lines, my colleague Pamina Firchow, who researches conflict resolution, reports how, in the Ugandan countryside, people would wonder: Are dogs barking at night? If they are, it means that there are strangers prowling around the village, and these strangers are usually up to no good. In a neighboring community, residents ponder: Can they go to the bathroom outside during the night? Their toilets are usually in the garden— not in the main house—but in times of trouble they prefer to use a chamber pot inside rather than risk stepping out. These, to them, are much more important markers of peace than the distant and abstract definitions that interveners use—and I feel the same.

In addition to reframing their definitions of progress, remarkable interveners know the local context well, they speak at least some of the local languages, and they have extensive local networks. Take for example my friend Banu Altunbas, a small Turkish woman with a big heart (and an even bigger mane of jet-black hair), who became the African Great Lakes manager for the peacebuilding organization International Alert in 2016. We met briefly in New York in the late 1990s and became friends when we both worked in Kosovo, but our friendship was truly cemented when we both fell in love with Congo in the early 2000s, and we have stayed in touch ever since. By the time Banu took on her leadership role in peacebuilding in Central Africa, she had already spent more than ten years in the region—primarily in Congo's Kivu provinces, with a few years in neighboring Burundi.

Banu is the kind of person who knows everybody in the area, from the rebel leader who keeps asking for her hand in marriage to the traditional chiefs in the remotest rural villages. And if I want to meet them? Easy: she'll give me their phone numbers, along with a briefing on their political and military situations—and the latest gossip on who's getting married, who's cheating on his wife, who's the brother or cousin or stepdad of this or that warlord, who has a huge fortune in mining, land, townhouses, restaurants, and so on. In addition to the usual network of fellow activists and interveners, she's also friends with many artists and businesspeople—so it's always great to dine with her in Goma; we get warm greetings from the chef, owner, and waiters.

Like Banu, remarkable interveners also cultivate not just professional, but personal and social relationships with local people—both elite and ordinary citizens. To do so, they build on their interests and activities, just like any of us does when we move to a new place and want to integrate in our surrounding community. They socialize with their local colleagues and counterparts, share meals and after-work drinks, or attend parties and outings on weekends. In addition, those who have children get to know the parents of their kids' local friends. Those who have hobbies, whether boxing or choir practice, join local clubs. And those who are religious get involved in their new congregation.

These kinds of informal relationships enable interveners to develop a different, more accurate picture of the place they're in and the conflict they want to address: one that reflects not only outsiders' perceptions, but also insiders' views—like James Scambary did in Timor-Leste, and like LPI and Urbain's peasant association did when they started working on the Rasta problem. Social networks also make it much easier for peacebuilders to obtain approval or cooperation for their programs, as officials tend to respond more positively to people they socialize with. Not to mention that personal contacts are useful in mitigating danger, as I've personally experienced. Multiple times, friends warned me ahead of time that a village I was traveling to was about to be attacked, and thanks to them I didn't get caught in the middle of the fighting. Likewise, several exceptional interveners told me gratefully how local residents had mobilized to keep them safe—by interceding with belligerents on their behalf, for instance.

Personal interactions with local people can make or break the success of peace initiatives. Mary Anderson—a well-known scholar-practitioner of international aid—and her colleagues talked with more than 6,000 people in 21 different conflict zones and concluded that every story of effective aid they heard involved a particular individual who had developed genuine, respectful, and trustful relationships with the people he or she intended to help. Likewise, the geographer Adam Moore found that the existence of informal and personal contacts largely contributed to the success of peacebuilding programs in Brčko (Bosnia), while the very same projects remained unsuccessful in the rest of the country, where interveners had only formal, professional, distant connections with local counterparts.

Despite all of that, the most effective interveners are perfectly aware of their limitations. Take Vijaya, for instance. She understands that no outsider will ever master the ins and outs of every single situation. To her, "you have to sit down with people, sift beans and babysit their kids" until you start having a sense of what might be going on. And then you don't decide how to address the problem, she said, but you let them do so.

During a visit to a school in Kitchanga (Congo), Major Van den Bergh, a United Nations peacekeeper, tells me about the strong relationships he has developed with the local community. Like other remarkable interveners, this South African officer speaks the local language (Kiswahili), and he acts kindly and respectfully toward Congolese people—in fact, he calls them all "warafiki" (friends).
Photo credit: Philippe Rosen, 2011

Banu too remains down-to-earth, a lot of fun, and modest. Her commitment to understanding local conditions is what allows her to see how much she still doesn't know. To me, she's the embodiment of a common joke between travelers, anthropologists, and interveners: Spend a day in a country, and you'll write a book about it. Spend a week, and you'll write an article. Spend a year, and you won't be able to write even a paragraph, because you'll realize how much you still don't understand. When Banu started her job as the African Great Lakes manager for International Alert, she spent the first year just listening to her local colleagues and counterparts—and telling me how much she was learning from them.

While we know that in-depth understanding of local conditions is essential, we must also remember that humility is just as crucial. Without it, an intervener with local knowledge and networks may still hold on to the assumption that outsiders can lead the peacebuilding process—like Hans (the first LPI country director) did.

The model interveners' humility is also evidenced by the fact that they don't place themselves at the forefront of peace efforts. They explain to their donors that the standard "branding" and "visibility" (which, in aid jargon, means publicizing your actions—like plastering your logos everywhere) is counterproductive: It makes host communities view projects as coming from the outside and, too often, as imposed by foreigners.

Instead, the remarkable interveners maintain a low profile and turn the spotlight on the achievements of their local partners. This is why you'd prob-ably never heard of the main organizations that use this approach (such as LPI, Peace Direct, International Alert, Interpeace, the Purdue Peace Project, and the Center for International Conflict Resolution) before you started reading this book. They don't claim credit for their achievements. Instead, they consider insiders—not outsiders—the stars.

For the past few years, the United Nations has asked me to participate in the training of the Peace and Development Advisors it deploys all around the world. Lawrence Lachmansingh, a long-time peacebuilder from Guyana, is one of the main facilitators. He often tells the story of his friend and former colleague Chris Spies, a South African national who served as one of the first-ever United Nations Peace and Development Advisors.

At that time, in the early 2000s, Lawrence was managing a program to build social cohesion in his home country. As so often occurs in Peaceland, Lawrence (the insider) had to report to Chris (the outsider) who then answered to the resident coordinator (another foreigner, and the person with top decision-making power). Shortly after his arrival in Guyana, Chris went to see his boss and told him: "I know I report to you [for official purposes], but Lawrence and his team are the real experts on Guyana, and they are already directing the work. Please allow Lawrence to be in the lead." And he did. For three years, while Chris remained formally in charge, it was Lawrence and the other Guyanese employees who actually ran the show, providing crucial support to Guyana's first-ever peaceful general election in 2006.

It is not only national staff or local elite who are the stars of successful peacebuilding efforts; ordinary people are too. When remarkable interveners design and implement their programs, they try to involve all of those affected—not just the government, local leaders, heads of armed groups, and prominent civil society activists that the cogs of Peace, Inc. favor.

For instance, Chris told me how, in Kenya, his local colleagues had found a way to avoid always meeting with the usual suspects—other foreign interveners, the village chief, the administrator, the chief of police, and so on, like most Peacelanders do. Instead, they would enter villages, gather residents, and ask them: "Who are the 20 most influential people in the community?" And then they would go and engage with these individuals, even when they included gang leaders and conmen.

Whenever possible, model peacebuilders rely on people from the exact area of intervention to carry out the programs on the ground, rather than on other outsiders from the capital city or from different provinces. Vijaya, for instance, told me proudly that she recruits her teams "from the community where they work." That way, they have the knowledge and networks necessary to make sure that their programs include all relevant stakeholders and tackle all salient issues. They can also get information that outsiders would never receive (as Urbain's local peasant association did when it worked on the Rasta problem).

Inhabitants of the Basali Chieftaincy (Congo) participate in an inter-community roundtable to discuss the conflict that divides them. It took Action Solidaire pour la Paix and LPI more than three years of low-profile, intensive Participatory Action Research to prepare this meeting.

Photo credit: Life & Peace Institute, 2013

Long-term involvement is key as well. Establishing trust and credibility with anyone takes years, as does developing an in-depth understanding of local conditions. Besides, like Vijaya, Déo, Urbain, and Banu, model peacebuilders know that, no matter how hard they try, a one-off reconciliation meeting or a month-long project won't immediately resolve problems that involve thousands of people and have taken years, and sometimes centuries, to develop. Instead, because they are humble and they listen, they understand that working at a gradual, steady rate is the key to success. (Remember that it took LPI and its partners nearly three years to complete just the first stage of their project on the Ruzizi Plain, the conflict analysis.) Operating at this pace in host communities takes patience—a *lot* of patience. Edward Rees, a peacebuilder who spent years in Timor-Leste, explained: You have to work "slowly," "consistently," and above all be "willing to accept the screw-ups."

All in all, remarkable interveners support and reinforce local efforts, as opposed to directing them. That's how things usually go in Somaliland, where—as a byproduct of its unrecognized sovereignty— international aid exists, but is limited and conducted on Somaliland's terms. Haroon Yusuf, the intellectual who has participated in the peace process from the 1980s onward, explained that, "besides the financial support, the international community did not interfere in the process: They did not set the agenda; they did not bring people together as such."

For instance, at the height of the post-independence violence, Yusuf was working for the international agency Action Aid in the city of Erigavo. Local residents organized a meeting to reestablish peace in their area, and Yusuf and his colleagues simply "brought essential but basic support." They supplied "fuel and food: fuel for bringing people together, because traditional leaders are scattered in all the villages, and food during the meeting." They did not even contribute all of the necessary provisions, because the participants came with their own livestock. However, they did provide nonperishable items, which were crucial because the gathering lasted about a month. The important point, Yusuf emphasized, was that outsiders "did not touch the process, the agenda, the outcome," or the duration of the meeting.

This kind of involvement is typical of the international support for Somaliland's broader peace process. When I met with Yusuf Weyne, an aid worker from Somaliland, and his colleague Robert Kluijver, a Dutch doctoral researcher, they listed all of the international contributions they had seen: the construction of roads and other essential infrastructure, the delivery of dozens of cars and planes full of food and other relief items, a contribution of more than a million dollars to cover the cost of disarming and demobilizing combatants, and an additional donation allocated for the creation of a compound to safely store the heavy military equipment. But in all of that, they explained, interveners treaded lightly. In Robert's words, "Since the internationals could not provide what Somaliland most needed (diplomatic recognition), they agreed to play a supporting role, backstage." Thankfully, he added, "Somaliland never became a 'sexy' place for internationals," and therefore foreign peace organizations maintained a nonintrusive presence. They "kept quite low levels of staff, some of them staying on for long periods of time. The disruptive international aid circus, with its experts that always know better, never fully hit" the region.

Many other analysts made the same point: Somalilanders may yearn for sovereignty, but the lack thereof spared them an onslaught of interveners who might have hijacked their locally-owned process and derailed their hard-won stability. Instead, they got to be the directors of their own show and lead the peace efforts as they saw fit.

Hard Choices

Letting the intended beneficiaries of international interventions decide for themselves is all the more important when you remember that quite often there are hard choices to be made between "good things"—like, for instance, choosing between peace and democracy, or peace and justice.

Nowhere was this dilemma more apparent than when I researched Wahat al-Salam – Neve Shalom, the "oasis of peace" that was created to show that Israeli Jews and Arabs could live side by side. I found the village so inspiring that I was puzzled at first when some of the peace activists I met dismissed it as irrelevant, or even got angry when they talked about it. How could a peacebuilder possibly object to living proof that reconciliation was possible? Why did they talk about this virtually utopian initiative as if it amounted to treason? And then I understood. To other activists, the inhabitants of Wahat al-Salam – Neve Shalom live in a bubble. They focus on the situation within their small village rather than that in the whole country. They don't put their lives on the line to fight against the issues at the heart of the conflict, such as (for Israelis) the security threats they face and (for Palestinians) the power differential and systematic discrimination. They prioritize village peace rather than broader justice.

I experienced something similar during my visit to San José de Apartadó in Colombia. I came in thinking that its inhabitants were exemplary citizens because they had managed to remain out of the conflict. And then I met with Antonia, Luis, and other members of the local farmers' union working nearby, outside the peace zone, and I realized that things were more complicated. As you may recall, the peace community stayed away from the state, the justice system, and all other governmental bodies. However, the farmers' association wanted to actually *change* these institutions. Their goal was to increase security and promote development for *all* of their fellow citizens. They emphasized national political reform over local peace. I left our meeting thinking that the positions of both the peace community and the union were admirable, respectable, and worthy of support.

These tensions between peace and justice, or peace and economic welfare, or peace and democracy, raise the kind of moral dilemma debated (though never resolved) in countless books and movies. Is my main moral obligation to protect my own life and well-being, along with those of my family and community, or to sacrifice them all in order to help strangers? What would you do? Personally, I still wonder how I would have reacted if I had had to decide whether to join the resistance against Nazis during World War II or keep my head low and try to survive. If I had been born in San José de Apartadó, would I have enrolled in the farmers' union or would I have moved to the peace zone? If I were Israeli, or Palestinian, would I prioritize justice or peace? I can't be sure. What I do know is that I would want to make the choice myself. I wouldn't appreciate it if someone tried to decide for me.

Unfortunately, given the power structure at work in Peaceland, foreign activists and diplomats are typically the ones who make these difficult decisions, rather than ordinary inhabitants. Many people living in conflict zones criticize this approach as a form of "neo-colonialism" and "neo-imperialism"—it's yet another instance of outsiders coming to tell them what to do. So, in recent years, there has been a new fad in intervention circles: the idea of bringing "African solutions to African problems" (or Latin American solutions to Latin American problems, and so on).

I used to love this idea, until the day I discussed it with Michel Losembe, the Congolese businessman who found that pretending to be Puerto Rican gave him more influence with foreign peacebuilders. "You know, Séverine, Africa is very diverse," he teased me, as if I was not aware of that already, but then went on to explain what he meant. What did he—a wealthy, highly educated man from a large city in Central Africa—have in common with, for instance, a West African villager whose way of life, colonial history, and culture are completely different? Why on earth would Losembe ever decide something for that person—or vice versa? A Japanese diplomat reacted the same way when we talked about his work in Timor-Leste. He kept hearing other interveners praise him for bringing "Asian solutions for Asian problems." But he constantly wondered why they saw him as better placed to decide on behalf of Timorese people, whose beliefs, outlook, values, and everyday lives were incredibly different from his.

I now firmly believe that outsiders should not be choosing between two worthy goals, even if those outsiders come from the same continent or country. The people who have to live with the consequences of a decision should be the ones making it.

This simple principle provides a moral compass for the dilemma that regularly haunts on-the-ground interveners: How can they possibly choose between, let's say, peace and democracy in Congo, or peace and women's equality in Somaliland? My answer: Let their intended beneficiaries decide, even if the result is unpopular, unfashionable, and uncomfortable, and even if it turns off some well-intended donors.

In response to this suggestion, Peacelanders often ask what they should do when the solutions reached by local people are at odds with international priorities, norms, and values. They'd love to support peace in Somaliland or in Idjwi, some of them add, but what about women and Pygmies? Communities are not monoliths, so what certain residents view as "peace" can mean oppression and exploitation for others. Should interveners help perpetuate abusive practices in the name of peace?

For years, I was stumped by this question. Eventually, I decided to brainstorm with some of my model interveners and with members of groups who get the short end of the stick. Here is the answer that we came up with, as one of my friends so strikingly encapsulated: "Some of these priorities can be step two—and yes, that sucks."

Take Somaliland. It is slowly starting to resemble the type of liberal, democratic states that the adepts of Peace, Inc. are trying to build in other parts of the world. This is a product of a gradual, locally-led process that, for years, has relied on illiberal customs and traditional authority structures. Step one was peace. Step two was democracy. Hopefully, steps three, four, and five will shepherd in gender equality and economic welfare.

Similarly, Idjwi's Pygmies told me that peace is what matters above all else, and that's why they haven't taken up arms. As for how outsiders can support the island's stability without condoning everyday discriminations, Livingston (the Pygmy representative) thought the answer was obvious: "Good Samaritans" should come and see his constituents so that, together, they can brainstorm, plan, and decide how best to proceed.

This is another instance where remembering the LPI model is so important. When the LPI team helped address the conflict in the Ruzizi Plain, they included *everyone* in the discussion: leaders and ordinary people, victims and perpetrators, powerful and powerless communities, peacemakers and warmongers. They also prioritized reaching a solution that satisfied all of those involved, even if that meant taking years, discussing the same issue over and over again, and adapting their strategies multiple times.

By the same token, if we want to help Somaliland's women, we have to include them in the discussions, so that *they* can consider what steps they could take to assert their rights, assess what the consequences would be for stability, and decide which, if any, are worth it. The same goes for marginalized people all over the world.

All of these processes take time. Not all good things come together, and we can't have it all tomorrow. Remarkable interveners understand that building peace sometimes requires baby steps, and they look to local people as a guide for which foot to start on.

Going Off-Script

There is one last characteristic that model interveners have in common: They are flexible. When I started researching for this book, I asked my assistants to review all of the evaluations of peacebuilding projects that they could find (they ended up with more than a hundred documents, some of them looking at multiple initiatives in various countries), and to list the main characteristics of all of the successful projects. "Flexibility in implementation" kept popping up in that list.

"Flexibility" also kept recurring in my discussions of successful initiatives, whether I was in Colombia or Timor-Leste. What this means in practice is avoiding coming in with an established set of ideas or project activities that you will implement in a given time frame. Instead, flexibility entails constantly revising your strategies based on the results you get, the obstacles you face, the feedback you receive from local residents and peace project implementers, the way the political, military, and social situation evolves, and so on. Remember, for instance, how adaptive LPI and its partners had to be when they worked in the Ruzizi Plain.

In fact, flexibility is so important that several former LPI staff members traced the start of the organization's decline in Congo to its effort to formalize the Participatory Action Research model: to put in place timelines, procedures, and standard templates, which eventually constrained what was—and should have remained—an organic process based on interpersonal relationships and constant adaptation to a changing environment.

Successful international peacebuilding programs often featured funders and main offices that, contrary to the Peace, Inc. norm, did not require a set project from the start, complete with a logical framework, timeline, deliverables, quantitative indicators, and the like. Instead, the headquarters gave significant autonomy to the field staff, and the donors agreed to support their work in a specific region, whatever form this action might take. In this manner, peacebuilders on the ground were able to adapt to the requests of communities and the demands of changing situations. This is how the Swedish International Development Cooperation Agency and the Belgian Ministry of Foreign Affairs funded LPI's peace initiative in the Ruzizi Plain.

Another major way in which donors help is by not requesting that their logos appear everywhere. For instance, a long-time intervener working for the Asia Foundation in Timor-Leste recalled:

The United Nations wrote fantastic standard operating procedures for the Timorese police: a set of 20 or 100 standard operating procedures in a big book with a big UN logo. On the day it was approved, the general commander of the police signed it in a big ceremony. And then the next day he wrote a memo to his staff saying: "Please ignore the standard operating procedures" . . . So the big book of standard operating procedures sits in a cupboard.

The Asia Foundation took over, and its staff started "a nitty-gritty get-people-involved process," which entailed "taking the logo off." Thankfully, their donor—the government of New Zealand—understood how crucial it was for foreign peacebuilders to take the back seat and shine the spotlight on local people's accomplishments. They preferred to see a Timorese Police logo on the final product and be sure that policemen would actually use the book, rather than having a New Zealand logo on a text that would get more attention from dust bunnies than police officers. In the trade-off between visibility and effectiveness, they chose the latter.

Donors can also ensure that the interveners they fund are accountable not only to them—as is the norm in Peaceland—but also to their intended beneficiaries. They can request, for instance, that their grantees measure the impact of the project on the ground or the satisfaction of the beneficiaries, rather than solely whether they have spent money appropriately and met their donors' expectations.

Unfortunately, given how Peace, Inc. operates, most peacebuilding funders and organizations lack this flexibility. So, for individuals caught in the bureaucracy, being effective may mean having to break the rules at times. For instance, the rules stipulating that you can't socialize with people of the opposite gender, because it could lead to accusations of sexual exploitation. Or the rules that prevent you from going to certain neighborhoods at night, and force you to remain in the rich and safe part of the town you live in. Basically, these are all rules that keep you inside the Peacelanders' bubble and hold you back from developing personal relationships with the inhabitants of the country you're in.

That's one of the most striking conclusions reached by my friend and fellow academic Susanna Campbell in her extensive research on peacebuilding. Her 20 years of work as an intervener and a scholar led her to make a case for calculated disobedience. In her analysis, the interveners who perform best are those who break or bend the rules and standard operating procedures imposed by their headquarters or donors. It's only by doing so that they can put local people in control and be held accountable for their actions by insiders, rather than solely by outsiders.

That's also what Josh Trindade, a Timorese peacebuilder, remarked: "The foreigners who really help local people, anywhere, are the ones who don't stick by the rulebook." To him, when diplomats and United Nations officials respect all of their organizations' regulations, "they have so many restrictions that they can't do anything." So, some of them don't follow their organizations' procedures, and others quit and move on to smaller agencies that provide their staff with more freedom.

That's the (undoubtedly not very popular) argument I developed when I briefed Australian diplomats on my research findings. My advice: You should not automatically sanction rule-breakers without first considering whether their actions actually led to good. "Or," one of the diplomats chimed in, "you could argue that we should change the rules." She was obviously right—we absolutely should.

Lastly, the biggest contribution donors can make is the gift of time: funding projects over the long term rather than over the usual six-month to two-year cycles. Remember how lengthy the reconciliation conferences were in Somaliland. Remember Luca's story (the former child soldier who kept fleeing to rejoin militias), and the years his mother Justine, Vijaya, and her colleagues took to reintegrate him into civilian life. Remember how long LPI needed to help address the conflict in the Ruzizi Plain—and the terrible consequences of cutting the initiative short before its achievements could be consolidated. In the words of Mauricio Paiz-Merino, a United Nations official I interviewed in Colombia, "Peacebuilding is not instant coffee." In fact, looking at the list of peacebuilding project evaluations that my research assistants compiled, those that external evaluators deemed "successful" were often projects that lasted five to ten years.

That peacebuilding requires a long-term commitment—up to two decades—is not only a standard research conclusion; it is also common sense. You can't resolve century-old conflicts that involve hundreds or thousands of people in a few days or months, or in a couple of one-off meetings. Deciding from the start that support will stop in a year, or two, or five, rather than whenever the objective has been achieved, is nonsensical. By contrast, multi-year funding enables organizations to work at the pace of local communities, and to deploy foreign staff over the long term.

Donors and diplomats blame political and financial constraints for preventing them from financing projects for more than a year or two at a time, but certain funding agencies have already managed to design long-term budgets. In late 2015, for instance, the European Union, the United Kingdom, and Australia established a Joint Peace Fund to help end the civil war in Myanmar. From the outset, they decided to accept only pledges from donors willing to make at least a five-year commitment, precisely for the reasons outlined above. Eleven countries have done so thus far—ranging from Italy to Finland and the United States. And there are several other such examples, like when the European Union funded the peace process in Northern Ireland through three successive six-year-long grants. While certainly still very rare, long-term investments such as these are far from impossible.

Recasting the Villains

You may wonder what is the point of continuing to send outsiders to conflict zones—why don't we just stop foreign interventions altogether and give all the resources directly to local populations? Given some of the news about Peacelanders, this question may have been on your mind even before you picked up this book.

In 2018, *The Times* reported that United Nations staff were "responsible for 60,000 rapes in a decade." "Sexual abuse 'endemic' in international aid sector," added CNN. Foreigners working in Haiti for the aid agency Oxfam turned "their guesthouse into what they allegedly called 'the whorehouse'" and threw "full-on 'Caligula' orgies," the *Washington Post* chimed in. The list goes on, to such a point that journalists have coined a new word for abusive expatriate interveners: "sexpats."

I bet that, when you see these kinds of stories in the popular press, your first thought may not be to question whether they are sensationalized, but rather whether it would be best to simply leave local people alone.

I wondered the exact same thing when I was working on a draft of my second book, *Peaceland*. In fact, for a while, I believed that interveners did more harm than good, so I tried to make the case that they should just get out. And then, in a twist, LPI invited me to present my draft manuscript at a conference in Burundi. It was a fantastic way for me to get feedback on the argument: In one room, LPI had gathered a sample of many people who had experience with the crux of my research. There were foreign peacebuilders, as well as native activists from Burundi, Congo, Somalia, Sudan, and a few other countries.

As I expected, the foreigners were less than thrilled by my criticisms of their work and were particularly upset by my conclusion that they should stop intervening, while the local activists praised my perspective. I was an outsider—someone whom other outsiders already took seriously—finally giving voice to their criticisms of international peacebuilders and saying that insiders have relevant skills and knowledge, too.

However, I received a lot of pushback from local activists as well. "Interveners bring essential things to conflict zones," they told me; "We don't want that to stop." To them, eliminating outside involvement would be a terrible, dangerous idea. In the following years, the more I researched, the more I discovered just how right they were—and the more grateful I became to the people who had confronted me, as their feedback enabled me to correct my argument in the later drafts of my *Peaceland* book.

Yes, there are many problems with the current aid system. Yes, certain interveners commit horrible acts like rape, torture, even human trafficking (although the 60,000-rapes-a-decade accusation is overblown: According to the UN's Conduct and Discipline Unit, the actual number is approximately 700 over the past ten years). And yes, these criminals have to be punished, harshly. But these bad actors do not represent all foreign peacebuilders. The bulk of their colleagues do not knowingly harm the population they're meant to help. Instead, the overall majority genuinely tries its best. Virtually all of the interveners I know are incensed by the atrocities committed by their coworkers.

By focusing exclusively on the perpetrators of violence, we're falling into the trap that my friend Loochi warned us about: We see only the black dots and ignore the white canvas. We're so obsessed with the problems, challenges, and failures that we overlook all of the things that foreign peacebuilders are doing right, and all of the assets outsiders bring into conflict zones.

First and foremost, foreigners contribute funding. Every time I meet with local associations, leaders, or authorities in any country, their number one request is that I help them financially. It's not only me, of course, and it reaches such a point that one of my friends complained of feeling like a walking money bag. But this financial support is crucial. Many domestic peacebuilders told me that without the money from international donors—funds that they rely on for initiatives of all shapes and sizes, both top-down and bottom-up—their efforts would never have succeeded.

Of course, this works only when outsiders behave like model interveners: by letting local activists decide when and how to use the money, rather than imposing their ideas, priorities, and solutions. Otherwise, an increase in funding becomes counterproductive, as you'll remember from the tragic story of LPI's decline, when an influx of money eventually destroyed local efforts rather than boosting them—something that I've also seen all over the world, from Kosovo to Timor-Leste.

In addition, in the eyes of domestic activists, it is essential that foreign peacebuilders transmit ideas from elsewhere. When I presented the first draft of *Peaceland* at the LPI conference in Burundi—during the time when I thought international interveners should just get out—the strongest push-back I received was from a Somali woman who told me very sweetly, very politely, that I was completely wrong on this point. It was crucially important for outsiders to share what has and hasn't worked in other conflict zones, because it gave her ideas for her own actions. Not that she would want to copy and paste their solutions, she explained, but knowing what kinds of initiatives had succeeded in other parts of the world helped her consider different approaches, different angles, and eventually come up with creative answers to the unique challenges she faced.

I heard the same argument many times afterward—proving just how wrong I had been. Take my meeting with Théoneste Buzakare. For years, Buzakare served as the military chief of the Mai Mai Nyatura—a Congolese militia responsible for countless killings and abuses. Then, one day he met a Congolese abbot; they began a series of in-depth, month-long discussions and, eventually, Buzakare decided to lay down his arms. Even better, he asked the people he had hurt to forgive him and, as a way to make amends, devoted his time to building peace. By the time I spoke with him in 2016, he was spending his days trying to convince his former colleagues to stop fighting and was attempting to reestablish collaboration between communities in conflict. As we chatted over tea, Buzakare kept telling me that what he most needed in terms of international support was first, money, and second, "other methods, other experiences." In his territory, he explained, "Our knowledge is limited, but when people have gone to other countries, they can tell us what happened elsewhere. It broadens our minds." His colleague Bertin Kibanja jumped in: "I can't tell you that because I'm from here and know the people here, I know everything. I need other types of knowledge too—foreign experiences."

A case in point: it was outsiders who first came up with the concept of "peace zones"—of the kind that we've seen in San José de Apartadó—but they let local people decide how to put this idea into action. And you may remember what Urbain Bisimwa (the farmers' union leader in Congo) saw as LPI's most important contributions to the local peace efforts during the Rasta crisis: first, training on the Participatory Action Research peacebuilding method and, second, money.

To Urbain, the third main contribution was the type of high-level connections that foreigners bring. Without LPI's support, he explained, he and his colleagues would never have been able to meet with the general of the Congolese army—or they would have been in danger during that meeting. They would also never have been able to talk to—much less convince—the head of the peacekeeping mission in South Kivu to change strategy.

Because of the power differential at work in conflict zones, local peacebuilders often lack credibility with and access to the military and political authorities of their own countries, not to mention diplomats and United

Nations officials. Foreigners can connect grassroots activists to domestic and international elites. In that sense, interveners are best situated to link bottom-up to top-down peace initiatives: They can help address the national and international dimensions of a local issue, like LPI attempted when it worked on the conflict in the Ruzizi Plain. Along the same lines, the residents of San José de Apartadó's peace community told me that the most useful contribution foreign supporters make to their cause is serving as liaison with—or putting pressure on—the Colombian government and state institutions.

Foreign peacebuilders are also best equipped to drum up international support for host populations' efforts, and this will remain the case until the adherents of Peace, Inc. start following the example of our model interveners. Because most Peacelanders share the same culture, they know how to whip up the key argument, the telling graph, the right language, or the precise piece of jargon that will resonate with their colleagues. They can navigate the intricate bureaucracy of the aid world, and use the proper form for requesting support, through the appropriate procedure. They can choose the best communication strategy, whether through websites, social media, or documentaries. They can help activists research, write reports, and argue in ways that other interveners find credible. They also have access to the spaces and information reserved exclusively for foreigners.

In addition to money, ideas, and connections, outsiders provide a certain level of security. For instance, they can take responsibility for sensitive decisions. The first day I served as acting country director for Médicos Sin Fronteras (in Congo), an army unit started harassing my staff. They asked for bribes and medicine, they wanted to use our radio and our cars, and they threatened to harm my colleagues and their families if they did not comply. As the head of our mission, my role was to step in and stand up to them. Admittedly, I did spend a very awkward moment, explaining to a tall, muscular, angry officer that no, he would not get his way. I was a bit scared (well... maybe more than a bit). But it did not matter: My family was safe, thousands of miles out of reach. And, if things really got ugly, my French passport enabled me to get out immediately. That's the kind of privilege that makes me feel incredibly grateful that I happened to be born in a stable, wealthy country, whose government and administration would try to protect me if the need arose. But it also makes me feel terrible, and at times, even guilty that so many people I know—my local allies, my foreign colleagues born in places like Turkey or China, my Arab neighbors in France, and my friends of color in the United States—have very different experiences.

On a similar note, outsiders can create safe spaces for people in conflict to meet without fearing that the gatherings may end in bloodshed, as you saw in the stories of Resolve and LPI. They can protect local activists from the harassment, pressure, and retaliation that so often comes from militias, local authorities, and national leaders—in short, all of those who stand to lose money or power should peace prevail. They can make it clear to potential perpetrators that someone is there to monitor abuses. In Colombia, this helps publicize peace communities' commitment to nonviolence, and thus deters attacks that would create public relations problems for combatants. In fact, armed groups are more restrained when they deal with peace zones that host foreigners. This is because an attack on these communities would likely have a negative effect on their reputation and credibility—two resources they cannot afford to squander.

For many local residents, moral and political support from foreigners means the difference between life and death. In the words of a leader of San José de Apartadó's peace community, "It's because of the international presence that we are able to live and stay alive . . . Simply put, foreigners are life; they are the life of the community." This reminded me of what Buzakare had told me in Congo: "If there were no interveners in this country, there would be many more cases of rape and human rights violations. People would be treated like animals."

Outsiders do not necessarily need to actively engage in conflict-resolution efforts; at times, their very presence helps deter some human rights abuses. When I worked with Médicos Sin Fronteras in Afghanistan and Congo, I often saw how, without having to do anything, my team provided some form of protection to surrounding populations, because combatants did not want us to witness or respond to the horrible things they usually did to local residents. Likewise, in San José de Apartadó, local activists told me that foreigners staying physically, 24/7, with the peace community leaders who have received death threats is one of the best protections they can get. And in Timor-Leste, the residents consider the foreigners in their country as "guests." Josh Trindade, a Timorese peacebuilder, explained to me that in the local culture, it's embarrassing to fight in front of a guest—it suggests a lack of respect. So, just by being there, outsiders stifle conflict.

Local residents are perfectly aware of this. Countless times, I've heard people criticize their resident interveners for staying in their bunker-like compounds all the time, wasting money and resources. But then the same individuals would take to the street, occasionally even riot, whenever someone hinted that the United Nations soldiers or the aid agency team might leave their village. Civilians in Bosnia, Cambodia, Indonesia, Kenya, Kosovo, and Sri Lanka have reacted the same way: The very presence of outsiders makes them feel safer.

Lastly, physical presence shows that outsiders care in a way that money, cars, and other purely material contributions cannot. In Colombia, for instance, the presence of foreigners in or around peace zones boosts the credibility and self-confidence of local activists, who think that if an international organization is interested in them then their efforts must be worth it.

To Err Is Human

Outsiders are also needed because nobody is perfect. Even those residents who, against all odds, manage to build and maintain peace in their communities are no saints. As mentioned earlier, too many Somalilanders regard women as second-class citizens and mere possessions. Domestic violence is rife in Idjwi, and most inhabitants treat their Pygmy neighbors horribly. This shouldn't come as a surprise: Ordinary citizens are just as likely as their local or national leaders to be violent, hateful, prejudiced, and corrupt. I'm sure we can all point to a neighbor or acquaintance who behaves just as badly as (or worse than) the president, prime minister, or opposition leader we most despise.

What's more, by dint of being from the place where the conflict is happening, insiders face challenges that outsiders are spared. Their kin often demand jobs, money, or other services in an attempt to escape the poverty and unemployment that characterize most war environments. This kind of pressure is frequently a door to patronage and corruption. Armed groups and political leaders regularly blackmail local residents into doing their bidding, using tactics such as threats against family members. Plus, as we all know, it's much harder to remain objective, calm, polite, and respectful—the kind of qualities we want from a mediator—when faced with a conflict that affects us personally.

In all of these situations, I've seen foreigners step in effectively. For instance, one of my friends took up a post as the financial and administrative coordinator for a non-governmental organization in Afghanistan—a position in which a local employee would have faced inordinate pressure to hire friends or family. An acquaintance became the representative of Human

Rights Watch in Congo, and another one became the head of the peace-keeping mission's political affairs section there—two jobs in which Congolese staff members would have worried about retribution when standing up to the government or a warlord.

Grassroots organizations are not the silver bullet to end war and violence either. Although I've heard (and told you) many stories of international failures, I've encountered an equal number of stillborn local initiatives.

In conflict zones, numerous local associations are "briefcase NGOs": non-governmental organizations set up to make (or divert) money, with no actual involvement in peace or aid work. Others are fronts for political or military groups. My favorite example is the association Tous Pour la Paix et le Développement (literally: "All for Peace and Development"). Officially, it promotes community reconciliation, resolves land conflicts, and builds roads, schools, and health centers in eastern Congo. In reality, for years in the early 2000s, it enabled Governor Eugène Serufuli to maintain his control over the province of North Kivu by diverting aid funds, co-opting local elites, and distributing arms to civilians and militias. So much for community reconciliation...

Thankfully, a majority of local organizations do actually work for peace and development, but still, they're far from perfect. Corruption and embezzlement are just as commonplace in grassroots associations as in international ones. And the consequences are just as serious, as you remember from the sad ending to the LPI story in Congo.

Therefore, it's crucial to have outsiders on site to help identify which local groups are worth supporting: which ones are *not* briefcase NGOs, which ones have legitimate, trained, competent, and honest staff, which ones actually promote peace rather than hatred. However, we need these outsiders to intimately know the ins and outs of the local politics, customs, stories, and histories, so that they can make the right call.

The Way Forward

Foreign peacebuilders have a lot to offer to conflict zones inhabitants. The catch is that, to really make all of these contributions, they have to focus on the resources or skills they have that local people *actually* need, as opposed to what they assume residents need. And they can't continue acting as typical Peacelanders.

To be successful, peace efforts must draw on the knowledge, perspectives, networks, and assets of both insiders and outsiders. The key to better peacebuilding is not simply "out with the old, in with the new." Rather, it is doubling down on those aspects that we already know to be effective and minimizing those that aren't. That's when it's helpful to remember the remarkable individuals who found another way to live and work in conflict zones—people like Leymah, Vijaya, Kaer, Alexandra, Déo, Pieter, Urbain, James, Banu, and so many others.

We need to ask, not assume. Follow, not lead. Support, not rule. And once we learn these principles, we can apply them to all conflict-resolution initiatives—even the ones in our own backyard.

7

The Home Front

You may wonder how lessons from war-torn places could possibly be useful to people who don't live or work in such environments. After all, you might think that gang fights, terror attacks, and domestic abuse in France or the United States are different from battles, massacres, and torture in Afghanistan or Congo. They are indeed, but all of these phenomena are related. Their roots are often the same, and even more importantly, so are their solutions.

Individuals exposed to violence, whether in their homes, in their neighborhoods, or in conflict zones, are much more likely to become perpetrators themselves. People who've witnessed wars tend to be more aggressive toward their families. Victims of abuse get disproportionately involved in gangs, shootings, and killings. In the words of Cure Violence, one of my favorite peacebuilding organizations in the United States, violence is "contagious."

I personally can attest to that. Do you remember what I told you about my dad—how he used to report on wars around the world for the French state radio? Sadly, the horrors he witnessed and the hardships he faced took a toll on his mental health. As a result, the violence he brought back home was not contained solely in the stories he told, or the tape recordings he gave me. It was also present in his behavior toward my mom and me.

I remember the fear that gripped us as soon as he was back, the sound of his voice when he yelled at us, the look in his eyes when we were cowering, the shame I felt when the insults poured in, the tension in my body when he touched me. He was unpredictable: loving, charming, and inspiring one minute, terrifying the next.

At age ten, I was finally strong enough to fight back. I stood up to my dad and, eventually, helped my mom bring an end to his abuses. From there, it was a natural step to try to protect others around me. In high school, I got involved in the student branch of SOS-Racisme (the leading French anti-racism organization). I learned to organize protests and strikes, and went on to join the national leadership committee.

Activism saved me. Traumatized kids often become violent when they grow up, whether against others or against themselves. Instead, after a few rocky years, I threw myself into countering violence in all its forms. I've since then realized that this is a common coping strategy: Taking care of other people is a powerful way to overcome your own fears.

Through my work, I've progressively realized that, no matter how hard it was, what I went through as a kid was nothing compared to what many victims of violence experience. In my case, the physical blows remained occasional. I could escape to safe places (school, my grandparents' home, etc.). And the whole ordeal eventually ended. In contrast, I've now seen so many bodies scarred with unescapable reminders of abuse. I've met so many individuals who have no place of refuge. I've grown to care for so many people who can't escape the traumatic situations in which they live.

Every time I think of them, I remember what it's like to be scared, day in and day out, every hour of every day. I empathize, automatically. I know how it is to feel trapped, to think that it's never going to end, that you're all alone, and that nobody cares. I'm out of this today, but I can't stand the idea that someone else, somewhere, is facing the same thing.

And unfortunately, violence is widespread, even in ostensibly peaceful nations. Most killings around the globe take place outside of conflict zones. Of the 30 countries with the highest homicide rates in the world, only half have ongoing wars. In Europe and North America, mass shootings have become commonplace, as have attacks against Jews, Muslims, and immigrants, and police brutality against people of color. Over the past few years, many interveners (myself included) have had a similar reaction to current events in the United States, France, Sweden, and neighboring states: Growing social tensions, divisive public discourse, demonization of political enemies, distrust of elected officials, increasing agitation, police violence—it all reminds us of what we see in war zones.

Thankfully, we also see a lot of peace work going on. Local activists may call it by a different name—like "social justice," "community empowerment," or "gang intervention"—but in essence, these are all efforts to confront violence.

The caveat is that many domestic programs suffer from the same kind of issues as do international peace efforts. I first realized this when talking with LPI staff member Cate Broussard.

Cate gets angry when outsiders don't take the back seat—when they design initiatives for local people, or when they speak and act on their behalf. In fact, when she mentioned this common behavior to me over tea, the typically soft-spoken American raised her voice, her gentle gaze becoming harsh and her calm demeanor giving way to visible agitation. This was clearly a hot-button topic for her. "It's because I'm from New Orleans," she said. She went on to explain that when Hurricane Katrina destroyed her home in 2005— while flooding 80 percent of the city and killing more than 1,800 residents— "it felt like the whole world converged on us to tell us how to rebuild." She also resented the people going on "disaster tours" and ogling her family when they were gutting their house. "That happens all the time in Africa," she concluded, "and I refuse to do that to other people."

That's why Cate decided to work for LPI. She first learned about this organization when she wrote a report on my book, *The Trouble with the Congo*, for one of her college classes. She liked that LPI didn't impose a pre-designed program—an approach she had resented so much as a teenager in her devastated city. Rather, LPI put the voices of people most affected at the forefront. So, although she had never considered moving to Sweden, when she received an offer to fill a temporary vacancy in the headquarters, she said yes. Seven years later, she is still there.

Cate has a goal. One day, she will go back home to New Orleans and use what she learned while working for LPI to help improve life in her own community.

Like Cate, many of the role models that you read about in this book started their journey right at home—in Australia, France, Turkey, and the United States. And like Cate, they can finish it there, too. In fact, organizations such as LPI, the Global Peace Foundation, and the Purdue Peace Project are now bringing the lessons they learned abroad to Sweden and the United States.

A few years ago, the Nobel Peace Prize winner Leymah Gbowee, whom you've met throughout this book, joined my own university and started a program to apply peacebuilding insights from war zones to America. Leymah is my kind of superstar. In the early 2000s, as fighting was ravaging her home country of Liberia (killing 250,000 people and displacing one million—out of a prewar population of slightly over two million), she banded with her neighbors to demand a ceasefire and peace negotiations. Their initiatives soon grew into a massive women's movement that used street protests, sit-ins, vigils—even a sex strike (practicing abstinence until their partners listened to their demands)—and eventually compelled leaders to sign a peace deal.

Leymah Gbowee stands next to a whiteboard as she briefs a group of fellow activists on local peacebuilding techniques. With her bright smile, inquisitive eyes, and vibrant dresses, Leymah is a fabulous public speaker—every time I've seen her address an audience, the room was spellbound.

Photo credit: Natalia Mroz for the Columbia University Program on Women, Peace, and Security, 2020

Today, Leymah is using the same strategies that helped her end war in Liberia to curb violence all over the world. In the United States, for instance, she supports women's organizations fighting against sexual abuse, racial tensions, unfair deportations, and mass incarceration. In parallel, she's building a global network of grassroots peace activists who can learn from each other and share unconventional ideas, effective approaches, and best practices. Leymah fires up my students whenever she comes to speak to my classes and motivates them to get involved. She's strong, courageous, purposeful—and witty!

What about you? Do you want to help address conflicts around you—whether they are private or public, local or global? If so, the journey you started when you opened this book can continue on your own turf.

Focus on What Works

It's not only in war-torn places that people ruminate over the negatives. We do it everywhere. My Facebook feed is rife with distressing stories shared by outraged friends and family members. The news on TV is so gloomy and depressing that I've stopped watching it.

As I wrote this book, I kept remembering Rebecca Solnit's uplifting message in her aptly-titled book *Hope in the Dark*: Activists have won many victories across the world, even if it has taken us years to feel their positive impact. It's high time we pay more attention to these accomplishments and emulate them. At home, just like in conflict zones, we should build on what works rather than obsessing over problems, challenges, and failures.

I know it's easier said than done. While researching for this concluding chapter, I had the same experience as the one I told you about at the beginning of this book—the one that ended in me meeting Vijaya. For the longest time, I desperately tried and failed to find peacebuilding success stories in France, the United States, or other Western countries. I would see organizations that worked like LPI and Resolve achieve fantastic results; they were bringing bottom-up solutions to various problems, but they focused on things that were unrelated to peace (like economic well-being). Or I would find ineffective organizations, many of which used a domestic version of Peace, Inc. to counter violence, with outsiders coming in and telling insiders what to do.

Thankfully, two of my colleagues at Barnard College (Matt Lacombe, an expert in gun politics, and Eduardo Moncada, a specialist on gang issues) read my draft manuscript and advised me to look at the initiatives that have managed to curb shootings in various American cities. This was a revelation. The more I read about these successful efforts, and the more I talked to the people involved in them, the more I saw striking parallels with the effective peace initiatives I've told you about.

Gun violence has been a huge problem in the United States for decades. More than 117,000 people are shot every year, resulting in roughly 33,000 fatalities. Gun injuries are the leading cause of death for young African-American men. When I read how residents of affected neighborhoods—usually impoverished minority communities—describe their everyday life, it reminds me of what I hear in war-torn places. A mother from Chicago sleeps on the floor to avoid bullets coming through her windows. A little girl from New Orleans has "one main goal in life": "to survive long enough to graduate from high school." Shooters and their victims are usually affiliated with gangs: loosely-structured armed groups that are often organized along ethnic lines and try to control a given territory—just like Congolese militias. And, like in Congo, the combatants do more than just shoot: stabbing, torture, abduction, rapes—guns enable a whole panoply of abuses.

The standard response to this problem is reminiscent of Peace, Inc.'s reliance on outsiders and top-down intervention. Politicians operating in the national and state capitals design policies based on what they view as the best solution: repression and punishment. Social workers, along with members of the police, justice, and intelligence services—most of whom are white, middle-class, well-educated people—implement these strategies on the ground. The result: mass incarceration and an increased sense of alienation among ethnic minorities, triggering more violence and shootings.

On the other hand, organizations like Cure Violence and Live Free are incredibly effective. Multiple independent evaluations show that the latter has cut homicides by 30 to 60 percent in metropolitan areas like Boston (Massachusetts), Cincinnati (Ohio), and Oakland (California). As for Cure Violence, it has worked in the violent neighborhoods of more than 20 cities in the United States, achieving a reduction in shootings and killings of up to 73 percent. It recently expanded its operations to other countries with similarly striking results: 53 percent fewer shootings in Cape Town's Hanover Park community (South Africa), 45 percent less violent crime in the Laventille area of Port of Spain (Trinidad), and 95 percent fewer group attacks in Cookham Wood Prison (United Kingdom). The reason? Both Cure Violence and the Live Free network use the same principles as those that promote peace in conflict zones. They rely on insiders, and they work from the bottom up.

From the Outside In

Too often, activists at home fall in the same trap as most Peacelanders and assume that their intended beneficiaries lack skills or expertise, just because they are uneducated, young, poor, unemployed, or on the margins of society. By contrast, effective individuals and organizations don't behave like the cogs of Peace, Inc. They don't over-assert themselves. They don't decide for insiders. They don't act or speak for them. They don't think they know better.

Instead, they work like Leymah, Vijaya, Kaer, Déo, Urbain, Pieter, and Banu: They listen. They are respectful and humble. They remain low-profile and stay in the back seat. They build on the expertise of the people they want to help, letting the latter decide how to analyze their own problems, and then choose the best solutions. They involve not only the elite, whether local or national, but also ordinary citizens. And they strive to be accountable to these people as much as possible, in addition to responding to their outside donors.

In the Cure Violence model, for instance, the community in which a given program takes place is in control. It is the city (or a local organization) that gets the funding, implements the project, and hires all of the "violence interrupters" and "outreach workers." Cure Violence staff provide guidance and training: They explain which core principles have proved effective and why, help identify competent employees, and remain on hand to troubleshoot issues. That way local community leaders and residents own the program, while Cure Violence gets to influence the overall strategy.

The core of this strategy is a reliance on "credible messengers": individuals who have a similar background with the people that they are trying to reach. Charlie Ransford, the organization's senior director of science and policy, explained to me that credibility is more than looking the part (by being from a specific race or ethnicity), having the right address (living in the community), or sharing a life experience (like having spent time in prison). These are all relatively superficial characteristics, which are useful but not enough to make individuals effective disrupters of violence. Instead, credibility means having respect and influence. It's being able to talk with people in such a way that they'll listen and actually change their behavior.

When Cure Violence set up its first project in Chicago's West Garfield Park, one of their violence interrupters was the man who used to run the area's drug trade. Another was a powerful former local gang leader. These two individuals had the kind of status that, when they went into the neighborhood, everybody listened to what they had to say. Likewise, when the organization expanded its operations to Baltimore, it hired Nathan "Bodie" Barksdale, a reformed drug dealer once so notorious that he served as an inspiration for the TV show *The Wire*.

The role of these credible messengers is to detect violent conflicts, prevent them if possible, and otherwise resolve them and make sure they don't escalate. To do so, these activists identify the individuals most likely to get involved in serious crimes, spend a lot of time with them, connect them to relevant social services, and try to convince them to make life changes. Cure Violence's interrupters also make sure that all residents know that they are on hand should any issue arise. And they mobilize clergy members, local business owners, school supervisors, political leaders, nonprofit directors, and others to help spread the message that the community won't tolerate violence anymore.

Let's take a typical example to see how this works. One day in Chicago, a mother overheard her teenage boy getting ready for a revenge attack on an enemy gang that had just killed one of his friends. Without Cure Violence, she would have faced a tough dilemma: Either allow her son to become a murderer (and, potentially, get injured or slain in the process) or call the police (which would land her boy in jail, unless he decided to resist his arrest, which could trigger a shooting). Thanks to Cure Violence, however, she had a third and much better option. She called the local violence interrupter, who came over, talked to her son for an hour, and tried to calm him down. Not by telling the boy that killing is bad—he knew that already. But by validating the teenager's feelings, notably his anger at the murder of his friend, and laying out what would happen if he decided to go ahead with his planned shooting: "They will come back, and murder more of your friends. You will retaliate, too, and eventually you will end up like me: I spent 20 years in prison, and because of that I missed my mom's funeral and my kid's graduation." Thankfully, the teenager decided to rethink his plan. So, the activist moved on to figuring out what the root of the dispute was—this time it was a killing; other times it can be an unpaid debt, a robbery, and so on. He then went to talk to the other side, and after a lot of back and forth he eventually found a peaceful solution that satisfied all of those involved.

Just like Cure Violence, numerous associations credit the success of their approaches to putting insiders in the driver's seat. The Live Free network relies on victims of gun violence, parents of victims, and former perpetrators, in addition to city officials, clergy leaders, and members of the local law enforcement agencies. Former gang members run the programs of Gangsline (in the United Kingdom) and A Better LA and Gang Rescue and Support Project (in the United States). They organize peer meetings, trainings, and workshops to convince at-risk youths to stay away from violence. Because they have led the same life, experienced the same fear and confusion, and intimately understand what it means to start over, they can build the trust and credibility they need to be effective.

By contrast, relying on outsiders and state institutions can actually make things worse. In countries such as France or the United States, calling the police may be most citizens' knee-jerk reaction when there is a problem, but it may not always be the best solution, given the widespread discrimination against people of color. In fact, rather than resolving conflicts, the involvement of police officials has repeatedly escalated what should have remained minor, localized issues. Too often, it has resulted in the death of unarmed civilians, like George Floyd in Minneapolis and Michael Brown in Ferguson (United States), or Adama Traoré in Paris and Aboubacar Fofana in Nantes (France). But there are many alternative ways to address such local issues, such as setting up safe havens with local businesses where people in harm's way can seek refuge, designing networks within communities to implement intervention activities outside of the police (like *Cure Violence* does), and more. These kinds of everyday behaviors can help defuse conflicts just as effectively in Western societies as they do in Idjwi and Somaliland.

There is one last reason why putting insiders in the driver's seat is so crucial. Remember the moral dilemma people face when they have to choose between peace and democracy in Congo, or peace and justice in Israel and the Palestinian territories. At home too, rather than maintaining that all good things come together, we have to acknowledge that we sometimes need to make hard choices. When our own countries oppress some of our fellow residents—people of color, LGBT+ communities, descendants of immigrants—is it best to remain law-abiding citizens and preserve stability, or to rebel and fight for justice and equality at the risk of triggering violence? And in the United States, do we want to protect free speech at all costs, or prevent extremists from fueling hatred and abuse against Black, Indigenous, LGBT+, Jewish, Muslim, and Latinx citizens? No matter what, whether at home or abroad, the people who have to live with the consequences of these decisions should be the ones making the choices.

Top-Down and Bottom-Up

The other lessons I learned from conflict zones are just as relevant for any kind of anti-violence efforts that we may undertake in outwardly peaceful societies. Many domestic activists focus their efforts on top-down changes such as national elections and state policies—and despair when they fail to reach their goals. Working with elites is certainly important, but, as you now know, so is working with your neighbors. Bottom-up activism can help address the racial, ethnic, religious, and political issues that divide not just places like Congo or Colombia, but also the societies of non-war countries.

Take the growing number of hate crimes around the world, for example. Fifty Muslim worshippers massacred in Christchurch (New Zealand), 11

Jewish congregants slain in Pittsburgh (United States), 77 participants slaughtered at a youth rally on Utøya Island (Norway): These are just three of the more than 400 deadly attacks that white supremacists have conducted in Australia, Europe, and North America over the past ten years.

Christian Picciolini used to be one of these extremists. Reading his memoirs, and then talking to him, reminded me of my discussions with combatants in Congo, Israel, Timor-Leste, and other war-torn places. White supremacists see themselves as part of a community (in this case, white people) that is threatened by minority groups (Blacks, Latinos, gays, Jews), so they believe that they have to use violence to protect their very existence and way of life. In their words, they are fighting a "race war."

A burly, bearded man with gentle eyes and many tattoos, Picciolini joined the Chicago Area Skinheads, a neo-Nazi group, in 1987, when he was 14. He soon became the group's leader, helping it grow from a band of dissatisfied youths to one of America's most violent hate movements. After a few years, Picciolini opened a shop to sell white power music—one of the main sources of revenue for his movement. However, he quickly realized he needed to broaden the genre selection to keep his business afloat. Thus, he started meeting clientele who challenged what he believed about them— people who were Black, gay, Jewish, Muslim, and showed him compassion at a time when he thought he least deserved it. Then came a growing disillusionment with the movement he'd helped build, the shock of losing friends to gang fighting, and a desire to take better care of his wife and sons. So not only did he abandon the neo-Nazi movement (in 1996), but he decided to make amends by helping others leave extremist groups.

He does so by building on his personal story, his intimate understanding of why one might join such movements, and the experience of the few existing organizations that counter white extremism in other parts of the world (notably Exit Sweden and Exit Germany). Picciolini develops personal relationships with the people he wants to assist, spends a lot of time listening to them, and eventually connects them to the resources they need to change their lives, from employment support to mental health treatments. He's quite effective: He has already convinced close to 400 extremists to forsake white power ideologies.

And he's not alone. Consider the case of the African-American blues musician Daryl Davis. The son of a State Department official, Davis spent his early childhood bouncing around the world, always in a multi-racial, multicultural environment. He encountered racism for the first time when he moved back home to the United States, and he never forgot his confusion upon realizing that certain people could hate someone they have never met. Once he became an adult, he decided to use his talents—his passion for music and his capacity for listening—along with interactions at his concerts, to improve race relationships. Over the last 30 years, Davis has persuaded dozens of individuals to leave the Ku Klux Klan. His method? Talking with these white supremacists extensively, befriending them, and eventually, over time, convincing them to renounce hatred. In other words, showing the kind of compassion that was so important in getting Christian Picciolini out of the white supremacist movement.

To Davis and Picciolini, change happens when we engage with the very people who disagree with us. Like them, and like the inhabitants of conflict zones you read about—people in Northern Ireland, Bosnia, Israel and the Palestinian territories—we can make great strides just by interacting informally with those who despise us or those whom we hate. Sports clubs, religious groups, arts associations, trade unions: These are all good places to start building common ground. A case in point: In the United Kingdom, studies have shown that the success of Mohamed Salah, an Egyptian forward for the beloved Liverpool football squad, has led to a decrease in anti-Muslim rhetoric and hate crimes across the city.

Everybody has skills, knowledge, and networks that can help them address their own predicaments—in non-war places just like in Colombia or Congo. We're all insiders somewhere. So, like the inhabitants of Idjwi, Liberia, and Somaliland, we can all build on the specific elements of our own cultures that can help smooth out tensions.

Every religion I know has teachings that direct us to love our neighbors as ourselves. In the United States, the participants of the Live Free network ground their activism in their identity as "people of faith." To them, "their most sacred texts"—including the Torah, the Bible, and the Quran—oppose the "racism, violence, and economic exploitation" that fuel gun violence.

Every tradition has features that help promote peace. For instance, the staff of the Non-Violence Institute draws on the teachings of Martin Luther King Jr. to prevent gang fighting in Providence and Chicago. Further afield, the inhabitants of Chéran (Mexico) used to face extortion, murders, and kidnappings on a daily basis. Illegal loggers affiliated with criminal cartels were plundering the communal forest, slowly destroying their main source of livelihood. So, in 2011, the residents—mostly poor Purhépecha indigenous people—revolted. They expelled the corrupt municipal officers and set up their own citizens' councils and local police. They built on indigenous laws, customs, and norms to maintain order. Over time, they managed to keep both the cartels and the state police at bay. The rate of homicides and serious crimes in their town dropped to zero.

We can also use our family ties to decrease violence. In Caracas (Venezuela), women put pressure on their sons who belong to warring gangs, and they band with other moms to negotiate and impose peace pacts. In the South Side of Chicago (United States), a group of women fed up with seeing so much bloodshed around them had a brilliant idea: They decided to hang out on street corners, bringing folding chairs and sitting on them for hours on end. And because nobody wants to kill someone in front of their own mothers, the number of shootings in their community slowly decreased. The association Mothers/Men Against Senseless Killings was born.

Just as bottom-up action has made a difference on a large scale in Somaliland, the results of similar efforts in the Western world need not remain localized either. It is thanks to a small group of suffragettes that all British women won the right to vote in 1928. When four African-American students refused to leave after being denied service at Woolworth's lunch counter in Greensboro, North Carolina, in 1960, they sparked national protests that eventually paved the way for the end of de jure racial segregation in the United States. Grassroots resistance movements have also led to the demise of British rule in India in 1947, communism in Czechoslovakia in 1989, apartheid in South Africa in 1994, Slobodan Milošević's dictatorship in Yugoslavia in 2000, Zine El Abidine Ben Ali's tyranny in Tunisia in 2011—and, as you remember from Leymah's story, war in Liberia in 2003.

That said, in ostensibly peaceful places, just like in war zones, it is often a combination of bottom-up and top-down efforts that can achieve the best results. To address gun issues in the United States, for instance, both Cure Violence and Live Free have expanded their work beyond the grassroots. They have joined a range of other organizations to fight for policy reforms at the city, state, and federal levels, requesting measures such as universal background checks, permit-to-purchase laws, minimum age restrictions, and the prohibition of large capacity magazines. The Californian towns that have benefited from both these top-down and bottom-up strategies have experienced a dramatic drop in gun violence.

All forms of activism, and not only peacebuilding, work best when top-down and bottom-up actions are combined. Take the different approaches to environmentalism in France and the United States in the

2000s—and my confusion when I moved from the former country to the latter. Growing up in Paris, my friends and I believed that saving the earth was our government's responsibility. Thus, our role was to vote for a Green party that would promote environmental protection domestically and internationally. To us, the United States was terribly behind on these issues, because they had no such representatives in government. So I was quite puzzled when Leigh, my roommate in New York, off-handedly told me she was appalled at how little French people cared about the environment, and how proud she was of American citizens for being sustainability trailblazers. After long chats, I finally understood that, to her, saving the earth was an individual responsibility: the kind you fulfill every day by recycling, turning off lights, etc. (things that I didn't think could make a difference). Today, thankfully, recycling is becoming mainstream in France, and green issues are becoming a high priority in American politics. On both sides of the Atlantic, those of us who want to halt the destruction of our planet have understood that we need to act both at the grassroots and at the treetops.

Rules of Thumb

All of these stories probably remind you of other key insights we've learned from remarkable peacebuilders in conflict zones. Just like Urbain Bisimwa when he worked on the Rasta problem in Congo and James Scambary in Timor-Leste, effective activists at home develop personal relationships with the people they want to help, in addition to professional ones. In fact, both Daryl Davis and Christian Picciolini constantly emphasize that listening, talking, finding common ground, and bonding over shared interests is essential in influencing white supremacists. Same for Cure Violence affiliates: They spend much of their time making connections and building trust with at-risk individuals.

Of course, effective peacebuilders at home do more than just talk—they also act. Dialogue is rarely enough, whether in conflict zones or in seemingly peaceful countries. As we saw in Congo, projects that address the specific needs of a community, whether by creating livestock paths or investing in small businesses, can keep the momentum of the initiatives going. In the same spirit, A Better LA runs job training and placement, and has walking patrols accompany students safely to and from classes. The Gang Rescue and Support Project helps participants get rid of tattoos—the ever-present physical reminders of gang membership—and they have set up an embroidery and print shop to employ interested youths and teach them marketable skills. Cure Violence and Live Free additionally connect at-risk individuals to organizations that provide mental health treatment, housing support, and tutoring to work toward a high school diploma. Exit Germany's services to help white supremacists start a new life are even more extensive: It not only provides psychotherapy, social skills development, and contacts with employers, but also helps those at risk of retaliation from their former comrades change their identity and move to new places.

In doing so, model activists at home remain wary of templates, checklists, and pre-determined strategies when they act—they don't want to end up in the same situation as the United Nations official who confused Kosovo and Liberia! Instead, they stay open to the practices and ideas that they may instinctively disdain or combat, like the superstitions that do so much to keep Idjwi peaceful, the idea of an African-American man (like Daryl Davis) befriending Ku Klux Klan members, or the sex strike that Leymah and her fellow activists used so effectively.

They also consider breaking bureaucratic rules when necessary. Thomas Sheldon, the founder of Gangsline, told me that he systematically ignores the risk assessment he's supposed to conduct before engaging with any new armed group. He already knows the evaluation will tell him the area is too dangerous and he should only go with a police escort. Not only is this obvious finding unhelpful—after all, if men were not shooting people on a daily basis, there would be no reason for Sheldon to get involved. It's also counterproductive because nobody would talk to him if he were accompanied by the police. So, in his view, it's better to ignore the self-defeating rule and have a chance at actually doing his job.

Above all, the best domestic activists focus on flexibility and adaptability throughout the course of their efforts. For instance, when Leymah started her program at Columbia University in the United States, her initial idea was to set up a global network of peacebuilders who would learn from each other. Then she and her colleague Mikaela Luttrell-Rowland spent two years figuring out what kind of support American and African activists needed to be more effective. They used Participatory Action Research—the same method LPI employed in Congo—along with countless discussions, workshops, and surveys. And they realized that many people actually prioritized very practical things, like website design and grant writing. So they obliged: They provided interns skilled in these areas, and they helped participants in their network share strategies to accomplish these very tasks.

Lastly, the most effective activists plan over the long term. I'm always amused (and annoyed) when I hear politicians running for elections and promising that they'll fix all of our societal ills during their short mandates—if only we would vote for them. It took decades—and a world war—to deal with the impact of the 1929 financial crisis. So how can we trust leaders who promise to bring our economies and societies back to their pre-COVID-19 glories in the few years of their presidential tenures? Germany and Italy spent most of the second half of the 20th century recovering from Nazism and fascism (and, given the current populist resurgence, it looks like they're still working on it), so why do we expect Russians and Eastern Europeans to overcome the legacies of communism any quicker?

Just understanding the roots of a problem takes a very long time, even when peacebuilders work in their home countries. LPI, for instance, first considered setting up a Sweden-based program in 2015, and officially started working on it in 2017. As of today, in 2020, they're still trying to grasp the ins and outs of the issues they want to address, decide what value they can bring to existing efforts, and identify the right local partners.

What's more, decreasing tensions takes years. We've seen this with LPI's experience in the Ruzizi Plain. Likewise, getting people out of gangs or white extremist groups in Europe and North America is a very slow process—it lasts up to four years, in Picciolini's experience.

And then, as the residents of Somaliland have shown us, maintaining social peace is a never-ending task. The city of Stockton (California) learned this the hard way. From 1997 to 2002, they implemented a version of the Live Free response to gun violence, and the monthly gun homicide rate decreased by 42 percent. But once the grassroots intervention ended, the number and severity of the shootings increased again, hitting an all-time high in 2011. So the city resumed the program in 2012, and the number of killings went down again.

Likewise, if you get involved, be patient. Remember that change happens slowly and progress must be continuously preserved. If you start getting antsy, keep in mind what Tobias, one of the LPI staff members who worked on the Ruzizi Plain, learned during his years in Congo: The process is just as important as the outcome—sometimes even more so. And when things get rough, remember how much of a difference a committed individual can make. Think about everything that Pieter, Loochi, Lena, and peacebuilders like them have accomplished over the years—even when they felt that the problems were piling up, their efforts were all for nothing, and they should just quit. So right when it's at its hardest, right when you want to give up most, *that's* when your commitment to the long term is most important. Because unlike you, the people you want to help can't just leave.

Above all, keep in mind that what you do matters. I still remember the surprise, relief, and gratitude I felt as a kid the day a complete stranger—a car salesman—stepped in and tried to protect me from my dad. We've all been there: When we feel frightened, isolated, or hopeless, knowing that we're not alone makes all the difference in the world.

Mic Drop

Chicago, Idjwi, Somaliland, San José de Apartadó, Wahat al-Salam – Neve Shalom, Cure Violence, Resolve, the Life & Peace Institute, Picciolini, Leymah, Vijaya, Justine, Kaer, Pieter, Déo, Urbain, Banu: You've now read their stories. There was violence, ordinary citizens and local leaders got involved, outsiders supported their efforts from the back seat, combatants met, talked, worked together, and residents praised peace. Then, a month or two later, sometimes even years later, there was still no violence. Often it never actually resumed, and in many cases, their peace continued for years after.

These individuals, organizations, and communities should have been the real heroes of the stories my dad used to tell me when I was a kid and my family gathered around our wooden living-room table. Because *they* are the people you and I should want to emulate. They stand on the frontlines of peace, and they get it right. They are the ones changing the world, one day at a time.

And now you and I have the tools to do the same.

Appendix: Sources

Some of the people I interviewed feared that they would be harassed, fired, or killed if I revealed their real names. I therefore promised them that I would use pseudonyms. Asterisks identify those pseudonyms upon first use. However, all of the village and city names I reference in this book are the real ones.

All foreign-language quotes used in this book are my own translations.

Preface—War, Hope, and Peace

Virginia Page Fortna's *Does Peacekeeping Work? Shaping Belligerents' Choices after Civil War* (Princeton University Press, 2008, pp. 2–4) and Lise Morjé Howard's *UN Peacekeeping in Civil Wars* (Cambridge University Press, 2008, pp. 2–3 and 284) first noted that the research on peacebuilding overwhelmingly concentrates on problems, challenges, and failures. For a review of this literature, see my article "Going Micro: Emerging and Future Peacebuilding Research," *International Peacekeeping*, vol. 21, no. 4 (2014). For the scholarly justification of the book project, read my article "International Peacebuilding and Local Success: Assumptions and Effectiveness," *International Studies Review*, vol. 19, no. 1 (2017).

The statistics about child soldiers are from the webpage "Lessons Learned and Best Practices" by the United Nations Office of the Secretary-General for Children and Armed Conflicts (https://childrenandarmedconflict.un.org/lessons-learned-and-best-practices) and the report *'Our Strength Is in Our Youth': Child Recruitment and Use by Armed Groups in the Democratic Republic of the Congo* by the United Nations Organization Stabilization Mission in Congo (2019, p. 13).

The statistics on the global budget allocated to peacebuilding come from the blog post "Reaping the Benefits of Cost-Effective Peacebuilding" by José Luengo-Cabrera and Tessa Butler on the International Peace Institute's website (2017). Those on the global cost and impact of wars were calculated from the figures compiled by the Uppsala Conflict Data Program, the Institute for Economics and Peace's *Global Peace Index 2018* (pp. 47–48), *Global Peace Index 2019* (pp. 58–59), and *Global Peace Index 2020* (pp. 42–44), and the Overseas Development Institute report *SDG Progress: Fragility, Crisis, and Leaving No One Behind* (2018, pp. 69–70). On the length of today's wars, see the report *Elite Bargains and Political Deals Project* by Christine Cheng, Jonathan Goodhand, and Patrick Meehan (United Kingdom Government, 2018, p. 7), and on the number of peacekeepers deployed around the world, see the United Nations website (https://peacekeeping.un.org/en/data).

Chapter 1—Island of Peace

On the global death toll of the Congolese conflict, see the International Rescue Committee's report *Mortality in the Democratic Republic of Congo: An Ongoing Crisis* (2008), the discussion of these findings in Joshua Goldstein's book *Winning the War on War: The Decline of Armed Conflict Worldwide* (Penguin, 2011, pp. 260–264), and the updated figures available in the Armed Conflict Database (International Institute for Strategic Studies, 2019).

The other statistics on Congo come from the United Nations Development Programme's *Human Development Report 2019—Beyond Income, Beyond Averages, Beyond Today: Inequalities in Human Development in the 21st Century* (2019, pp. 25, 314, 320, and 336) and *Human Development Indices and Indicators: 2018 Statistical Update* (2019, pp. 53, 56, and 64). I found the information about citizens' priorities and perceptions of their government in Patrick Vinck, Phuong Pham, and Tino Kreutzer's yearly *Poll Reports* (Harvard Humanitarian Initiative, 2008 to 2019).

On gun violence and economic opportunities in the United States, see the report *Healing Communities in Crisis: Lifesaving Solutions to the Urban Gun Violence Epidemics* by the Law Center to Prevent Gun Violence and the PICO National Network (2016).

The statistics on Idjwi come from Michael Hadley, Dana Thomson, and Thomas McHale's *Health & Demographics of Idjwi Island, DRC: Key Findings of a Multidisciplinary Assessment* (Harvard Humanitarian Initiative, 2011), except for those on the percentage of Pygmy children enrolled in school, which I found in Kalegamire Bahozi Kaer's thesis *La Faible Scolarisation des Peuples Autochtones Pygmées et son Incidence sur leur Développement Socio-Économique dans la Chefferie Rubenga* (Institut Supérieur de Developpement Rural, 2012), and those on life expectancy, which I quote from Ruth MacLean, " 'Everybody Thought it Was Witchcraft, So He Died': Doctors Fight to Change Beliefs and Save Lives on Remote DRC Island" (*Vice News*, 2015).

For historical background on Idjwi, including its fraught relationships with Belgian, Congolese, and Rwandan authorities, and the roots of its North-South conflict, see David Newbury's books *Kings and Clans: Ijwi Island and the Lake Kivu Rift, 1780–1840* (University of Wisconsin Press, 1991) and *The Land Beyond the Mists: Essays on Identity and Authority in Precolonial Congo and Rwanda* (Ohio University Press, 2009, pp. 65–188).

My sources on the fighting in Nyunzu are interviews and field observations I conducted in North Katanga, as well as the report *Off the Record: Documentation of Massacres and Mass Rapes Committed from 2016 to 2018 Against the Indigenous Batwa People in the Province of Tanganyika, Democratic Republic of the Congo* (Initiative for Equality, 2019).

Chapter 2—Role Models

In addition to all of the reports and publications available on LPI's website (http://life-peace.org), three particularly useful sources were Thania Paffenholz's book *Community Based Bottom-Up Peacebuilding: The Development of the Life and Peace Institute's Approach to Peacebuilding and Lessons Learned from the Somalia Experience* (Life & Peace Institute, 2003), Carol Jean Gallo and Pieter Vanholder's paper *From the Ivory Tower to the Boots on the Ground: Conflict Transformation Theory and Peacebuilding in the Democratic Republic of Congo* (presented at the annual meeting of the International Studies Association, New Orleans, 2015—the quote in the section "The Fall" comes from p. 23), and François Van Lierde, Winnie Tshilobo, Evariste Mfaume, Alexis Bouvy, and Christiane Kayser's report *Collaborative Learning from the Bottom Up: Identifying Lessons from a Decade of Peacebuilding in North and South Kivu through Bottom-Up Evaluation (2009–2019)* (Life & Peace Institute, forthcoming 2021).

On the research ideas that influenced LPI's vision, see John Paul Lederach's many publications; the book *Building Peace: Sustainable Reconciliation in Divided Societies* (United States Institute of Peace Press, 1998) provides a particularly clear and accessible synthesis. For more background on Participatory Action Research, reference these seminal texts: Paolo Freire's *Pedagogy of the Oppressed* (Herder and Herder, 1970), Stephen Kemmis, Rhonda Nixon, and Robin McTaggart's *The Action Research Planner: Doing Critical Participatory Action Research* (Springer, 2013), Kurt Lewin's "Action Research and Minority Problems," *Journal of Social Issues*, vol. 2, no. 4 (1946), and Alice McIntyre's *Participatory Action Research* (Sage Publications, 2007).

The statistics on the impact of renewed conflict in the Ruzizi Plain come from the article "In Eastern Congo, a Local Conflict Flares as Regional Tensions Rise" by Philip Kleinfeld (*The New Humanitarian*, 2019) and the report *Genocide Warning: The Vulnerability of Banyamulenge "Invaders"* by Rukumbuzi Delphin Ntanyoma (Genocide Watch, 2020). On corruption, see *Le Monde Diplomatique*'s "Dossier: À Qui Profite la Lutte Anticorruption?" (2019) and *The New Humanitarian*'s "Leaked Review Exposes Scale of Aid Corruption and Abuse in Congo" (2020).

Chapter 3—Insiders and Outsiders

I describe foreign peacebuilders' way of living and working in *Peaceland: Conflict Resolution and the Everyday Politics of International Intervention* (Cambridge University Press, 2014). This book provides more details and analysis about all of the topics discussed in Chapter 3, as well as additional statistics and examples.

On better ways to understand and address wartime sexual violence, see the article "Rape as a Practice of War: Toward a Typology of Political Violence" by Elisabeth Jean Wood, *Politics and Society*, vol. 46, no 4 (2018), the book *Sexual Violence as a Weapon of War? Perceptions, Prescriptions, Problems in the Congo and Beyond* by Maria Eriksson Baaz and Maria Stern (Zed Books, 2013), the report *Wartime Sexual Violence: Misconceptions, Implications, and Ways Forward* by Dara Kay Cohen, Amelia Hoover Green, and Elisabeth Jean Wood (United States Institute of Peace, 2013), and the forum "Peacekeeping Prevention: Strengthening Efforts to Preempt Conflict-related Sexual Violence" by Louise Olsson, Angela Muvumba Sellström, Stephen Moncrief, Elisabeth Jean Wood, Karin Johansson, Walter Lotze, Chiara Ruffa, Amelia Hoover Green, Ann Kristin Sjöberg & Roudabeh Kishi (*International Peacekeeping*, vol. 27, no. 4, 2020).

In the paragraph discussing the fact that foreign peacebuilders rarely speak local languages, the Haiti example comes from Sarah Jane Meharg's *Measuring What Matters in Peace Operations and Crisis Management* (McGill-Queen's University Press, 2009, p. 136), and the Afghanistan example is from Roger Mac Ginty's *International Peacebuilding and Local Resistance: Hybrid Forms of Peace* (Palgrave Macmillan, 2011, p. 112).

Numerous authors have analyzed the relationships between 20th-century colonialism and today's peace interventions. My favorite texts include Michael Barnett's *Paternalism Beyond Borders* (Cambridge University Press, 2016), Gabrielle Dietze's "Mythologies Blanches: Découvreurs et Sauveurs du Congo" (in *Repenser l'Indépendance: La R.D. Congo 50 Ans Plus Tard*, Pole Institute, 2010), Kevin Dunn's *Imagining the Congo: The International Relations of Identity* (Palgrave Macmillan, 2003), Kimberly Zisk Marten's *Enforcing the Peace: Learning from the Imperial Past* (Columbia University Press, 2004), Anne Orford's *Reading Humanitarian Interventions* (Cambridge University Press,

2003), Roland Paris's "Saving Liberal Peacebuilding," *Review of International Studies*, vol. 36, no. 2 (2010), pp. 344–346 and 348–350, and Meera Sabaratnam's *Decolonizing Intervention: International Statebuilding in Mozambique* (Rowman & Littlefield International, 2007). For the seminal texts on legacies of colonialism and imperialism, see Franz Fanon's *The Wretched of the Earth* (Grove Press, 1963), Edward Said's *Orientalism* (Pantheon Books, 1973), and Gayatri Spivak's "Can the Subaltern Speak? Speculations on Widow Sacrifice," *Wedge*, no. 7/8 (Winter/Spring 1985, pp. 120–130). My alternative peacebuilding approach also echoes classic works of anti-colonial literature, notably Paulo Freire's *Pedagogy of the Oppressed* (Herder and Herder, 1968).

Chapter 4—Designed Intervention

The most helpful publications on the benefits and limitations of top-down peacebuilding in Northern Ireland are Landon Hancock's "The Northern Irish Peace Process: From Top to Bottom" (*International Studies Review*, vol. 10, no. 2, 2008) and Roger Mac Ginty's *Elite Bargains and Political Deals Project: Northern Ireland Case Study* (United Kingdom Government, 2018).

The statistics on the United States' budget to promote democracy around the world come from the written testimony "Electoral Assistance: A Cost-Effective Investment in a More Stable, Prosperous World," submitted by J. Kenneth Blackwell to the United States House Committee on Appropriations (2018) and the bill *H.R.2839 - Department of State, Foreign Operations, and Related Programs Appropriations Act*, 2020 by the 116th Congress of the United States (1st session, 2019, section 7032).

The most useful analyses of the liberal peace agenda are the books *At War's End: Building Peace after Civil Conflict* by Roland Paris (Cambridge University Press, 2004) and *The Transformation of Peace* by Oliver Richmond (Palgrave Macmillan, 2005), as well as the articles "The Responsibility to Protect? Imposing the 'Liberal Peace'" by David Chandler, *International Peacekeeping*, vol. 11, no. 1 (2004), and "Indigenous Peace-Making Versus the Liberal Peace" by Roger Mac Ginty, *Cooperation and Conflict*, vol. 43, no. 2 (2008).

My book *The Trouble with the Congo: Local Violence and the Failure of International Peacebuilding* (Cambridge University Press, 2010), provides more information on the Congo-specific issues mentioned in this chapter, including a thorough historical background, an in-depth analysis of local dynamics of violence, and an extensive discussion of the international response to grassroots tensions.

The figures on the budgets of the Congo-focused peace conferences come from the report "The Agreement on a Cease-Fire in the Democratic Republic of Congo: An Analysis of the Agreement and Prospects for Peace" by the International Crisis Group (August 1999) as well as the news articles "Congo Factions Gather for Peace Talks" by Norimitsu Onishi (*New York Times*, 2002) and "Militants, Civil Groups Boycott Congo's Peace Talks" by Eddy Isango (*Associated Press International*, 2008).

The statistics on the extent of sufferings in Congo come from the factsheets "Democratic Republic of Congo: Internally Displaced Persons and Returnees" by the United Nations Office for the Coordination of Humanitarian Affairs (2017) and "UNHCR DR Congo Factsheet – August 2020" by the United Nations High Commissioner for Refugees (2020), the report *Year in Review: 2019* and the factsheet "Sexual Violence in Conflict" by the Armed Conflict Location & Event Data Project (2020), and the webpage "Democratic Republic of the Congo" by Reliefweb (https://reliefweb.int/country/cod?figures=all#key-figures, 2020).

Drew Cameron, Annette Brown, Anjini Mishra, Mario Picon, Hisham Esper, Flor Calvo, and Katia Peterson reviewed all available impact evaluations of peacebuilding initiatives for the Evidence for Peace Project and published their overall findings in the *Evidence for Peacebuilding Evidence Gap Map* (International Initiative for Impact Evaluation, 2015; the quote comes from p. 55). You can find more information about Pamina Firchow's alternative evaluation method in her book *Reclaiming Everyday Peace: Local Voices in Measurement and Evaluation After War* (Cambridge University Press, 2018).

On the relationships between democracy and peace, the most prominent sources include two articles published in the *American Political Science Review*: Zeev Maoz and Bruce Russett's "Normative and Structural Causes of the Democratic Peace, 1946–1986" (vol. 87, no. 3, 1993) and Michael Doyle's "Three Pillars of the Democratic Peace" (vol. 99, no. 3 , 2005). On the dangers of democratization, look at the work of Jack Snyder, notably his books *From Voting to Violence: Democratization and Nationalist Conflict* (Norton, 2000) and *Electing to Fight: Why Emerging Democracies Go to War* (co-authored with Edward Mansfield, MIT Press, 2005), as well as his article "Time to Kill: The Impact of Election Timing on Postconflict Stability" (co-authored with Dawn Brancati, *Journal of Conflict Resolution*, vol. 57, no. 5, 2012). The 31 percent statistics come from pp. 839–840, and the 2.7 years statistic from p. 823 in the latter article. Three other useful publications are Thomas Flores and Irfan Nooruddin's "Democracy under the Gun: Understanding Postconflict Economic Recovery" (*Journal of Conflict Resolution*, vol. 53, no. 1, 2009) and "The Effect of Elections on Postconflict Peace and Reconstruction" (*The Journal of Politics*, vol. 74, no. 2, 2012), as well as Zachary Jones and Yonatan Lupu's "Is There More Violence in the Middle?" (*American Journal of Political Science*, vol. 62, no. 3, 2018). The statistics on the recurrence of conflict were calculated from p. 20 of the first article, and the information on economic recovery comes from p. 560 in the second article. *Theories of Democratic Change Phase III: Transitions from Conflict*, by Jennifer Dresden, Thomas Flores, and Irfan Nooruddin (USAID, 2019) is a white paper that presents a useful synthesis of all of these debates. For the clearest and most convincing argument in favor of building institutions prior to holding elections, see Roland Paris' book *At War's End: Building Peace After Civil Conflict* (Cambridge University Press, 2004).

Elisabeth King's *From Classrooms to Conflict in Rwanda* (Cambridge University Press, 2014) is a fantastic book on education and conflict. Kenneth Bush and Diana Saltarelli's report *The Two Faces of Education in Ethnic Conflict: Towards a Peacebuilding Education for Children* (UNICEF, 2000) and Jeaniene Spink's "Education and Politics in Afghanistan: The Importance of an Education System in Peacebuilding and Reconstruction," *Journal of Peace Education*, vol. 2, no. 2 (2005) are two other useful sources on this topic.

On the counterproductive consequences of statebuilding programs, see my article "Dangerous Tales: Dominant Narratives on the Congo and their Unintended Consequences," *African Affairs*, vol. 111, no. 43 (2012). The paragraph on Iraq summarizes the arguments of Charles Tripp's "The United States and State-Building in Iraq," *Review of International Studies*, vol. 30, no. 4 (2004) and Harith Hasan Al-Qarawee's "Political Violence and Failures of Nation-Building in Iraq" (World Peace Foundation's blog *Reinventing Peace*, 2013).

If you want more details regarding how "good things" (e.g., peace and democracy) counteract one another—or, more broadly, how assumptions spread among interveners and influence peace action—look at my article "International Peacebuilding and Local

Success: Assumptions and Effectiveness," *International Studies Review*, vol. 19, no. 1 (2017).

Christine Cheng, Jonathan Goodhand, and Patrick Meehan led the team of experts who worked on the *Elite Bargains and Political Deals Project* I reference in Chapter 4. Their synthesis paper, along with all of their case studies, are available on the United Kingdom government's website (www.gov.uk/government/publications/elite-bargains-and-political-deals, 2018).

Stathis Kalyvas' *The Logic of Violence in Civil War* (Cambridge University Press, 2006) is the seminal book on local causes of violence in armed conflicts. The Timorese example is based on James Scambary's book *Conflict, Identity, and State Formation in East Timor 2000–2017* (Brill, 2019), the Afghanistan one on Christopher Coyne and Adam Pellillo's article "The Art of Seeing Like a State: State-Building in Afghanistan, the Congo, and Beyond," *Review of Austrian Economics*, vol. 25, no. 1 (2012) and Mike Marten's book *An Intimate War: An Oral History of the Helmand Conflict, 1978–2012* (Oxford University Press, 2014), the South Sudan one on Jana Krause's article "Stabilization and Local Conflicts: Communal and Civil Wars in South Sudan," *Ethnopolitics*, vol. 18, no. 5 (2019), the Bougainville one on John Braithwaite, Hilary Charlesworth, Peter Reddy, and Leah Dunn's book *Reconciliation and Architectures of Commitment: Sequencing Peace in Bougainville* (Australian National University Press, 2010), the Nigerian one on International Crisis Group's report *Stopping Nigeria's Spiralling Farmer-Herder Violence* (2018), the Burundi one on Stephanie Schwartz's doctoral dissertation *Homeward Bound: Return Migration and Local Conflict After Civil War* (Columbia University, 2018), the Indonesia one on Jana Krause's book *Resilient Communities: Non-Violence and Civilian Agencies in Communal Wars* (Cambridge University Press, 2018), the Nepal one on Tobias Denskus' article "The Fragility of Peacebuilding in Nepal," *Peace Review*, vol. 21, no. 1 (2009, pp. 54 and 57), the Mali one on Yvan Guichaoua and Matthieu Pellerin's report *Faire la Paix et Construire l'État: Les Relations entre Pouvoir Central et Périphéries Sahéliennes au Niger et au Mali* (Institut de Recherche Stratégique de l'École Militaire, 2017) and International Crisis Group's report *Central Mali: An Uprising in the Making?* (2016), the Somalia one on Hussein Adam's "Somalia: International Versus Local Attempts at Peacebuilding" (in *Durable Peace: Challenges for Peacebuilding in Africa*, eds. Ali Taisier and Robert Matthews, University of Toronto Press, 2004, p. 270); Mark Bradbury's *Becoming Somaliland* (Indiana University Press, 2008); Afyare Abdi Elmi's *Understanding the Somali Conflagration: Identity, Islam, and Peacebuilding* (Pluto Press, 2010, pp. 21–22 and 141); and Ken Menkhaus's "International Peacebuilding and the Dynamics of Local and National Reconciliation in Somalia" (in *Learning from Somalia: The Lessons of Armed Humanitarian Intervention*, eds. Walter Clarke and Jeffrey Herbst, Westview Press, 1997, pp. 54–56), and the Sudan one on Gunnar Sørbø's article "Local Violence and International Intervention in Sudan," *Review of African Political Economy*, vol. 37, no. 124 (2010).

The statistics on the number of armed groups in today's conflicts come from the report *The Roots of Restraint in War* by Fiona Terry and Brian McQuinn (International Committee of the Red Cross, 2018, p. 13), as well as the article "Reducing Community Violence in the Central African Republic—The Case of Bria" by Robert Muggah and Jean de Dieu Ntanga Ntita (*Small Wars Journal*, 2018) and the *Armed Groups Maps* periodically released by Christoph Vogel on the Suluhu blog (https://suluhu.org/congo/mapping).

If you're interested in the debate on elections and peace in Congo that *Foreign Affairs* ran online in 2017, see my original essay "What the Uproar Over Congo's Elections Misses," the response "Congo's Inescapable State" by Jason Stearns, Koen Vlassenroot, Kasper Hoffmann, and Tatiana Carayannis, and my follow-up "The Right Way to Build Peace in Congo."

Chapter 5—Peace by Piece

The statistics on Somalia come from the *Fragile State Index 2020* (The Fund for Peace, 2020), the *Corruption Perceptions Index 2019* (Transparency International, 2020), and the *Appropriation Act for 2019 Budget* (Federal Republic of Somalia, 2019, p. 8). Those on the differing security situation in Somalia and Somaliland are based on Uppsala University Conflict Data Program's *Fatalities View* (Department of Peace and Conflict Research, 2020), those on the money spent on peacebuilding come from the World Bank report *Federal Republic of Somalia Security and Justice Sector PER* (2017, p. ix), and I found those on the percentage of unemployed people in the report *Unemployment in Somaliland* by Mohamed Muse Haji Abdi (Somaliland's Ministry of Labor and Social Affairs, 2014).

For the casualties attributed to al-Shabaab, I used the Armed Conflict Location & Event Data Project's page *Al Shabaab in Somalia and Kenya* (https://acleddata.com/2020/01/15/ acled-resources-al-shabaab-in-somalia-and-kenya, 2020), and for those of Somaliland's "independence" war, *Past Human Rights Abuses in Somalia: Report of a Preliminary Study Conducted for the United Nations (OHCHR / UNDP-Somalia)* by Chris Mburu (2001).

Mark Bradbury's *Becoming Somaliland* (Indiana University Press, 2008) is the book I referenced extensively for the history and culture of this territory. The story of fathers and uncles taking away young men's guns comes from p. 113. Other useful analyses of the recent political and security situation in Somaliland include the books by Marleen Renders, *Consider Somaliland: State-Building with Traditional Leaders and Institutions* (Brill, 2012) and by Gérard Prunier, *The Country that Does Not Exist: A History of Somaliland* (Hurst Publishers, 2020), the book chapter by Ken Menkhaus, "International Peacebuilding and the Dynamics of Local and National Reconciliation in Somalia" (in *Learning from Somalia*, eds. Walter Clarke and Jeffrey Herbst, Westview Press, 1997), the report by Nicholas Eubank *Peace-Building without External Assistance: Lessons from Somaliland* (Center for Global Development, 2010), the paper "On Ethical Retreat: Lessons from Somaliland" by Olivia Rutazibwa (presented at the annual meeting of the British International Studies Association, Dublin, 2014), and the articles "Making Peace in Somaliland" by Ahmed Farah and Ioan Lewis (*Cahiers D'Études Africaines*, vol. 37, no. 146, 1997), "A Better Approach to Statebuilding: Lessons from 'Islands of Stability'" by Michael Harsch (*Foreign Affairs* online, 2017), "Internally Driven Post-War Reconstruction and Development" by Salvo Heleta (*Africa Insight*, vol. 44, no. 3, 2014), "Somaliland: Where There Has Been Conflict but No Intervention" by Rakiya Omaar and Mohamoud Saeed (*Prism: A Journal of the Center for Complex Operations*, vol. 5, no. 2, 2015), and "When Less Was More: External Assistance and the Political Settlement in Somaliland" by Sarah Phillips (*International Affairs*, vol. 92, no. 3, 2016). For the clearest version of the argument that Somaliland's peace is due in part to its colonial history, see Gérard Prunier's "Benign Neglect Versus La Grande Somalia: The Colonial Legacy and the Post-Colonial State" (in *Milk and Peace, Drought and War: Somali Culture, Society and Politics*, edited by Markus Hoehne and Virginia Luling, Hurst and Co., 2010).

The statistics on the Colombian conflict and the cost of top-down efforts come from the infographics *Balance del Conflicto Armado* and *Violencia Sexual* by the Centro Nacional de Memoria Histórica (2018), as well as the reports *Colombia: Background and U.S. Relations* by the Congressional Research Service (2019) and *World Report 2020* by Human Rights Watch. For more on peace communities in Colombia, see the books *Opting out of War: Strategies to Prevent Violent Conflict* by Mary Anderson and Marshall Wallace (Lynne Rienner Publishers, 2013), *Local Peacebuilding and National Peace: Interaction between Grassroots and Elite Processes* edited by Landon Hancock and Christopher Mitchell (Bloomsbury Academic, 2012, chapters 3 and 4), and *Resisting War: How Communities Protect Themselves* by Oliver Kaplan (Cambridge University Press, 2017), the article by Philipp Naucke "Peacebuilding Upside Down? How a Peace Community in Colombia Builds Peace Despite the State," *Social Anthropology*, vol. 25, no. 4 (2017), as well as the doctoral dissertations *A Theory of Civilian Noncooperation with Armed Groups: Civilian Agency and Self-Protection in the Colombian Civil War* by Juan Masullo (European University Institute, 2017) and *Neutrality in Internal Armed Conflicts: Experiences at the Grassroots Level in Colombia* by Pedro Valenzuela (Uppsala University, 2009).

The figures for the Israeli-Palestinian conflict were calculated from the fatalities data available on B'Tselem's website (www.btselem.org/statistics/fatalities/after-cast-lead/by-date-of-event, 2020).

Regarding local successes in other parts of the world, my sources are Mary Anderson and Marshall Wallace's book *Opting Out of War: Strategies to Prevent Violent Conflict* (Lynne Rienner Publishers, 2013), as well as, on Afghanistan and Iraq: Michael Harsch's article "A Better Approach to Statebuilding: Lessons from 'Islands of Stability'" (*Foreign Affairs* online, 2017); on Indonesia and Nigeria: Jana Krause's book *Resilient Communities: Non-Violence and Civilian Agencies in Communal Wars* (Cambridge University Press, 2018); on Rwanda: Scott Straus's book *The Order of Genocide: Race, Power, and War in Rwanda* (Cornell University Press, 2006, pp. 65 and 85–87); on Mali: Yvan Guichaoua's blog post "A Northern Knot: Untangling Local Peacebuilding Politics in Mali" (Peace Direct, 2016); on Bosnia: Ioannis Armakolas's article "The 'Paradox' of Tuzla City: Explaining Non-Nationalist Local Politics During the Bosnian War," *Europe-Asia Studies*, vol. 63, no. 2 (2011), and Adam Moore's book *Peacebuilding in Practice: Local Experience in Two Bosnian Towns* (Cornell University Press, 2013).

The crucial involvement of local activists and communities has been emphasized by: on Bougainville, John Braithwaite, Hilary Charlesworth, Peter Reddy, and Leah Dunn's *Reconciliation and Architectures of Commitment: Sequencing Peace in Bougainville* (Australian National University Press, 2010); on Burundi, Myanmar, Nepal, South Sudan, Sri Lanka, and Ukraine: Phil Vernon's *Local Peacebuilding: What Works and Why* (Peace Direct, 2019); on Cambodia, Kosovo, the Solomon Islands, and South Africa: Diana Chigas and Peter Woodrow's *Adding Up to Peace: The Cumulative Impacts of Peace Programming* (CDA Collaborative Learning Projects, 2018); on Colombia: Oliver Kaplan and Enzo Nussio's "Explaining Recidivism of Ex-Combatants in Colombia," *Journal of Conflict Resolution*, vol. 62, no. 1 (2018); on Congo: Sara Hellmüller's "The Power of Perceptions: Localizing International Peacebuilding Approaches," *International Peacekeeping*, vol. 20, no. 2 (2013) and François Van Lierde, Winnie Tshilobo, Evariste Mfaume, Alexis Bouvy, and Christiane Kayser's *Collaborative Learning from the Bottom Up: Identifying Lessons from a Decade of Peacebuilding in North and South Kivu through Bottom-Up Evaluation (2009–2019)* (Life & Peace Institute, forthcoming 2021); on Indonesia and Nigeria: Jana Krause's *Resilient Communities: Non-Violence and Civilian*

Agencies in Communal Wars (Cambridge University Press, 2018); on Iraq, Israel and the Palestinian Territories, Lebanon, Myanmar, Northern Ireland, and Timor-Leste: Zachary Metz's *The Intimacy of Enemies: The Power of Small Groups to Confront Intractable Conflict and Generate Power and Change* (New School, 2019—the quotation comes from p. 108); on Northern Ireland: Avila Kilmurray's *Community Action in a Contested Society: The Story of Northern Ireland* (Peter Lang, 2017); on Sierra Leone: Rebekka Friedman's *Competing Memories: Truth and Reconciliation in Sierra Leone and Peru* (Cambridge University Press, 2017, pp. 114–126); on Sri Lanka: Craig Valters's *Building Justice and Peace from Below? Supporting Community Dispute Resolution in Asia* (Asia Foundation, 2016). Peace Direct's mapping of grassroots conflict resolution efforts is available on its website www.peaceinsight.org.

On informal, everyday peace practices, the Northern Ireland example comes from Roger Mac Ginty's "Everyday Peace: Bottom-Up and Local Agency in Conflict-Affected Societies," *Security Dialogue*, vol. 45, no. 6 (2014), the Israeli and Palestinian one from Zachary Metz's *The Intimacy of Enemies: The Power of Small Groups to Confront Intractable Conflict and Generate Power and Change* (New School, 2019), and the Bosnian one from Jelena Obradovic-Wochnik and Louis Monroy Santander's *Power and Governmentality in "the Local": Donors, NGOs and Peacebuilding Projects in Bosnia* (paper presented at the annual meeting of the International Studies Association, 2017).

Many scholars have written about the need to support *both* bottom-up and top-down initiatives. The most useful sources on this topic are the books *Confronting War: Critical Lessons for Peace Practitioners* by Mary Anderson and Lara Olson (Collaborative for Development Action, 2003); *Building Peace: Sustainable Reconciliation in Divided Societies* by John Paul Lederach (United States Institute of Peace Press, 1998); *A Crucial Link: Local Peace Committees and National Peacebuilding* by Andries Odendaal (United States Institute of Peace Press, 2013); and *Building Peace: Practical Reflections from the Field* by Craig Zelizer and Robert Rubinstein (Kumarian Press, 2009).

Chapter 6—Recasting Roles

The report that emphasizes the importance of listening and developing personal relationships was authored by Mary Anderson, Dayna Brown, and Isabella Jean, and entitled *Time to Listen: Hearing People on the Receiving End of International Aid* (CDA Collaborative Learning Projects, 2012).

The Ugandan examples of local criteria for peace come from Pamina Firchow's book *Reclaiming Everyday Peace: Local Voices in Measurement and Evaluation After War* (Cambridge University Press, 2018). You can find Susanna Campbell's case in favor of rule-breaking in her book *Global Governance and Local Peace: Accountability and Performance in International Peacebuilding* (Cambridge University Press, 2018).

Many scholars have shown that having local people author, design, and implement initiatives is a key to peacebuilding success. Among them, see especially the book chapter by Jean Paul Lederach and Scott Appleby, "Strategic Peacebuilding: An Overview" (in *Strategies of Peace: Transforming Conflict in a Violent World*, edited by Daniel Philpott and Gerard Powers, Oxford University Press, 2010), and the books by Mary Anderson, Dayna Brown, and Isabella Jean, *Time to Listen: Hearing People on the Receiving End of International Aid* (CDA Collaborative Learning Project, 2012), Susanna Campbell, *Global Governance and Local Peace: Accountability and Performance in International*

Peacebuilding (Cambridge University Press, 2018), Adam Moore, *Peacebuilding in Practice: Local Experience in Two Bosnian Towns* (Cornell University Press, 2013), and Rosie Pinnington, *Local First in Practice: Unlocking the Power to Get Things Done* (Peace Direct, 2014).

The research on the importance of long-term funding includes, among many others: my book *Peaceland: Conflict Resolution and the Everyday Politics of International Intervention* (Cambridge University Press, 2014, pp. 271–273), Stephanie Kerr's doctoral dissertation *The Northern Ireland Conflict: Conditions for Successful Peacebuilding* (University of Manitoba, 2010, pp. 29–31, 146, and 153–155), John Paul Lederach's book *Building Peace: Sustainable Reconciliation in Divided Societies* (United States Institute of Peace Press, 1998, pp. 74–84 and 170–178), Roland Paris and Timothy Sisk's book *The Dilemmas of Statebuilding: Confronting the Contradictions of Postwar Peace Operations* (Routledge, 2009, pp. 83–90 and 313–14), and Craig Zelizer and Robert Rubinstein's book *Building Peace: Practical Reflections from the Field* (Kumarian Press, 2009, pp. 12, 18–28, and 267–270).

The news articles cited at the beginning of the section "Recasting the Villains" are: "Charity Sex Scandal: UN Staff 'Responsible for 60,000 Rapes in a Decade,'" by Henry Zeffman (*The Times*, 2018), "Sexual Abuse 'Endemic' in International Aid Sector, Damning Report Finds," by Sheena McKenzie (*CNN*, 2018), "Oxfam Prostitution Scandal Widens to at Least Three Countries," by Avi Selk and Eli Rosenberg (*Washington Post*, 2018), and "Humanitaire: Le Fléau des 'Sexpats,'" by Aude Massiot (*Libération*, 2018). The source for the actual number of abuse allegations is the UN's Conduct and Discipline Unit's website (https://conduct.unmissions.org/sea-overview, 2020).

In addition to my own interviews, the sources for the Colombia examples are the book *Opting Out of War: Strategies to Prevent Violent Conflict* by Mary Anderson and Marshall Wallace (Lynne Rienner Publishers, 2013, pp. 85–86 and 129–142) and the doctoral dissertation *A Theory of Civilian Noncooperation with Armed Groups: Civilian Agency and Self-Protection in the Colombian Civil War* by Juan Masullo (European University Institute, 2017).

On the importance of the foreign interveners' presence in the eyes of Bosnian, Cambodian, Indonesian, Kenyan, Kosovar, and Sri Lankan citizens, see *The Listening Project Issue Paper: The Cascading Effects of International Agendas and Priorities* (CDA Collaborative Learning Projects, 2008, pp. 6–7).

Chapter 7—The Home Front

The narrative builds extensively on information from the websites of the various organizations I mention in this chapter. The source of the *Live Free* quote is their webpage www.livefreeusa.org/ourcalling. I also draw on the memoirs of the individuals I feature, including Leymah Gbowee's *Mighty Be Our Power: How Sisterhood, Prayer, and Sex Changed a Nation at War* (co-authored with Carol Mither, Beast Books, 2013), Christian Picciolini's *Romantic Violence: Memoirs of an American Skinhead* (Goldmill Group, 2015) and *Breaking Hate: Confronting the New Culture of Extremism* (Hachette Books, 2020), and Daryl Davis's *Klan-destine Relationships: A Black Man's Odyssey in the Ku Klux Klan* (New Horizon Press, 2005).

The book *Contagion of Violence: Workshop Summary* by the Institute of Medicine and National Research Council (National Academies Press, 2013) explains in detail why violence is "contagious." Keith Krause's article "From Armed Conflict to Political Violence: Mapping & Explaining Conflict Trends," *Daedalus*, vol. 145, no. 4 (2016), includes numerous statistics supporting the statement that most lethal violence around the world occurs in non-war states.

The classic books on community organizing, whose principles bear a strong resemblance to the LPI and Resolve approach, are: Saul Alinsky's *Rules for Radicals: A Pragmatic Primer for Realistic Radicals* (Random House, 1971) and Aaron Schutz and Mike Miller's *People Power: The Community Organizing Tradition of Saul Alinsky* (Vanderbilt University Press, 2015).

The statistics on the Liberian conflict come from the *Final Report of the Truth and Reconciliation Commission of Liberia* (2009, p. 61).

Rebecca Solnit's book *Hope in the Dark: Untold Histories, Wild Possibilities* (Haymarket Books, 2004) served as a special inspiration for *The Frontlines of Peace*. My other model was Steven Pinker's *The Better Angels of Our Nature: Why Violence Has Declined* (Viking, 2011).

The report *Healing Communities in Crisis: Lifesaving Solutions to the Urban Gun Violence Epidemics* by the Law Center to Prevent Gun Violence and the PICO National Network (2016) was particularly useful to assess the magnitude of the problem as well as the most effective responses to it. The statistics on shootings and deaths come from pp. 6 and 52, the stories told by residents from pp. 6 and 11, the information on successes in California from p. 12, and the Stockton example from p. 26. The links listed at the end of Aaron Rose's blog post "What to Do Instead of Calling the Police" (www.aaronxrose.com/blog/alternatives-to-police, 2018) present various alternatives to contacting the police in the United States.

The figures on white extremist attacks come from the article "Attacks by White Extremists Are Growing. So Are Their Connections" by Weiyi Cai and Simone Landon (*New York Times*, 2019), and the Global Terrorism Database (National Consortium for the Study of Terrorism and Responses to Terrorism, 2020).

My source on the Mohamed Salah effect is the working paper "Can Exposure to Celebrities Reduce Prejudice? The Effect of Mohamed Salah on Islamophobic Behaviors and Attitudes" by Ala' Alrababa'h, William Marble, Salma Mousa, and Alexandra Siegel (Immigration Policy Lab, 2019). On the role of women in fostering peace in Venezuela, it was "Micropolitics in a Caracas Barrio: The Political Survival Strategies of Mothers in a Context of Armed Violence" by Verónica Zubillaga, Manuel Llorens, and John Souto (*Latin American Research Review*, 2019). On Chéran, I used the articles "Indigenous Resistance to Criminal Governance: Why Regional Ethnic Autonomy Institutions Protect Communities from Narco Rule in Mexico" by Sandra Ley, Shannan Mattiace, and Guillermo Trejo (*Latin American Research Review*, 2019), "One Mexican Town Revolts Against Violence and Corruption. Six Years In, Its Experiment Is Working" by Patrick McDonnell (*Los Angeles Times*, 2017), and "The Women and Youth of Chéran: Choosing Non-Violence and Nature" by Karla Medrano (presented at the workshop "Where Are the Women after Resolution 1325," Leiden University, 2019).

Acknowledgments

My deepest thanks go to . . .

. . . all of the individuals and communities I mention in this book (for being who they are, for the work that they do, and for patiently answering my endless questions)

. . . Leigh Allen, Fanny Azema, Catherine and Alan Dumait-Harper, Ayten Gündoğdu, Elisabeth King, Kimberly Marten and Jack Levy, Ariane Warlin, my French and Belgian families, and all of my friends (for making sure I didn't give up)

. . . Hiram Cody, Tierra Hurd, Mario Lacouture, Jun Mao, Shanu Modi, Simon Powell, Anthony Rossi, Lisa Travis, and all of the dedicated staff of the Memorial Sloan Kettering Cancer Center (for giving me the chance to finish this book)

. . . Devon Halliday, Susanna Lea, Laura Mamelok, Noa Rosen, Lauren Wendelken, and the staff of Susanna Lea Associates (for fabulous representation)

. . . Alexcee Bechthold, Elizabeth Bortka, Angela Chnapko, Cayla DiFabio, Don Larson, Rob McCaleb, Rachel Perkins, Niko Pfund, Katelyn Phillips, Amy Whitmer, and the Oxford University Press team (for fantastic editing, production, marketing, and publicity)

. . . Sajdah Bey, Maia Bix, Mary Soledad Craig, Mário da Costa Silva, Graham Glusman, Clara Harter, Kalegamire Bahozi Kaer, Emmanuel Kandate Musema, Jennifer Kaplan, Rekha Kennedy, Erik Lin-Greenberg, Miradji Saidi Milla, Meena Roldan Oberdick, David Quintas, Annie Renas, and Juliette Verlaque (for superb research assistance)

. . . Nancy Gerth (for preparing such a useful book index)

. . . Barnard College, the Carnegie Corporation of New York, Columbia University, the Folke Bernadotte Academy, and the Gerda Henkel Foundation (for generously funding my research)

. . . Michel Alligier, Naazneen Barma, Denise Douart, Michele Farley, Gabriella Ginsberg-Fletcher, Caroline Hartzell, Joseph Ho, Carolina Jimenez, Elisabeth King, Laura Kunstler, Timothy Longman, Zachariah

Mampilly, Anne Pitcher, Karen Reppy, Elisabeth Jean Wood, and the students of my 2019 and 2020 colloquia and seminars (for invaluable feedback on the manuscript)

...Fanny Azema, Laia Balcells, Charles Call, David Chandler, Sarah Zukerman Daly, William Durch, Dan Fahey, Pamina Firchow, Rebekka Friedman, Kenedid Hassan, Lauren Hirsch, Steven Hirsch, Peter Katzenstein, Adam Kochanski, Janosch Kullenberg, Matthew Lacombe, Mikaela Luttrell-Rowland, Roger Mac Ginty, Sara Mael, Judy McCallum, Antonia Miller, Eduardo Moncada, Dipali Mukhopadhyay, Juan Carlos Muñoz-Mora, Michael Nest, David Newbury, Georges Nzongola-Ntalaja, Timothy Pachirat, Jordan Palmer, Roland Paris, Radhe Patel, Lianne Pedersen, Lexie Russo, Stephanie Schwartz, Sarah Shore, Jessica Steinberg, Vijaya Thakur, Kerstin Tomiak, David-Ngendo Tshimba, Pieter Vanholder, Stephen Winkler, and the participants of all of the seminars, lectures, workshops, briefings, and events at which I presented this project (for insightful comments on parts of the argument)

...Philippe Rosen (for all of the above, and so much more)

Lastly, I thank *you* for reading until the end. If you want to continue this journey and learn more about any of these topics, you can find a lot of additional resources on my website www.severineautesserre.com. And I have a favor to ask you: Would you post a review of this book on your favorite webpage, please? I would love to read what you thought of *The Frontlines of Peace*!

Index

For the benefit of digital users, indexed terms that span two pages (e.g., 52–53) may, on occasion, appear on only one of those pages.

Note: Names followed by an asterisk (*) are pseudonyms. An italicized *f* following a page number indicates a figure.